THINKING WITH SHAKESPEARE
COMPARATIVE AND INTERDISCIPLINARY ESSAYS

LEGENDA

LEGENDA, founded in 1995 by the European Humanities Research Centre of the University of Oxford, is now a joint imprint of the Modern Humanities Research Association and Maney Publishing. Titles range from medieval texts to contemporary cinema and form a widely comparative view of the modern humanities, including works on Arabic, Catalan, English, French, German, Greek, Italian, Portuguese, Russian, Spanish, and Yiddish literature. An Editorial Board of distinguished academic specialists works in collaboration with leading scholarly bodies such as the Society for French Studies and the British Comparative Literature Association.

MHRA

The Modern Humanities Research Association (MHRA) encourages and promotes advanced study and research in the field of the modern humanities, especially modern European languages and literature, including English, and also cinema. It also aims to break down the barriers between scholars working in different disciplines and to maintain the unity of humanistic scholarship in the face of increasing specialization. The Association fulfils this purpose primarily through the publication of journals, bibliographies, monographs and other aids to research.

MANEY
publishing

Maney Publishing is one of the few remaining independent British academic publishers. Founded in 1900 the company has offices both in the UK, in Leeds and London, and in North America, in Boston. Since 1945 Maney Publishing has worked closely with learned societies, their editors, authors, and members, in publishing academic books and journals to the highest traditional standards of materials and production.

Portrait of Tony Nuttall by Richard Hamilton

*Reproduced with the permission of the artist and the
Warden and Scholars of New College, Oxford*

Thinking with Shakespeare

Comparative and Interdisciplinary Essays
for
A. D. Nuttall

❖

EDITED BY WILLIAM POOLE AND RICHARD SCHOLAR

Modern Humanities Research Association and Maney Publishing
2007

Published by the
Modern Humanities Research Association and Maney Publishing
1 Carlton House Terrace
London SW1Y 5DB
United Kingdom

LEGENDA is an imprint of the
Modern Humanities Research Association and Maney Publishing

Maney Publishing is the trading name of W. S. Maney & Son Ltd,
whose registered office is at Suite 1C, Joseph's Well, Hanover Walk, Leeds LS3 1AB

ISBN 978-1-904350-84-2

First published 2007

Printed in Great Britain

Cover: 875 Design

Copy-Editor: Michael Wood

CONTENTS

ACKNOWLEDGEMENTS

This collection of essays arises from a symposium on 'Shakespeare and Philosophy' held in honour of A. D. Nuttall in New College, Oxford, in October 2004. The editors are most indebted to the College for its generous financial support of the event and this volume. The speakers — Colin Burrow, Gabriel Josipovici, Charles Martindale, Stephen Medcalf, Subha Mukherji, and Noël Sugimura — were given the opportunity to develop and revise their texts following the symposium. The editors are grateful to all six of them. Terence Cave and A. D. Nuttall agreed to write afterwords to the essays: they too have our thanks. We thank also Benjamin Crabstick for compiling the index. Many people in and outside Oxford, too numerous to mention here, offered further practical help, financial support, and assistance of various kinds: we thank them warmly.

W. P. & R. W. S.

Tony Nuttall, to whom this volume is dedicated, wishes to add: 'To Will Poole and Richard Scholar, and also to Noël Sugimura who, I know, worked hard in the background, I can only say how touched I am, and how grateful.'

LIST OF CONTRIBUTORS

Colin Burrow is Senior Research Fellow in English, All Souls College, Oxford.

Terence Cave is Emeritus Fellow in French, St John's College, Oxford.

Gabriel Josipovici is Research Professor of English at the University of Sussex.

Charles Martindale is Professor of Latin at the University of Bristol.

Stephen Medcalf is Emeritus Reader in English at the University of Sussex.

Subha Mukherji is Fellow in English, Fitzwilliam College, Cambridge.

A. D. Nuttall is Emeritus Fellow in English, New College, Oxford.

William Poole is Fellow in English, New College, Oxford.

Richard Scholar is Fellow in French, Oriel College, Oxford.

N. K. Sugimura is Research Fellow in English, Gonville and Caius College, Cambridge.

INTRODUCTION

William Poole and Richard Scholar

'Who's there?' says Barnardo the sentry, his voice ringing out in the chill night air across the battlements of Elsinore. These are the first words of *Hamlet*, and, as A. D. Nuttall observes at the opening of his 1989 essay on the play, 'it is hard to see how they could be bettered'. Nuttall goes on to explain why:

> They carry, as often in Shakespeare, both an immediate meaning and a larger meaning, which is not simultaneously present but can grow in the mind as the play unfolds. Barnardo means only, 'Who goes there?', the sentry's challenge. The larger meaning is, 'Who is there, in the darkness, among the dead?' As I struggle to paraphrase, I find myself in the danger of opting too easily for the more usual phrases: 'Is there life beyond the grave?' 'Are there human existences on the far side of what we call death?' But these fail to take account of a certain grammatical peculiarity in Shakespeare's words; the sentry's challenge, though formally in the third person singular, is partly infiltrated by a sense of second person singular, arising from the fact that the question posed is addressed to its presumed subject. In which case we must modify our paraphrase, perhaps to 'Who, of you that are dead, is there?' The very awkwardness of the sentence is instructive. The English language naturally resists such a combination of second and third persons. Yet some such phrasing is needed, because *Hamlet* is not a cool treatise on death but is instead about an encounter with a dead person.[1]

Barnardo's words, as analysed by Nuttall, exemplify the defining characteristic of Shakespeare's work that the present volume sets out to identify and examine. Shakespeare's plays and poems alike may be said to draw their audiences and readers into thinking with them — and, like the ghost of old Hamlet, to haunt that thinking — because they dramatize with a peculiar intensity certain questions that concern us to this day. This volume attempts to show, through a series of detailed case studies, what those questions are, how they are expressed and explored, and what kinds of thinking they set in motion. It suggests that the questions raised by Shakespeare's work may be called 'philosophical' in so far as they have to do with ethical, political, epistemological, and metaphysical matters of general human concern. For three reasons the term 'philosophical' needs to be understood here in its broadest, most inclusive sense. The first is that the questions raised by Shakespeare's work also relate to other modes of thinking (those of theology and law, for example). The second is that while at times such questions draw upon and engage with recognizable philosophical ideas and traditions, at other times they appear innocent of any such frame of reference (the opening of *Hamlet* is one example of this). The third is that, whatever their provenance, those questions are invariably pursued by Shakespeare not according to the established procedures of philosophy as an intellectual discipline, but rather by poetic, dramatic, and imaginative — in short, *literary* — means. Barnardo's challenge is a case in point: slotted into the first foot of an iambic pentameter, it gives rise to larger philosophical preoccupations only because it opens the drama. Thinking 'with' Shakespeare means, then, both thinking about the questions that Shakespeare's work explores and thinking through the modes of their exploration.

This is the approach to Shakespeare that A. D. Nuttall has consistently advocated and practised over the last four decades. According to Frank Kermode, Nuttall is 'probably the most philosophically-minded of modern literary critics, and he has the additional merit of assuming that at some level philosophical (or theological) problems are of importance to everybody'.[2] Nuttall has by no means applied his mind in this manner to Shakespeare alone; his bibliography testifies to the breadth of his applications and interests. Kermode's remark, indeed, was occasioned by *The Alternative Trinity* (1998), Nuttall's study of the presence of Gnostic thinking in Marlowe, Milton, and Blake. It is true to say, however, that Shakespeare is the writer with whom Nuttall has done most of his thinking and to whom he has most consistently returned.[3] This may be because, as Nuttall suggests in *A New Mimesis* (1983), 'Shakespeare, more perhaps than any other writer, creates a cloud of alternative or overdetermining explanations round his figures', using his literary intelligence not so much to solve difficulties as to start them for his audiences and readers.[4] Shakespeare is viewed here as what Terence Cave calls 'a paradigm of literary thoughtfulness'. Thinking with Shakespeare has taken different forms for Nuttall. In some instances, such as in the 1989 essay on *Hamlet*, his critical enquiry starts from the Shakespearean text before moving away from it to examine the philosophical ideas with which it converses. In other instances, such as his first book *Two Concepts of Allegory* (1967), the Shakespearean text (in that case *The Tempest*) functions as no more than the central example of a broader investigation, although Nuttall stresses in his preface to that book that 'the investigation is intended incidentally to increase our understanding of the play, much as crystals can be used to reflect light back on their source'.[5] The contributors to the present collection prove to be equally diverse in their understanding of what thinking with Shakespeare might mean in critical and historical terms. In that sense they take part here in a dialogue with Nuttall about the value of different approaches to Shakespeare; and Nuttall himself responds at the end of the volume.

These approaches might usefully be aligned with certain rediscoveries taking place in both Shakespearean studies and in early modern studies at large: the rediscovery of the text, particularly the dramatic text, as a readerly object, not merely coextensive with its dramatic performance; and the associated reappraisal of the playwright as no longer the 'committee member' shackled to the exigencies of the stage, but also as a textual artist. Furthermore, the creation of this understanding is coming to be viewed as a late Elizabethan moment and not a modern imposition. Ben Jonson has long been celebrated for his 1616 folio *Works* and the contribution it made to the elevation of playwrights and playtexts to literary status. The 1600 quarto of Jonson's *Every Man out of his Humour* and the 1605 quarto of *Sejanus his Fall* likewise both attempted to emphasize their difference from, and indeed advance upon, the dramatic event. Jonson is thus rightly celebrated for his 'possessive authorship' and for the shaping effect this attitude has had on literary and artistic history.[6] Nevertheless, Jonson's efforts did not come 'out of nowhere'. Lukas Erne's recent study *Shakespeare as Literary Dramatist* (2003) has persuasively argued that the shift from playbook as ephemeral, the record of a performance, uninterested in literary posterity, to the quarto as appealing to a new kind of literary reader, and emanating from the pen of a known and named author, took place very rapidly after 1590 and was more or less complete by the date of the Jonsonian folio.[7] The effect of this revaluation, argued in minute detail from the evidence of early printed editions, is to dismantle the usual opposition between Shakespeare and Jonson, the former the man of the stage, the latter the writer for states unborn. Erne's backdating of the move from stage to page crucially times this transition as coterminous with Shakespeare's writing career. Shakespeare as literary dramatist, in other words, was by no means a posthumous creation, marked by the appearance of the First Folio in 1623.

If, then, the time is ripe for the reintroduction of Shakespeare the thinker, what are the conditions of encounters with Shakespeare's thought? The first thing to say is that any approach to Shakespeare and the philosophical attitude must operate on the conviction that literature has a part — and a unique part — to play in wider philosophical discussions; that one understands literature best by placing it in dialogue with non-literary, philosophical modes of thinking; and that the result of this dialogue must be to show what it is that literature — especially Shakespearean literature — *uniquely* allows one to think and express, and how it does so. The second, rather different observation that must follow this is that such a project is by no means 'unhistorical'. The history of philosophy, particularly early modern philosophy, is written in terms of competing traditions and their recurrences; and notions such as 'Shakespeare could not have thought that' have come to seem overbold in terms of what is now emphasized about the rhetorical culture of Shakespeare's age, a culture that prized disputation *in utramque partem*, the classroom-originating exercise on why Brutus was right to kill Caesar and why he was also wrong.[8] A similarly important literary activity was the construction of *paradox*, then a more profound business that its pale modern equivalent of 'contradiction in terms'. Renaissance paradox meant, following its etymology, thinking against, alongside, even beyond current teaching, and as such provided both the apology and the model for thinking of more things in heaven and earth. But Horatio *could* have learned that 'in [his] philosophy' — that is, at Wittenburg university — paradox was a flourishing genre in the academe, a form that reminded its users of the provisionality and ductility of apparently stable systems of thought.[9]

In other words, we can work with the hypothesis that the intellectual culture of Shakespeare's age is robust enough to bear many speculations that we might too hastily deny it, and we can expect historical riches when we do so. Yet we should also not neglect the possibility that Shakespearean text can allow us to reflect on philosophical issues that may really have been uncodified in his age. Several of the essays in this volume are *both* discussions of Shakespeare's philosophical encounters *and* philosophical encounters with Shakespeare in their own right. By dramatizing philosophical encounters, Shakespeare offers models for later appropriation, means by which Shakespeare can be used as a tool for the discussion of modern philosophical problems. Comparativist criticism replicates this movement at one or more removes, and hence in the following pages Shakespeare will be discussed against the background of the ancient Greek novel, Senecan Stoicism, Mozartian aria, or the ideas of Heidegger, Sartre, and Rorty. There are two types of apology for this work, then: the first appeals to a more generous estimation of the rhetorical and philosophical cultures of Shakespeare's time; the second appeals to an equally generous but slightly different project — the appeal of literature as a peculiar kind of thinking, and one that can and should be used to forward the 'new mimesis'.

Colin Burrow opens the volume with a provocative essay that does exactly what its title promises: it explains 'Why Shakespeare is not Michaelangelo'. In so doing, he examines various possible approaches to the idea of thinking with Shakespeare. He proves less than keen on so-called 'philosophical' approaches to literature that adopt what he terms either 'interior' or 'posterior' perspectives: the former 'tries to find a philosophical system embedded in literary works', whereas the latter tends to 'a minor time-warp in intellectual history' — as when Milton, for instance, is subjected to an explicitly Kierkegaardian reading. While Burrow strongly resists the interior approach, he admits that all criticism partakes in weak forms of the posterior approach, under the guise of aesthetic advice — a provisional 'see it this way'. But what he regards as the major pitfall of both approaches in their extreme modes is that they operate on an understanding of aesthetics that concerns itself with art *objects* rather than artistic *processes*. Burrow, conversely, appreciates the mobility of text as an aesthetic value in itself, as it is this property that allows literary text to resist, or rather elude, both internalist and posterior methods. Through a close examination of two of Michaelangelo's *Rime* (151 and 237) and two of Shakespeare's *Sonnets* (60 and 124), Burrow argues that while Michaelangelo's vision of poetry is dominated by the ideal of sculpture, of fixed form, Shakespeare's *Sonnets* reveal 'a profoundly unsculptural aesthetic', and 'in doing that they turn thinking into an aesthetic experience'. That, Burrow contends, is what makes Shakespeare better than Michaelangelo.

Where Burrow celebrates art for eluding the stasis of philosophical thought, Josipovici goes further, suggesting that art in fact outstrips philosophy in its fundamental task of understanding the 'unbridgeable gap between life and thought'. Where philosophy refuses to acknowledge that such a difference exists, 'works of art [...] can help us grasp the nature of that difference, and so help us in our philosophical task of understanding ourselves and the world'. What, though, is Shakespeare's distinctive contribution to this kind of thinking? Josipovici addresses here what Terence Cave describes as the 'vast and intractable question' raised by the title of this volume: 'is thinking with Shakespeare in any sense different from thinking with literature in general?' Josipovici takes *Twelfth Night* as his example and contrasts it with its prose source, Barnabe Rich's *Apolonius and Silla*, while maintaining a running comparison with Mozart's opera *The Marriage of Figaro*.

He examines what gives Shakespeare's play its peculiar signature, and shows how 'the spectator or reader is led into areas of experience he or she has always known existed but could never, by themselves, have arrived at'.

Charles Martindale concludes the first section of the book by examining the ways in which Shakespeare's plays, while primarily works of imaginative literature, might also be said to perform philosophical work. Martindale makes his case by contrasting Shakespeare's attitude towards the content and style of philosophy with that of conventional philosophers. He criticizes the style currently deemed appropriate by analytic philosophers and also their way of reading the philosophers of the past, offering Plato, Hume, and Kant as examples. He examines the merits and shortcomings of those philosophers such as Richard Rorty, Martha Nussbaum, and Stanley Cavell who work with literary texts. Martindale goes on to trace in Walter Pater and Michael Oakshott the appearance of an attitude towards ethics that sees it not as the formulation of general principles or a fixed intellectual system but, rather, as the creation of a vernacular language. It is in this sense that we may speak of Shakespeare as a philosopher, Martindale argues with particular reference to *Antony and Cleopatra*, for there and elsewhere he 'shows us a vernacular language, and thereby, perhaps, teaches us, if we will let him, to think, to choose, to act, and, above all else, to utter'.

Subha Mukherji, in the first of a series of 'investigations', discusses the phenomenon of the 'false trial' in Shakespeare and various other contemporary dramatists; the trial in which one person is subjected to a quasi-legal testing that is not strictly necessary. Her opening example is the scene in *Macbeth* (IV. 3) in which Macduff is 'tried' by Malcolm, who pretends that he is after all an unworthy candidate for the crown. Malcolm, of course, is deceiving Macduff in order to try his integrity. Mukherji argues that such trials are used in the drama to interrogate the potential perversity of certain epistemologies. Such false trials also exploit movements in the legal philosophy of the time, especially the shift in the common law towards a probabilistic, precedent-based procedure, where civil law and legal philosophy still held to the idea of demonstrable certainty. Mukherji dwells particularly on the writings of Francis Bacon, notably his principle that 'the passages and variations of nature cannot appear so fully in the liberty of nature, as in the trials and vexations of art'. This notion of trials and vexations is then traced through Shakespeare's *Cymbeline*, Massinger's *The Picture*, and Ford's *The Lady's Trial*. Mukherji concludes that the charge of the false trial in such texts resides in the 'fertile intermediate space between actual legal procedure and general thinking about ways of knowing'.

N. K. Sugimura, returning to a play discussed more briefly by Martindale, considers the opposing conceptions of reality by which Antony and Cleopatra live and die. Her essay also situates Shakespeare's thinking in a 'fertile intermediate space', in Mukherji's phrase, but in Sugimura's case the space lies between the earlier and later histories of metaphysical thought. Sugimura suggests that where Antony's thinking is largely determined by Stoic paradigms, his preparations for suicide cause him to drift towards a state that can better be understood by recourse to Sartreian ideas. In contrast to Antony, Cleopatra is always seen to exceed roles and representation by creating herself out of herself, since for her, 'being and meaning are derived from the power of the imagination'. The play, Sugimura argues, tests out and ultimately assents to this 'experimentation with a wholly new mode of art and concept of reality that transforms art into nature, dreams into realities'.

Stephen Medcalf's essay investigates the double myth of death and resurrection throughout Shakespeare, and the manipulation of what T. S. Eliot calls 'the ultra-dramatic'. He locates this pattern against Shakespeare's reading of and evident love for the Hellenistic romance *The History of Apollonius of Tyre*, and traces his double motif through *The Comedy of Errors* to *Pericles Prince of Tyre*. The heart of his analysis, however, is *King Lear*, in both its surviving texts, the *History* and the *Tragedy*. Medcalf treats the Folio text of this play as a revision of the Quarto text, partially powered by Shakespeare's desire to revisit and recomplicate on stage a moment many of the audience had already seen — the apparent death of Cordelia. Shakespeare's revised text gives to Lear last lines that no longer signal flat despair and hence the assumed deadness of Cordelia, but the possibility that Lear at his own moment of demise sees (or thinks he sees) Cordelia alive, resurrected. Shakespeare's revisions 'give a shiver to the whole fabric of the play' as the audience struggles to decide which way to understand this difficult scene. Shakespeare's revisions recharge his play and force new interpretative problems on its audience.

Finally, Terence Cave and A. D. Nuttall himself offer two responses to the foregoing material. Cave cuts the Gordian knot of an old question — what did Shakespeare think about Montaigne? — by imagining a meeting between the two men. Nuttall, in contrast, responds directly to the preceding chapters. He does so with a characteristically engaging mixture of generosity and resistance.

Notes to the Introduction

All references to Shakespeare, unless otherwise stated, are to the Riverside edition.

1. A. D. Nuttall, '*Hamlet*: Conversations with the Dead', in *The Stoic in Love: Selected Essays on Literature and Ideas* (Hemel Hempstead: Harvester Wheatsheaf, 1989), pp. 27–40 (p. 27).
2. Frank Kermode, 'O How Unlike the Father', *London Review of Books*, 15 October 1998, p. 14.
3. See most recently A. D. Nuttall, *Shakespeare the Thinker* (New Haven: Yale University Press, 2007).
4. A. D. Nuttall, *A New Mimesis: Shakespeare and the Representation of Reality* (London: Methuen, 1983), p. 180.
5. A. D. Nuttall, *Two Concepts of Allegory: A Study of Shakespeare's 'The Tempest' and the Logic of Allegorical Expression* (London: Routledge & Kegan Paul, 1967), p. xi.
6. Joseph Loewenstein, *Ben Jonson and Possessive Authorship* (Cambridge: Cambridge University Press, 2002).
7. Lukas Erne, *Shakespeare as Literary Dramatist* (Cambridge: Cambridge University Press, 2003).
8. Russ Macdonald, *Shakespeare and the Arts of Language* (Oxford: Oxford University Press, 2001).
9. Ian Maclean, 'Foucault's Renaissance Episteme Reassessed: An Aristotelian Counterblast', *Journal of the History of Ideas*, 59 (1998), 149–66, esp. pp. 163–64.

PART I

❖

APPROACHES

CHAPTER 1

Why Shakespeare is not Michelangelo

Colin Burrow

This frivolous title invites a frivolous response. Yes, Shakespeare did not, so far as we know, paint; and yes, it is very unlikely indeed that he ever attacked a piece of stone with a chisel. *Hamlet* is visibly not the roof of the Sistine Chapel, whatever its hero may say about majestical roofs fretted with golden fire. So Shakespeare is not Michelangelo at all.

The question I would like to consider, however, is not perhaps so much why Shakespeare is not Michelangelo as how he is not: that is, Michelangelo has been, since the 1540s and certainly since the first publication of his *Rime* in 1623, regarded as a philosophical poet, whose work manifests a set of ideas about truth and about beauty.[1] Shakespeare is a profoundly different kind of writer. In making a comparison between the two poets I will engage with some of the many things which A. D. Nuttall has thought about during his long and continuing career, although I will consider more the relationship between Shakespeare and that branch of philosophy known as aesthetics than the ethics, metaphysics or theology which have consistently lain beneath Tony's criticism. I will ask what sort of attitude we should take to Shakespeare's *Sonnets* as art objects, and I will do so from the perspective of someone who suspects that the word 'object' is not the right one to use of poems. I am also going to return to the kind of literary criticism which no-one now is allowed to do any more, and seek to explain in a primitive way not only why Shakespeare's *Sonnets* are not like Michelangelo's, but also why I think they are better than Michelangelo's. This will entail thinking about what we do with the word 'philosophy' when we use it in literary contexts.

Broadly speaking, there are two kinds of philosophical approach to literature, which are often found blended in the wild. The first might be called the 'interior approach'. This tries or claims to find a philosophical system embedded in literary works. The most naive version of this way of talking about literature philosophically would be to make a claim of this sort: 'in this sonnet Shakespeare expresses his philosophy of love', or 'Shakespeare here explores his view of friendship'. The 'his' here might then be qualified by reference to an anterior philosophical tradition — Platonism, say, or Neoplatonism, or Plutarch — and the critic might go on to argue that for various reasons Shakespeare either modifies or distorts the prevailing premises of that tradition. A reductive version of this method could lead to the extraction of a more or less simple set of precepts from the works ('love the form of the good'). The interior approach, unless it is used with great delicacy, tends to make philosophy emerge as the master discipline, as texts get crunched into propositions to which, it would be claimed, the author of the text under discussion would have given assent. The core problem with this kind of approach in its cruder forms is its predictive poverty. It is probably the case that all agents have a complex set of beliefs, at least some of which could be formulated in language appropriate to a United Nations charter ('all people are entitled to respect', for instance; or 'aspire to winning the respect of your superiors'). It is also probably the case that a sophisticated account of those beliefs could be worked out from our words and behaviour. It is, however, extremely improbable that any level of sophisticated mapping out of those propositions could issue in a mind map of the philosophical systems in play in any text sufficiently sophisticated to enable the reader to predict what would come next. A complex model might enable a careful reader to know what the next sentence would be about, perhaps; but it is in the nature of writing to resist the predictive, to provide a next word which is not the inevitable word.

'Toffee apples are over-rated.' Could any model of the premises of a mind be sufficiently highly developed to predict that that would have been my next phrase? If we are to talk about literature philosophically, with a view to describing the interior structuring beliefs that shape a given work, we ought to do it in a way that accepts the complex relationship between dispositions ('Shakespeare admired the nobility') and acts (the creation of Claudius). We need also to accept that literary acts are convention-bound and dispositionally mappable only to an extent, and that a central principle of literary acts might be a conceptual version of the figure of *variatio*, whereby slight shocks, surprises, impromptu departures from a philosophical script are not just incidental but structural principles. Aesthetics here has a major advantage over philosophy as an approach to the literary, since it allows for surprise. Interior philosophical analysis tends implicitly to deny that we read things that both make and break patterns, and that the breaking of a pattern, or a moment of unpredictable revolution against the principles that have apparently been followed in a text up to that point, is usually the moment that provokes amazement, or delight, or whatever we are to call the experience that makes most of us (except most dons) read.

The second way of thinking about literature philosophically, broadly speaking, is an 'exterior approach'. Critical studies of this type tend to make a philosophical system into an adjective, and present an Aristotelian, or Kierkegaardian reading of a given author. The major risk of this kind of approach is that a historically posterior philosophical position is adopted, and Shakespeare, or whoever it might be, is then taken as having anticipated that philosophical system. But the main claim of such approaches is usually, implicitly, not that this kind of time-warp in intellectual history has occurred, but that posterior philosophical impositions can give us an aspect under which to view a particular work of art. The exterior philosophical approach in this form is potentially very close kin to most forms of critical activity which seek to be more than purely historical. Exterior philosophising can be a form of aesthetic advice: it takes a philosophical system or idea and a text and it invites readers to see the text under the aspect of that philosophy; and as it does so it claims that if readers do view it under that aspect they will hear it or see it in a new way ('if you read this line as an existentialist it can be heard as one which enacts a lurch into freedom'). In some minimal way all criticism is doing this kind of posterior aesthetic philosophising: it commends a view of a text to its readers, and that view might incorporate all or some of the critic's philosophy. The principal risk of most exterior philosophising, though, is that it tends to end up making universalisable claims; that Donne's poems make signs slide, as they always do, say, or that Milton shows us man being appellated by a subjecthood that is always (already) before him. The exterior approach, with its posterior application of philosophies to texts, has a tendency to end up claiming to be interior—that is, to have shown us something in some sense there in the work that its analysing; and it too can seek earnestly to look the other way when a text resists or shocks or surprises by not quite doing what it should be doing if it exactly fitted the philosophy through which it is being read.

The value of the shocking is the central reason why philosophical approaches to literature (and here one could also include many theoretical approaches to literature) need to be more aesthetic than they have tended to be in the past. Criticism partly is an improvised interplay between interior and exterior philosophising: it is an activity which involves thinking with a text as well trying to work out the thinking that lies behind a text. Part of that process might lead a critic to say 'read this philosopher: it will make you see things in Shakespeare'; another part of that process might lead another or even the same critic to say 'take this provisional view of some of the dispositional preferences which are manifested in this work; it will help you to understand even moments which do not appear directly to manifest them.' Both of these forms of philosophising start to lose touch with art when they begin to see literature as the exoskeleton which takes its warped form from the real philosophical structures beneath it. Philosophical responses to literature should be mobile and accommodating; they should sharpen the gaze, but they should also let you apprehend moments of bluriness in your vision, and they should not prevent you seeing moments which thwart attempts to turn them into principle.

Beliefs tend to hunt in packs. This is to say more than that someone who holds directly contradictory beliefs (that God exists; that God cannot exist) is in a bit of a mess; rather, it is to say that beliefs about one area of human activity can have a foreseeable companionship with beliefs about another area. My argument so far is about the relationship between literature and philosophy, but underlying it is a clear dispositional preference that accompanies my beliefs in those areas. I have been briefly and sweepingly critical of attempts either to extract philosophical systems from literature, or to impose posterior philosophical systems on fictions. Implicitly in these arguments I have been attaching aesthetic value to something we might call mobility: that is, texts that resist the extreme forms of exterior or interior philosophical approaches are texts that I am implicitly valuing.

This claim about value takes me to why Shakespeare is better than Michelangelo and why he is not Michelangelo. Blandly, one could state that obviously both wrote love sonnets, some of which were or which appear to be directed to a younger man; both were widely recognized as geniuses more or less as soon as the category of 'genius' came into being; and both were at various points bowdlerized by their editors to change the sex of the addressees of several of their poems.[2] Some critics have pressed the comparisons further than this. John Kerrigan has argued that both poets produce 'Sonnets of Art', that is, poems that reflect on the processes of their own making, and are in significant ways *about* art.[3] Leonard Barkan has argued for a large-scale analogy between Michelangelo and Shakespeare, and has suggested that Michelangelo's interest in sculpture as a manifestation of an idea that is beyond anything present in nature carries across to the ending of *The Winter's Tale*. For Barkan Shakespeare transcends sculpture by providing a 'four dimensional' reality in the final transformation of Hermione from a statue into life, but 'for narrative and thematic purposes, Shakespeare depended upon all those traditions which saw sculpture as both prime among the arts and closest of all the arts to real life.'[4]

Michelangelo is a poet of whom it is possible to say that he has an aesthetic and probably also a philosophy (at least one can say this with some confidence about his poems that are likely to date of the mid-1540s). Much of his verse also has what one might call an internal aspiration towards 'the hard'. He likes things, and things that are of physically resolved form. In the first quatrain of the poem numbered 63 in Girardi's edition of the *Rime*,[5] Michelangelo imagines a spark being struck from marble; he then describes the calcination of marble into lime by fire; but then the tendency towards the hard comes in, and the lime becomes plaster, which in turn becomes a building, which, like a soul purged by fire, lives on.

> Sì amico al freddo sasso è 'l foco interno
> che, di quel tratto, se lo circumscrive,
> che l'arda e spezzi, in qualche modo vive,
> legando con sé gli altri in loco etterno.

[So friendly to the cold stone is the fire within it that if, when drawn forth from it, the fire so surrounds it that it burns and breaks it, the stone lives on in a certain way, binding with its substance other stones into an eternal place.]

To say that Michelangelo wants a poem to be a thing is perhaps not quite right; but he is interested in objects that are of one physical shape, that can be grasped in a moment, and are durable. Several of his poems, and especially poems that editors are prone to say were directed to Vittoria Colonna (his close friend and image of loveliness from the mid-1540s), take sculpture as the prime art, the one to which all other arts aspire. It is often said too that sculpture is for Michelangelo the prime art in that what the sculptor seeks to do is to find within the stone the 'concetto', or the pre-existent form of the beautiful thing that lies within it.[6] Now the primacy of this aspect of Michelangelo's thought is deeply entrenched in, perhaps partly constituted by, his reception history. On March 7th 1547 Benedetto Varchi gave a learned lecture on Sonnet 151 that presented Michelangelo as a kind of Neoplatonist whose verse is substantially about the transcendent fixity of the form of the beautiful.[7] (Varchi also saw in the poem something of Aristotle's conception of a potentiality within matter, rather than a Platonic form). The poem that Varchi analysed was printed first in sequence in 1623, in the volume of *Rime* that Michelangelo's grand-nephew Michelangelo the Younger edited, expurgated, and carefully designed to highlight the artist's philosophical side. In Girardi's chronological reconstruction of the *Rime* it is number 151; but it is important to remember that for most early readers this was their first encounter with Michelangelo's *Rime*:

> Non ha l'ottimo artista alcun concetto
> c'un marmo solo in sé non circonscriva
> col suo superchio, e solo a quello arriva
> la man che ubbidisce all'intelletto.

[The greatest artist does not have any concept which a single piece of marble does not itself contain within its excess, though only a hand that obeys the intellect can discover it.][8]

Varchi's interpretation of the poem as Aristotelian in its philosophy has been said to reflect Michelangelo's own views:[9] a great artist liberates the form which pre-exists in his *concetto* from the stone's massy superfluity. Ever since Varchi this poem has consistently been seen as one that is, as it were, on the side of the *concetto* rather than its opposite, the *superchio*: as Saslow puts it 'the essential sculptural act is "taking away" (*levare*) — that is a subtractive process of carving away parts of a stone block to reveal the "preexisting" form within'.[10] The word *superchio* means 'abundance', but Michelangelo uses it to mean 'the redundant bits of stone that have to be chipped away'.[11] We should remember, of course, that Michelangelo had learned about the *superchio*, or the mass of stone that has to be carved away in order to liberate the *concetto* within, the hard way. In April 1506 he had left Rome, and with it a hundred tons of Carrara marble that had been painstakingly imported into the city in order to be carved into the *Prigioni* for the tomb of Julius II.[12] That work, consisting of forty-five life-sized figures, remained pure *concetto* that remained buried until 1545 in *superchio*. Julius had turned his attention to the rebuilding of the Sistine Chapel and failed even to pay the artist for the stone, although he did, of course, later engage Michelangelo as painter to work on his Chapel.

  In 'No ha l'ottimo artista', the *superchio* is where philosophically minded critics, and perhaps also Michelangelo the philosophically minded poet, get themselves into problems. The fineness of this poem lies in its refusal to deliver the philosophy with which it is apparently aligned, in its residual alignment with *superchio*. The singular forms ('solo', 'solo') create an impression that a singular, pre-existent form lurks within the marble, and that a man of skill (again 'l'ottimo artista' is singular) can chisel it forth. But the poem also allows for a contradictory abundance along with and around this single *concetto*. When it says 'Non ha alcuno concetto', it implies that the sculptor can have as many *concetti* in his head as he likes, but however many he has, the stone will have that one and more 'col suo superchio', within its massive bulk. It is the relative pronoun 'quello' — 'that one' — that re-establishes the illusion that a stone's bulk contains only one form. What this part of the poem mainly gives us is a sense of that one form wrestling with other potential forms, and struggling with matter that is both capacious and chaotic. The next part of the poem is one that commentators tend to ignore; neither Barkan, nor Kerrigan, nor Ryan quote past the first four lines, and in this they follow Varchi, who spent the majority of his *lezzione* interpreting those first four lines.[13] As the poem continues, it widens out again the possibility that there are various forms hidden within the stone:

> Il mal ch'io fuggo, e 'l ben ch'io mi prometto,
> in te, donna leggiadra, altera e diva,
> tal si nasconde; e perch'io più non viva,
> contraria ho l'arte al disïato effetto.
>   Amor dunque non ha, né tua beltate
> o durezza o fortuna o gran disdegno,
> del mio mal colpa, o mio destino o sorte;
>   se dentro del tuo cor morte e pietate
> porti in un tempo, e che 'l mio basso ingegno
> non sappia, ardendo, trarne altro che morte.

[The evil which I flee, and the good to which I aspire, gracious, noble and divine lady, lie hidden in you in just this way; but that I may not live hereafter, my art brings about the opposite of what I desire. It is not love, then, nor your beauty, nor harshness, nor fortune, nor haughty disdain that is to be blamed for my evil, nor my destiny nor fate, if within your heart you carry at the same time death and mercy, and my low mind, in its burning, does not know how to draw forth from it anything but death.]

The point here is that the lady, like the massy stone, contains all potentialities, and the poet's art will not pull out of those possibilities the one thing it should find. 'E perch'io più non viva' seems to me to mean both what Ryan's translation says it means ('that I may not live hereafter'), but also it means 'because I am no longer alive' (*perché* functions as both a cause and as an expression of future result). The world of possibilities in the stone chokes both present and future life because the artist cannot realize that elusive one form within the multiplicity.

Michelangelo here is *wanting* poetry to be like sculpture, but he is watching that aesthetic and philosophic aim fail in his verse. With that failure comes a version of Neoplatonism that is surrounded by material blocks to its realization: I cannot chisel the *concetto* from the *superchio*; its abundance chokes. The outcome — the poem — is wonderful; but it is wonderful because it fails when judged against the philosophical framework that it establishes for itself: it fails to make one thing fixed, and it fails to be what philosophical critics want it to be. The poem (could one say?) outwits both the philosophical critic and the artist who made it.

Another poem, this time not a sonnet but a double quatrain poem (often thought of as a stunted sonnet, and often for Michelangelo the form is one for registering the incomplete), tussles over a similar problem. It is 237 in Girardi's edition (again it is pushed up the order in 1623; there it is the fifth poem):

> Molto diletta al gusto intero e sano
> l'opra della prim'arte, che n'assembra
> i volti e gli atti, e con più vive membra,
> di cera o terra o pietra un corp' umano.
>   Se po' 'l tempo ingiurioso, aspro e villano
> la rompe o storce o del tutto dismembra,
> la beltà che prim'era si rimembra,
> e serba a miglior loco il piacer vano.

[To one whose taste is healthy and unspoiled, the work of the first art brings great delight: in wax or clay or stone it makes a likeness for us of the face, the gestures, the whole human body, and indeed gives greater life to the body's

members. If destructive, harsh and boorish time then breaks, distorts, or dis-
members such a work, the beauty which first existed is remembered, and keeps
for a better place the pleasure that here proved vain.]

I admire sculpture this side idolatry. I find it a limitation that in classical sculpture
one's viewpoint is literally where one stands in relation to it, rather than being
formed by the illusion of the artwork. In this poem I hear the verse, its word
order, its structure, and its internal echoes working against sculpture, as though the
medium is resisting what Michelangelo is trying to make it say, and is becoming
almost aggressively more complicated than sculpture. There is a sort of *paragone*
going on within the poem, in which the temporally extended disorderly medium
of verse wins. The energy of a sculpted form comes first, 'i volti e gli atti', then the
medium enters in an ascending triplet of hardness (wax, clay, stone). But then in
'un corp' umano' I hear a corpse, something dying; and by line three the rhymes
are starting nigglingly to make 'dismembra' seem inevitable: the body is breaking
up even before time actually does dismember it, as rhyme pre-empts time. The
argument of the poem is that 'la beltà' remains remembered after time's destruction
— and it registers the kinds of active and creative response to fragments of Roman
statuary discovered in the early sixteenth century;[14] but it leaves us with a heavily
carnal sound emerging from 'rimembra' (memory puts the limbs — *membra* — back
together again) and that last word, 'vano'. Ryan, a close and careful translator, adds
'that here proved' to the simple 'vano' in his version of this poem. He is being
too philosophical in doing this: that is what a Neoplatonic poem would say ('it
was vain passion here, and so it will appear in the afterlife'), but it is not what this
poem says. There is in that word *vano* a nostalgia for the body at the same time
as its renunciation; the disembodied pleasure offered in the future is as *vano* as
the embodied pleasure that precedes it. And there is an extraordinary consonance
between that dissonance and the way that the poem seems to have taken over
from the sculpture, as though the medium, fickle and changeable, of words rather
than stone has won this round of the *paragone* between the rival arts of poetry and
sculpture.

  Now it will be clear from this that I admire Michelangelo's verse for its deep
unhappiness, for setting itself a sculptural goal of permanence and transcendent
beauty, which it fails to realize. But its beauty is the result of something like a
category error. It is the work of a sculptor who wanted to produce works of art
that could be viewed as a single material object, who found himself operating in
a medium that is temporal and labile. Unhappiness can be beautiful sometimes;
but what seems to be enacted in Michelangelo's *Rime*, if they are read through
and in the chronological sequence in which they appear in Girardi's edition, is an
interior philosophy that is trying to carve stillness out of a medium that is at home
with process. The poems written to Vittoria Colonna in about 1545 come closest
to articulating a vision of poetic process as one of carving a *concetto* of beauty (236
describes how she files away the *superchio* from the poet); the poems seem to be
moving one way — to stone, to beauty, to a difficult realization of the *concetto*
within — up until about that date. After that date (if one accepts Girardi's ordering,
which may in part be motivated by a belief that poems of this kind are clustered in

this period) there is much to repent and regret: in their recantations of carnality, and entanglement with earth, the later *Rime* turn against the earlier attempts to see the divine through craftsmanship. And in a sense those later poems acknowledge that the process of attempting to find divine beauty in stone may have been wrong all along. The earlier poems were, perhaps, too optimistic about matter.

If having a philosophy means having a set of beliefs that issue in fixed and pre-dictable modes of behaviour, then it is not clear to me that Shakespeare had a philosophy. Certainly his aesthetics do not really allow for a gradual convergence of the processes of art with the divine; neither do they lead naturally to a single representation of a perfect idea in a fixed form. And in that respect he is about as unlike a Platonist as any writer could be. If we look, for example, at the way he tends to represent metamorphoses in his work, we see a truly profound difference from Michelangelo at the level of aesthetic priorities and practice. Shakespeare likes metamorphoses that are reversible, and in which people do not finally become objects that express what they intrinsically are. Bottom, of course, becomes an ass; but then he changes back into a weaver. Hermione seems a statue; but then she is revealed to be a person. There is no form here (in the Platonic sense) that people finally attempt to realize. This goes along with a profoundly unsculptural aesthetic, and one that is likely to appeal perhaps more to lovers of the written or spoken arts than of the plastic arts. It can also go along with a way of writing that can sometimes suggest that objects of beauty might finally emerge from processes of writing, but that it is the changeful processes of reading that matter more than the eventual emergence of an object for static contemplation. Poets who are imaginatively committed to this form of open-ended metamorphing writing tend to want their readers to keep on living with a changing set of textual signals rather than resting comfortably in a fixed thing — they tend to be uneasy with statues and with final changes of shape. John Kerrigan's essay 'Shakespeare's Sonnets of Art' presents a strong case for the philosophical seriousness of the *Sonnets*, and for regarding them as works which bear comparison with Petrarch and Michelangelo. But the price of this attempt to raise the status of Shakespeare's *Sonnets* can be that of overemphasising their aesthetic completeness and sculptural solidity. Sonnet 24 ('Mine eye hath played the painter and hath stelled | Thy beauty's form in table of my heart') imagines the lover as a painter, and this poem prompts Kerrigan to observe that 'this "eye" has the strength to sketch and apparently engrave ... to depict images in hard matter, like Michelangelo's "arco" [bow used in carving stone]'.[15] This risks presenting the poem as one which seeks to make a thing of beauty which is a joy for ever, rather than as a work which is about the perceptual warpings which a mind can perform when it sees a work of art from an odd angle, and which is primarily focused, not on sculptural engraving, but on the ways in which eyes cannot see hearts. Sonnet 24 ends in a dazzle of perspectives, as lover sees himself in the eyes of the beloved, and then strangely and obliquely sees the sun peeping at the image of the beloved within his own breast:

> Mine eyes have drawn thy shape, and thine for me
> Are windows to my breast, wherethrough the sun
> Delights to peep, to gaze therein on thee.[16]

'Thine' is a characteristically unbalancing note: the Sonnets frequently do not do what you expect them to do with pronouns. Here 'thine' must mean 'thine eyes', rather than 'thy shape'; the syntax refuses symmetry as it moves surprisingly on from artistic representation to the reflection of eye in eye. And that leads it on to present a half-shared, or checked, intimacy here: the sun is the only power which can see into the breast, and even then it only 'peeps' furtively into the image of the beloved which hides within the lover's breast. The reflectiveness of the beloved's eyes reveal not what the beloved thinks or feels, but the lover's own breast, within which only the sun can see. This is not a sonnet of art so much as a sonnet of perceiving, a work caught not in representing representation, but in evoking the endless elusiveness of emotion and thought within.

Shakespeare's *Sonnets* are more than a little in love with how things change, how things change with their viewer, and how they cannot hold one form. It is therefore not surprising that if, as it were, one looks at them from a great height, it is very notable how free they are from the tales from Ovid which issue in final and reversible change or which sculpt emotion into form. Philomela puts in a brief appearance as a nightingale in Sonnet 102, but then rapidly shifts her sex from male to female, as though to insist that there is to be no fixity of form in this so unsculptural medium. The other Ovidian characters sometimes encountered in Elizabethan sonnet sequences — Adonis, Narcissus, Myrrha — find no place at all in Shakespeare's, except as incidental images or occasional buried allusions. This is not just an accident; it is a symptom of the way that sonnet writing for Shakespeare is profoundly counter-objectifying. What I mean by this is that his sonnets do not want to be simply statuesque aesthetic objects. They rather admit a rapid succession of forms and varying stories in such a shower of energy that their readers cannot hold the objects described by the poems, or the poems themselves, as material objects, at all. The aesthetic power of these poems does not come from being in any simple sense *objects* of beauty, or static forms; it comes from their mobility. This makes them not 'comfortable' with their medium — the word 'comfortable' smells too much of leather armchairs and Volvos to be right for Shakespeare. But they are welcoming of it. It also makes them accommodating of shifts and turns in time. A famous example (Sonnet 60) shows this well:

> Like as the waves make towards the pebbled shore,
> So do our minutes hasten to their end,
> Each changing place with that which goes before,
> In sequent toil all forwards do contend.
> Nativity, once in the main of light,
> Crawls to maturity, wherewith being crowned
> Crookèd eclipses 'gainst his glory fight,
> And Time that gave doth now his gift confound.
> Time doth transfix the flourish set on youth,
> And delves the parallels in beauty's brow,
> Feeds on the rarities of nature's truth,
> And nothing stands but for his scythe to mow.
> And yet to times in hope my verse shall stand,
> Praising thy worth, despite his cruel hand.

Much of the poem has been thought out of Ovid's discourse of Pythagoras in Book xv of the *Metamorphoses*, which in Golding's version runs as follows:

> And sith on open sea the winds do blow my sails apace,
> In all the world there is not that that standeth at a stay.
> Things ebb and flow, and every shape is made to pass away.
> The time itself continually is fleeting like a brook.
> For neither brook nor lightsome time can tarry still. But look
> As every wave drives other forth, and that that comes behind
> Both thrusteth and is thrust itself; even so the times by kind
> Do fly and follow both at once and evermore renew. (15.196-203)[17]

Shakespeare's poem has its origins not in a philosophy of change, but in a great passage dramatizing the voice of a philosopher of change, so it is doing its philosophy at several removes by imitating an imitation of it. It relishes the transformation of philosophy into a self-consciously rhetorical performance. There are little buried fragments of the Ovidian source in the poem: the near neologism of 'sequent' surely nods back to 'pariter pariterque sequuntur' (*Metamorphoses*, 15. 183), but the change from verb to adjective keeps that allusion as just a nod, a gesture to a past text that is partly being swept away by the changeability of the environment that the poem describes. And the poem very pointedly does not give us a fixed object of beauty to contemplate. Image follows image: waves are followed by a baby that crawls and grows, but as soon as it is grown it is attacked by time. By lines 9 and 10 there may be an object of fully-grown beauty emerging from the poem, but it is registered only in the moment of its destruction. Time carves away at this grown body, and does not carve creatively as a sculptor would — to get at the *concetto* within — but carves to erode: 'transfix the flourish' suggests both that Time carves the engaging ornaments (flourishes) away from the face of youth by causing pain ('transfix' usually means 'stab' or physically pierce), *and* that Time chips away the flourishing signs of youth on beauty's face. Time makes and mars at once. Eroding and making, those two processes so awkwardly at war in Michelangelo, seem here to be working together. And, to make sure that that a statue of beauty does not emerge from the restless sequent change of the poem, Time's chisel turns into his scythe, and the object of beauty becomes as frail as a flower. 'My verse shall stand' pulls something back — a sense of solidity, of the monumental Horace, or the coda to the *Metamorphoses* and their sense of writing as at least potentially marmoreal — but its consolation is qualified by the repetition of 'stands' from line 12. If the poem 'stands' like a monument, it also participates in the botanical frailty of 'nothing stands but for his scythe to mow'. What comes out of this poem is not an object on which one can focus one's desires, but a sense of the impermanence that follows from trying to represent or retrieve bodies in texts. It is as though we are in a world in which as soon as we make something it is unmade again — as though all we can make are things that are subject to time's power, and all an artist can hope to present readers with is change. What the poem gives us is *not* art as the refinement of the material towards beauty. It does not imprint an experience in a material form or petrify an image of a lover with a Medusa's gaze. Rather, it changes everything so continually that even the material form of the poem seems vulnerably exposed to the processes it describes.

This means that in thinking about poems as aesthetic objects, perhaps part of the pleasure is profoundly unsculptural: part of the pleasure of reading a poem comes from not being able to see an object that one can desire, or of seeing that object change as soon as one focuses on it. That is, poems can register change not as the emergence of a fixed form about which a number of tales and points of view cling, but as a process that repeatedly takes away an object from us and gives us finally a process instead of a thing. This is an obscure point, or obscurely put, perhaps. I shall attempt to clarify what I am saying in relation to another of Shakespeare's *Sonnets*, number 124, a poem, it seems to me, that is very insistent that poems can deal in a kind of mobile aesthetic experience that does not stop in a statue. This particular poem, though, seems almost to have a nostalgia for stone, as though it quite wants the love it describes to enjoy a marmoreally fixed form, but it cannot quite fix it that immovably:

> If my dear love were but the child of state
> It might for Fortune's bastard be unfathered,
> As subject to time's love, or to time's hate,
> Weeds among weeds, or flowers with flowers gathered.
> No, it was builded far from accident,
> It suffers not in smiling pomp, nor falls
> Under the blow of thrallèd discontent,
> Whereto th' inviting time our fashion calls.
> It fears not policy, that heretic,
> Which works on leases of short-numb'red hours,
> But all alone stands hugely politic,
> That it nor grows with heat, nor drowns with show'rs.
> To this I witness call the fools of Time,
> Which die for goodness, who have lived for crime.

Botany and biology, both subject to perishable growth, are here what the poem starts from. As so often in the *Sonnets*, plants and men, growing and dying at once, interweave their lives and their decay into the language of the poem. The 'love' described by this poem is, however, not a person, but something that grows to be powerfully abstract — an 'it' rather than a 'he'. In line 5 'builded' adds something monumental to the scale of the love, suggesting that it is in the process of metamorphosing into a palace or a statue. Still, the poem's 'it' is refused a local habitation and a name: it was 'builded far from *accident*' rather than 'far from Rome' or 'seven miles from Stratford'. It 'stands hugely politic' like a Colossus, but it is a statue or building with no clear face or shape. The love changes its being, becoming child, plant, stone, or animal as occasion suits, and seeks to stand outside historical scheming by separating itself from 'policy' and 'thrallèd discontent'. The love is trying to become what a post-Enlightenment audience might call an 'aesthetic' object, in that it is trying to be simply itself and to separate itself off from its surroundings. It is partly trying to achieve that end by turning into a piece of monumental statuary or masonry. However, it perhaps finally becomes valuable to its reader as an object of enquiry and devotion rather than as a thing of fixed shape. We are left with something that is described as 'hugely politic' rather than 'hugely aesthetic', as though the love-monument-continually-shifting-morphic-thing seeks to recycle and to purify the language used to describe what it is trying to escape from. 'Policy, that heretic' is not simply avoided by the love: by the echo of 'Policy' in 'politic', our beloved object seems to *absorb* rather than simply escape from the nasty political things that it is not.

This is a poem that has not attracted philosophical-minded critics. But historical critics have had a variety of opinions about it. Most of the commentary on it tries to locate it, fix it down, as though it were a monument to a particular time or to particular people. The 'fools of time' have variously been identified with Jesuits, the Earl of Essex, the Gunpowder plotters, or even the Marian Martyrs of the mid-sixteenth century.[18] Fashions for melancholy in the 1590s have been invoked to explain its discontents. The poem simply does not offer enough definite allusion to a particular time for it to be readable simply as a testament to a moment, and seems as a result to be dancing through time. It is describing what an aesthetic object might be when it is freed from the constraints of material being: a thing struggling to be free from its present but knowing it is not free from its present; a love that is striving to become something monumental but is aware of its biological frailty. The poem is trying to be changeable, to open up a space between the immediate circumstances of its production and its future reception by describing something that is mutable and ungraspable. It is a poem that gets its readers running through various shapes or forms for the love it describes, while never fixing itself in a single shape. In this respect it is a poem that relishes the kind of open-ended aesthetic, responsive to shocks and reluctant to seek fixity, that I am advocating. It is thinking about a triumphal statue or palace, but does not wish to fix the love in such an objective form.

Is there a philosophy here? There is certainly something productive of thinking, and produced by thinking; but it is thinking as a process rather than as a result. There also might be something like an aesthetic of mobility: that beauty lies in change rather than chiselling. That goes along with a profound difference from Michelangelo. Shakespeare's sonnets do not aspire to realize a *concetto*. They rest only fleetingly in things, and relish a process of startling, continually revisionary thinking. And in doing that they turn thinking into an aesthetic experience, which moves and rests and moves again, and might make us remember that the root of the word 'aesthetic' lies in the Greek verb 'to perceive'. It is writing by someone who wants percept and concept to be running a continual race against each other, as perception makes itself by an understanding that is then unmade. These *Sonnets* were made by someone who could relish a cloud 'that's dragonish, | A vapour sometime like a bear or lion, | A tower'd citadel, a pendant rock' (*Antony and Cleopatra*, IV. 14. 3–5), or the dislimning of a cloudscape. They were made by someone for whom beauty is a matter of sequentially seeing new forms emergent before you, rather than carving out one pure conceit of the beautiful. And that is why Shakespeare is not Michelangelo, and why too he is better than Michelangelo.

Notes to Chapter 1

1. 'His writing takes the form of philosophical discourse prompted by the particulars of his experience', *The Poetry of Michelangelo*, trans. by James M. Saslow (New Haven and London: Yale University Press, 1991), p. 23. An edition of Michelangelo's verse was planned in 1542-6 but never completed; the first printed edition, in which Michelangelo the younger, the poet's grand-nephew, altered and completed many poems is *Rime; raccolte da Michelangelo suo nipote* (Florence, 1623).

2. Michelangelo Buonarotti, *Rime*, ed. by E. N. Girardi (Bari: Laterza, 1967), nos 76 and 81, derive from drafts originally addressed to a woman, and 246 began as an address to a woman, then was revised for a male addressee (possibly Febodi Poggio), and was then readapted for a female when Michelangelo revised it for publication. On John Benson's modification of masculine pronouns to feminine on three occasions in Shakespeare's Sonnets, see William Shakespeare, *The Sonnets*, ed. by Hyder Edward Rollins (Philadelphia: Lippincott, 1944), 2 vols., ii. 20; and Margreta De Grazia, 'The Scandal of Shakespeare's Sonnets', *Shakespeare Survey* 46 (1993), 35–49.

3. John Kerrigan, 'Between Michelangelo and Petrarch: Shakespeare's Sonnets of Art', in *On Shakespeare and Early Modern Literature: Essays* (Oxford: Oxford University Press, 2001), pp. 23–40.

4. Leonard Barkan, '"Living Sculptures": Ovid, Michelangelo, and *The Winter's Tale*', *English Literary History*, 48 (1981), 639–67; 658.

5. Michelangelo Buonarotti, *Rime*. For arguments against Girardi's ordering of the poems, see Guglielmo Gorni, 'Casi di filologia cinquecentesca: Tasso, Molza, Da Porto, Michelangelo', in *Per Cesare Bozzetti: Studi di letteratura e filologia italiana, a cura di Siimone Albonico, Andrea Comboni, Giorgio Panizza, Claudio Vela* (Milan: Mondadori, 1996), pp.425–42.

6. Glauco Cambon, *Michelangelo's Poetry: Fury of Form* (Princeton, N.J.: Princeton University Press, 1985), p. 77: 'Michelangelo sees the world *sub specie sculpturae*.'

7. Benedetto Varchi, *Due lezzione, nella prima delle quali si dichiara un sonetto di M. Michelangelo Buonarroti* (Florence, 1549). See David Summers, *Michelangelo and the Language of Art* (Princeton: Princeton University Press, 1981), pp. 203–33.

8. Texts and Translation from Michelangelo Buonarroti, *The Poems*, trans. by Christopher Ryan (London: Dent, 1996).

9. Summers, *Michelangelo and the Language of Art*, p. 203 supposes that 'it is ... likely that Varchi went to the trouble of gathering Michelangelo's opinions before publishing them for all the world and Michelangelo to see.' Michelangelo's letter to Luca Martini in March 1547 may indicate that the artist did not consider himself worthy of the praise Varchi lavished on him; alternatively it might hint that Varchi's philosophising went beyond what the poet thought he was saying: 'And as I perceive from his words of praise that I appear to be what I am not, I beg you to express my acknowledgements to him in terms befitting such devotion, affection and courtesy.' Michelangelo Buonarroti, *The Letters of Michelangelo, translated from the Original Tuscan*, trans. by E. H. Ramsden, 2 vols (London: Peter Owen, 1963), II.72.

10. *The Poetry of Michelangelo*, p. 35.

11. Summers, *Michelangelo and the Language of Art*, p. 219, notes it can also mean the overflowing bounty of love and grace from his mistress. Love finally directs the hand of the artist to fashion the *concetto* into material form.

12. 'So great was the quantity of the blocks of marble that, when they were spread out on the piazza, they made other people marvel and rejoiced the pope, who conferred such great and boundless favours on Michelangelo that, when he had begun to work, he would go more and more often all the way to his house to see him.' Ascanio Condivi, *The Life of Michelangelo*, trans. by Alice Sedgwick Wohl (London: Phaidon, 1976), p. 30. See further Ross King, *Michelangelo and the Pope's Ceiling* (London: Pimlico, 2003), pp. 7–10, 282–5, 289.

13. Christopher Ryan, in *The Poetry of Michelangelo: An Introduction* (London Athlone, 1998), says blithely: 'Perhaps the opening image may serve as a reminder of the entire poem' (p. 150). Robert John Clements, in *The Poetry of Michelangelo* (London: Peter Owen, 1966), glosses the philosophy thus: 'Although the notion corresponds exactly to the Platonic view of art, it

reflects also the notion held by some Aristotelians of the Renaissance that (in the words of a contemporary Latin version of the *Metaphysics*): "In lapide est forma Mercurii in potentia"' (p. 65).

14. See Leonard Barkan, *Unearthing the Past: Archaeology and Aesthetics in the Making of Renaissance Culture* (New Haven and London: Yale University Press, 1999).

15. Kerrigan, *On Shakespeare and Early Modern Literature: Essays*, p. 37.

16. Texts from William Shakespeare, *The Complete Poems and Sonnets*, ed. by Colin Burrow (Oxford: Oxford University Press, 2002).

17. *Ovid's Metamorphoses Translated by Arthur Golding*, ed. by Madeleine Forey (London, 2002), pp. 440-1. 'Et quoniam magno feror aequore plenaque ventis | vela dedi: nihil est toto, quod perstet, in orbe. | cuncta fluunt, omnisque vagans formatur imago; | ipsa quoque adsiduo labuntur tempora motu, | non secus ac flumen; neque enim consistere flumen | nec levis hora potest: sed ut unda inpellitur unda | urgeturque prior veniente urgetque priorem, | tempora sic fugiunt pariter pariterque sequuntur | et nova sunt semper; nam quod fuit ante, relictum est, | fitque, quod haud fuerat, momentaque cuncta novantur.' (*Metamorphoses* 15.178-185).

18. See Rollins, ed., *The Sonnets*, I. 313–14.

CHAPTER 2

The Opinion of Pythagoras

Gabriel Josipovici

CLOWN	What is the opinion of Pythagoras concerning wild fowl?
MALVOLIO	That the soul of our grandam might happily inhabit a bird.
CLOWN	What thinks't thou of his opinion?
MALVOLIO	I think nobly of the soul and no way approve of his opinion.
CLOWN	Fare thee well. Remain thou still in darkness.

(Twelfth Night, IV. 2. 51–55)

It used to be a quarrel between philosophers and poets: Plato against Homer, St Augustine against Virgil and Ovid. But in recent times it has become a quarrel within philosophy itself: Kierkegaard against Hegel, Nietzsche against Plato, Nussbaum against Kant. What, in their different ways, Kierkegaard and the rest are saying is that there is an unbridgeable gap between life and thought, one that philosophy has always refused to recognize, has even, in effect, conspired to hide. Works of art, though, can help us grasp the nature of that difference, and so help us in our philosophical task of understanding ourselves and the world. To read Chapter 22 of Genesis, to listen to Mozart's *Don Giovanni*, to enter the world of Dante's *Commedia* or Mahler's *Kindertotenlieder*, these philosophers say, is to understand something about our condition that philosophers have not simply failed to recognize, but have been instrumental in occluding.

Does the example of Shakespeare have anything to offer this debate? In this essay I shall look at *Twelfth Night*, the play that shows up, perhaps more so than any other he wrote, the difficulty discursive thought has when faced with a work of art. This is not an arcane subject. It simply results from the fact that we, as viewers or readers of the play, experience far more than our critical or philosophical vocabulary seems able to articulate. The problem, in other words, does not come with our immediate responses (the plural is important) to the play, but with our attempts, after the fact, to make sense of that experience to ourselves and to others. The task of criticism, as I see it (and as A. D. Nuttall, I am sure, does too), is to break down that critical response, to articulate better what we all feel as we watch or read.

One way to set about the task is to see what Shakespeare made of his source, which here, as so often, is well known and, at first sight, rather faithfully followed. Barnabe Rich's *Of Apolonius and Silla*, published in 1581, is itself distantly derived from *Gl'Inganni* ('The Deceived'), a Plautine comedy produced in Siena in 1531. Rich begins with a generalization: that all love is folly, although there is such a thing as 'reasonable love', namely, love that depends on 'desert' or reciprocity. To illustrate this he tells a tale, which he carefully anchors in time and place: 'During the time that the famous city of Constantinople remained in the hands of the Christians, amongst many other noblemen that kept their abiding in that flourishing city, there was one whose name was Apolonius'.[1] This 'Duke', having led a valiant band against the Turk and triumphed, on returning home is shipwrecked on the island of Cyprus, where he is welcomed by its ruler, who has two children, a son Silvio and a daughter Silla. Silla falls in love with Apolonius, who, more interested in war than in women, ignores her. This only feeds her passion, so that when Apolonius sails for home, she, disguising herself as a serving maid, and with a faithful servant whom she now calls her brother, follows him. The captain of the ship takes a fancy to her; she manages to keep him at bay for a while, but then, as he is about to have his way with her (the Mills & Boon phrase is appropriate to the tone of this tale), a storm wrecks the ship and washes her up on dry land.

Disguising herself now as a man and taking her brother's name Silvio, she makes her way to Constantinople, where she enters the service of her beloved Apolonius, who in the meanwhile has begun to pay court to a noble lady called Julina: 'So my Duke,' says Rich,

> who in all the time that he remained in the Isle of Cyprus had no skill at all in the art of love, although it were more than half preferred to him, was now become a scholar in Love's school, and had already learned his first lesson, that is, to speak pitifully, to look ruthfully, to promise largely, to serve diligently, and to please carefully; now he was learning his second lesson, that is, to reward liberally, to give bountifully, to present willingly, to write lovingly.

To this end he sends 'his man' Silvio, in whom he now 'reposed his only confidence', 'to go between him and his lady'.

The lady, of course, falls in love with the go-between. Meanwhile, the real Silvio comes to Constantinople in search of his sister, happens upon Julina, and willingly responds to her advances. Invited to her house for supper, he is easily persuaded to remain for the night. '[T]hey passed the night in such joy and contentation', says Rich — and the laddish wink and nudge is typical —

> as might in the convenient time be wished for; but only that Julina, feeling too much of some one dish above the rest, received a surfeit, whereof she could not be cured in forty weeks after, a natural inclination in all women which are subject to longing and want the reason to use a moderation in their diet.

The next day Silvio goes his way, leaving the city in search of his sister. Julina, however, now tells the insistent Duke that she is betrothed to someone else, none other, in fact, than his serving man. Confronted by the furious Duke, Silla/Silvio protests 'his' innocence, utterly baffled by the accusation. In a scene worthy of Kleist, but of course rendered here wholly without the metaphysical anxiety characteristic of the German writer, Rich tells us that,

> hearing an oath sworn so divinely that he had gotten a woman with child, [Silvio] was like to believe that it had been true in very deed; but remembering his own impediment, thought it impossible that he should commit such an act.

By now 'he' has succeeded in turning both the Duke and Julina against him, and finally has no option but to prove the truth of his denial:

> And herewith loosing his garments down to his stomach, showed Julina his breasts and pretty teats, surmounting far the whiteness of snow itself, saying: Lo, madam, behold here the party whom you have challenged to be the father of your child; see, I am a woman.

The Duke, when apprised of this, and moved by Silla's subsequent story of her love and devotion to him, proposes to her and is accepted. The real Silvio, hearing of the strange events that have occurred in Constantinople, returns to find his sister, whereupon everything is made clear and he and Julina also marry. '[T]hus Silvio, having attained a noble wife, and Silla, his sister, her desired husband, they passed the residue of their days with such delight as those that have accomplished the perfection of their felicities.'

I have recounted the plot of this insignificant romance at length because it is important to get the feel of it, so as to grasp both what Shakespeare saw in it and how vastly it differs from *Twelfth Night*. Rich is clearly interested solely in the confusions of the plot and in the titillation afforded by the false accusation. On the way, he provides Shakespeare with the scaffolding for his play and a hint as to how he might treat the Duke. But it is important to recognize that Shakespeare has little interest in what is at the centre of Rich's story — the final revelation. It is also important to grasp that Shakespeare has not simply taken over the story and added a comic subplot. Already, in *A Midsummer Night's Dream*, he had hit on how to integrate main plot and subplot, nobles and commoners, but in that play the distance between the two was still retained. Here they are fused into a seamless whole. In fact it is a mistake, in my opinion, even to speak of a subplot. The play, after all, is not called *Of Orsino and Viola* but *Twelfth Night or What You Will*. Critics have always been aware of the fact that this hints that we are dealing with a carnival play, a festive comedy; but even C. L. Barber, the author of a superlative book on Shakespeare's festive comedy, fails, when it comes to this play, to rise to the challenge of its title.

The key thing to note is how, as we watch or read, we find ourselves embarked on a roller-coaster ride whose effect is quite different from that of reading Rich's romance. In Rich there is a single narrative voice, ironic, titillating, omnipresent. By contrast, in Shakespeare the register changes abruptly in every new scene, and sometimes within a scene itself. We might be tempted to say that this is simply the difference between a play and a work of prose fiction. But that is not so. A play by Racine or Ibsen affects us quite differently, and even Shakespeare's other plays, whether in the genres of comedy, tragedy, or romance, do not change register quite as violently as *Twelfth Night*.

One way of approaching the characterization within the play is to say that some characters, notably Orsino, Olivia, Sir Toby, and Sir Andrew, have only one register, while others, notably Viola and Feste, seem protean, and that this is a clue as to their characters and how we respond to them. The following is a quotation from Muriel Spark's early novel *The Bachelors* (1960):

'I shall never believe he's guilty', she said. 'Never.'

Ronald thought: 'How that second, histrionic "never" diminishes her — how it debases this striking girl to a commonplace.'

It shows how we reveal ourselves in what we say — sometimes in the content, but more often in the manner of our saying. Barnabe Rich, who does not on the whole go in for dialogue, presents us with flat characters, characters who are given certain traits and then put through the hoops of the plot. In Rich, the Duke and Silla are both equally examples of 'unreasonable love', a love that is hopeless since it is not based on reciprocity. In Shakespeare the gulf between Orsino and Viola is enormous. Orsino is the embodiment of self-love:

> If music be the food of love, play on,
> Give *me* excess of it (*Twelfth Night*, I. I. 1–2)

is his first sentence, and his last words are:

> Cesario, come
> For so you shall be while you are a man,
> But when in other habits you are seen,
> *Orsino*'s mistress and *his fancy's* queen.
> (V. I. 387–90; my emphases)

Viola, by contrast, has little thought for herself. When we meet her she is concerned only for her brother; later, constrained by her disguise, she can speak her thoughts only by indirection.

Orsino, locked in himself, will never surprise us or himself. Viola, by contrast, does both, and she does this because Shakespeare, like Mozart, has the resources to change gear suddenly:

> VIOLA   If I did love you in my master's flame,
>   With such a suff'ring, such a deadly life,
>   In your denial I would find no sense;
>   I would not understand it.
> OLIVIA   Why, what would you?
> VIOLA   Make me a willow cabin at your gate
>   And call upon my soul within the house;
>   Write loyal cantons of contemned love
>   And sing them loud even in the dead of night;
>   Hallo your name to the reverberate hills
>   And make the babbling gossip of the air
>   Cry out 'Olivia!' O, you should not rest
>   Between the elements of air and earth
>   But you should pity me. (I. 5. 265–77)

This is quite as rhetorical as 'If music be the food of love, play on, | Give me excess of it'. But it knows itself to be rhetoric, much as Mozart's Cherubino in *The Marriage of Figaro* knows when he sings 'Voi che sapete', whereas neither Orsino nor the Count is in control of his words, since both imagine they come 'from the heart'. Paradoxically, then, it is precisely because both Viola and Cherubino consciously 'sing' that we feel their sensibility vibrating in their words. The act of singing liberates them, allows them to discover who they are. Olivia clearly picks this up as much as the audience does, for here is surely the moment at which she falls in love with Cesario.

But varieties of rhetoric are not all that Shakespeare has at his command. Everything Viola does and says conveys her character to us; we respond to her not as to a set of characteristics, but as we respond to someone we meet and who makes a powerful impression upon us. For, as A. D. Nuttall said in a splendid early essay, to try to turn a Shakespeare play into a late story by Henry James is to bark up the wrong tree.[2] Her willingness to trust to time — 'O Time, thou must untangle this, not I' (II. 2. 40) — in contrast to the desperation of Orsino, Olivia, and Malvolio to reach their different goals as soon as possible; her feminine fear of physical danger; her secret love, which she will not allow to interfere with her duty to her master: all this conveys a sense of her quality, of a balanced recognition of the complexities of the world and the fact that it rarely fits in with our desires, which gives her a kind of wisdom and moral authority.

There is more. (With Shakespeare, as with Mozart, there is always more.) Is it a coincidence that two of the most charged images of classical mythology employed in the play come in the first and second scenes? In the first, Orsino dramatizes himself as Actaeon, the hunter turned prey, allegorizing the story in good Renaissance fashion to make it describe his inner state:

> O, when my eyes did see Olivia first,
> Methought she purged the air of pestilence,
> That instant was I turned into a hart,
> And my desires, like fell and cruel hounds,
> E'er since pursue me. (I. 1. 20–24)

In the second scene the captain describes to Viola how he saw her brother escape the shipwreck:

> When you, and those poor number saved with you,
> Hung on our driving boat, I saw your brother,
> Most provident in peril, bind himself
> (Courage and hope both teaching him the practice)
> To a strong mast that lived upon the sea;
> Where, like Arion on the dolphin's back,
> I saw him hold acquaintance with the waves
> So long as I could see. (I. 2. 10–17)

This is Sebastian, not Viola; but in Shakespeare, as in Mozart, the 'music' has the habit of migrating from character to character. The brother and sister, as alike as two peas, and both miraculous survivors of the cruel sea, are in a sense one, and what holds for Sebastian will hold for Viola. Where Orsino is torn by his inner demons, the brother and sister have the spiritual and bodily agility to breast the seas; they survive because they know how to 'hold acqaintance' with both inner and outer waves. With the image of Arion, as with that of Actaeon, Shakespeare gives us the tools, so to speak, to make sense of what we are witnessing, gives us one key to character. Of course, it would not work if he then failed to provide us with characters to embody those traits. But neither Shakespeare nor Mozart fail us in such circumstances; their grasp of character is as sure as their grasp of verbal and musical form.

If scenes 1 and 2 give us very different registers, then scene 3 continues the process. After 'If music be the food of love' (I. I. I) and 'What country, friends, is this?' (I. 2. I), we have 'What a plague means my niece to take the death of her brother thus? I am sure care's an enemy to life' (I. 3. 1–3). This is as great a leap in register as we find in the shocking transition from *Combray* to *Un amour de Swann* in the first volume of Proust's *A la recherche du temps perdu*. Yet Toby and Andrew are as limited in their view of the festive spirit as Orsino is in his view of love; all of them are blind to the springs of their own characters, are locked in a particular and limited view of who they are and what they want out of life.

But what of Feste? Talk of 'Shakespeare's clowns and fools' does us a disservice. We fail to see the particular *kind* of fool Feste is, why we respond to him with much more sympathy than we do, for instance, to Launce in *The Two Gentlemen of Verona* or Lancelot Gobbo in *The Merchant of Venice*. 'Well, God give them wisdom that have it, and those that are fools, let them use their talents' (I. 5. 14–15), he tells Maria, who is quite capable of sparring with him. Indeed, the exchanges between the two of them remind us of how the ideal conversation should perhaps be conducted. Georg Simmel, in his 1910 essay on 'Sociability', helps us out. According to Rosalind Krauss, in an essay on Picasso's 1912–13 collages,

> Simmel wants to project a social space in which signs circulate endlessly as weightless fragments of repartee, stripped of practical content — that of information, argument, business — taking as their content, instead, the functional play of conversation itself, conversation whose playfulness is expressed by the speed and lightness with which its object changes from moment to moment, giving its topics an interchangeable, accidental character.[3]

It is in this way, Simmel says, that conversation is 'the purest and most sublimated form of mutuality among all sociological phenomena', since conversation 'becomes the most adequate fulfilment of a relation which is, so to speak, nothing but relationship, in which even that which is otherwise the pure form of interaction is its own self-sufficient content'.[4] Conversation of this kind is, in fact, a way of being Arion in a social setting, and it contrasts markedly with the attitude to dialogue of so many of the other characters. Olivia, for example, has too great a sense of herself and her worth to show the suppleness required. Feste teases her:

> Those wits that think they have thee do very oft
> prove fools, and I that am sure I lack thee may
> pass for a wise man. For what says Quinapalus?
> 'Better a witty fool than a foolish wit.'
> God bless thee, lady! (I. 5. 28–32)

She tries half-heartedly to play the conversation game: 'Take the fool away' (33). And Feste responds: 'Do you hear, fellows? Take away the lady' (34–35); whereupon she brings the conversation to a close by reasserting her authority, her social superiority: 'Go to, y'are a dry fool! I'll no more of you. Besides, you grow dishonest' (36–37).

Like Viola, Feste's strength comes from the fact that he expects nothing from life. Hence he has the suppleness to respond, both verbally and physically, to any situation; those, on the other hand, who are always expecting life to give them what they want are helpless before its blows. Like Viola too, he has a role, a mask, that helps him be himself. And also like Viola, Feste can change register. We shall see below how he does so in the song that concludes the play. But first let us glance at a non-musical change of register by referring back to the passage of dialogue quoted at the beginning of this essay. Here we see Feste as the curate Sir Topas in catechetical mode. The exchange is funny for many reasons. One is the surrrealist fantasy of the dialogue, the way the history of philosophy is translated into the demotic: the Clown does not ask Malvolio's opinion of Pythagoras's view of the transmigration of souls. What he says is: 'What is the opinion of Pythagoras concerning wild fowl?'. Malvolio does not bat an eyelid, but answers his question in the appropriate idiom: 'That the soul of our grandam might happily inhabit a fowl'. And for once it is Feste who brings the dialogue to an end with the authoritarian: 'Fare thee well. Remain thou still in darkness'.

Of course, one source of our laughter depends on the fact that neither participant, if we are being realistic, could possibly say what he does. We are in the world of Ionesco's *Bald Prima Donna* or the browbeating catechism in Pinter's *The Birthday Party*, where the real dialogue is going on between the playwright and the audience. But with art many things can go on at the same time, and here the balance of our sympathies shifts towards Malvolio precisely because he can match Feste sentence for sentence. That is why Malvolio is such a troubling figure. Unlike Olivia and Orsino, Toby and Andrew, he has a kind of integrity; and, like Shylock, he acquires, through his ordeal, a disquieting dignity.

As I have said, the *raison d'être* for Rich's narrative is the revelation at the end, which sorts out the confusions and makes possible the happy ending. But *anagnorisis* in the great artists is rarely so simple. As Terence Cave points out at the start of his monumental study of the subject,

> In Aristotle's definition, anagnorisis brings about a shift from ignorance to knowledge; it is the moment at which the characters understand their predicament fully for the first time, the moment that resolves a sequence of unexplained and often implausible occurrences; it makes the world (and the text) intelligible. Yet it is also a shift *into* the implausible: the secret unfolded lies beyond the realm of common experience; the truth discovered is 'marvellous' (*thaumaston*, to use Aristotle's term), the truth of fabulous myth or legend. Anagnorisis links the recovery of knowledge with a disquieting sense, when the trap is sprung, that the commonly accepted co-ordinates of knowledge have gone awry.[5]

As Cave recognizes, *Twelfth Night* fits well into his argument. When, in Act v, Sebastian and Viola appear on stage together for the first time, Orsino speaks for all the characters when he says: 'One face, one voice, one habit, and two persons — | A natural perspective, that is and is not' (v. 1. 216–17). Although commentators are still arguing about the precise meaning of 'a natural perspective', everyone agrees that even in the most derivative plays, such as *A Comedy of Errors*, a supernatural frisson attaches to the moment of anagnorisis: we know that it is the result of plot manipulation, yet nevertheless it seems — Shakespeare makes it seem — the result of some supernatural force at work in the doings of men. My own feeling is that we should not make too much of it here. Shakespeare, as so often in his work, is slipping in something that does not quite belong, that will be fully recognized and developed only in the later romances, especially *The Winter's Tale*, where very great care is taken to liken the revelation to 'an old tale' in order to mine its mythic potential. Shakespeare, for example, reserves his 'If this were played upon a stage now, I could condemn it as an improbable fiction' merely for Malvolio making a fool of himself before Olivia, in stark contrast to the appearance of this topos at the climax of *The Winter's Tale*. In *Twelfth Night*, on the other hand, little is made of Orsino's remark, and the exchange between brother and sister leading to their certainty that they are who they are is treated as comedy, and perfunctory comedy at that. In fact, in this play Shakespeare seems to be at pains to *defuse* the sense of climax and revelation, to show us that little of significance is resolved or crucially changed: Viola remains dressed in her man's attire till the end; Malvolio leaves the scene with his curse on the assembled company, profoundly hurt by the treatment he has received and in no mood to forgive and change; and we do not feel that Orsino and Olivia are altered in any deep way. In fact every character remains much as he or she was at the start.

The play ends too not with an image of change but with one of sameness:

> When that I was and a little tiny boy,
> With hey, ho, the wind and the rain,
> A foolish thing was but a toy,
> For the rain it raineth every day.
>
> But when I came to man's estate,
> With hey, ho, the wind and the rain,
> 'Gainst knaves and thieves men shut their gate
> For the rain it raineth every day.
> […]
> A great while ago the world begun,
> Hey, ho, the wind and the rain;
> But that's all one, our play is done,
> And we'll strive to please you every day.

How are we to explain this? Why does Shakespeare make use of a plot that seems to derive its sole *raison d'être* from its denouement, if he is not only not concerned with denouement but seems to wish actively to subvert it? And how are we to explain the fact that the viewer and the reader do feel that he or she has been through something transformative; that, having paid attention, he or she is not quite the same person at the end as at the start?

Of course, this is the opposite of what happens to the reader of Rich, who is only confirmed in his attitudes and prejudices. But I think that Shakespeare, by denying us the comfort of closure, has made us aware that from the first moment we have been not so much following a story as exploring a field; and that when the field is completely covered — the space saturated, as it were — the play must end, but end in such a way that we are once more returned to the field.

By talking about 'field', I want to try and bring out the way this play is both a unity and not a unity; that although it certainly does not feel unresolved, it somehow also feels open. I think that what Bakhtin has to say about Dostoevsky may be of help here:

> What unfolds in his works is not a multitude of characters and fates in a simple
> objective world, illuminated by a single authorial consciousness; rather, *a*
> *plurality of consciousnesses, with equal rights and each with its own world*, combine but
> are not merged in the unity of the event.[6]

Bakhtin goes on to show that although sympathetic and sensitive critics of
Dostoevsky recognize that his work is multivoiced and polychronic, they invariably
grant this only to take it back again. Either they take the polyphony present in the
novels as a reflection of the multivoicedness found in the real world and thus transfer
explanations directly from the plane of the novel to the plane of reality. Or they
'remonologize Dostoevsky's dialogical invention by identifying it with an entity
called a reflection of the dialogical progression of the idea.' 'Each novel', Bakhtin
goes on, would then 'form a completed philosophical whole, structured according
to the dialectical method. We would have in the best instance a philosophical novel,
a novel with an idea [...] [Or] in the worst instance we would have philosophy in
the form of a novel.'

In reality, says Bakhtin, in Dostoevsky every thought is 'accompanied by a
continual sideways glance at another person'; every thought 'senses itself from the
beginning to be a *rejoinder* in an unfinalized dialogue'. 'Such thought', Bakhtin
splendidly says, 'is not impelled towards a well-rounded, finalized, systematically
monologic whole. It lives a tense life in the borders of someone else's thought.'
Note that the critic has himself to fight for his insight, to find the words to express
what he experiences as he reads his chosen author. With that last sentence Bakhtin
triumphantly scores.

In Feste's last song, which ends *Twelfth Night*, we are given access to the world as
beyond the understanding of any single person, a world multiple yet unchanging;
transformed, held in suspension by the voice, the rhythm, the music. Like a
firework it rises up into the sky and then spreads, as it falls, over the whole of the
play we have just experienced.

Shakespeare and Mozart convey in their mature stage works, and especially in
Twelfth Night and *The Marriage of Figaro*, a joy quite alien to Dostoevsky, and, indeed,
to almost any other art known to me. I think that joy has to do with the fact that
the spectator or reader is led into areas of experience he or she has always known
existed but could never, by themselves, have arrived at. It reminds me of what Virginia
Woolf said about Proust: that, reading him you become, for a while, more intelligent,
more sensitive, more aware than you ever are in your normal life; that you do not
feel as though you have been transformed, but simply made to realize your possibilities, the possibilities of human life, more fully and with more intensity than ever
before or after, until, that is, you start reading Proust — or Shakespeare —
once again.

Notes to Chapter 2

This essay also appears in Gabriel Josipovici, *The Singer on the Shore: Essays 1991–2004* (Carcanet,
2006), 60–77. I am grateful to Carcanet Press Ltd for allowing me to reprint this essay here.

1. All references to Rich's *Apolonius and Silla* follow the text provided in the Signet Classic edition
   of *Twelfth Night*, ed. by Herschel Baker (New York, 1965).

2. A. D. Nuttall, 'The Argument about Shakespeare's Characters', *Critical Quarterly*, 7 (1965), 107–20.
3. Rosalind Krauss, 'The Circulation of the Sign', in *The Picasso Papers* (London: Thames & Hudson, 1998), pp. 25–85 (pp. 63–64). Krauss's essay stimulated much of the thought behind the present chapter.
4. Georg Simmel, 'Sociability', in *On Individuality and Social Forms* (Chicago: Chicago University Press, 1971), pp. 127–40.
5. Terence Cave, *Recognitions: A Study in Poetics* (Oxford: Clarendon Press, 1988), pp. 1–2.
6. This and subsequent quotations from Bakhtin are taken from Krauss, pp. 43–48.

CHAPTER 3

Shakespeare *Philosophus*

Charles Martindale

My question in this essay is whether there is any critical mileage in figuring
Shakespeare as a philosopher. No self-respecting analytic philosopher of the old
school would countenance such an idea, clearly. And yet. We know from Plato's
Ion and other sources that many Greeks saw Homer as a sort of *uomo universale*, an
expert in almost everything (what Homer doesn't know isn't knowledge) — in
seafaring, for example, or the arts of war; interpreters allegorized Homer's poems as
repositories of encoded wisdom, 'physical' and philosophical. We may laugh at such
pretensions, even if we no longer bother to condemn them with Platonic passion
('the old quarrel'). Yet for the committed bardolater, among whom I emphatically
count myself, Shakespeare's works constitute a kind of sacred book, endlessly
repaying meditation, and part of a world of belief and cognition (A. D. Nuttall once
told me that he was prepared to take chastity seriously only because Shakespeare
had done so). Such a reader will constantly play off her encounter with the world
against her encounter with Shakespeare's plays. Accommodation, appropriation
— these once fashionable terms in no way give a sufficient sense of the potentially
dialogic and sometimes fraught character of such a process. It is not so much, or not
only, that Shakespeare imitates, effectively, an extra-literary world; rather, for the
lover of Shakespeare the experience of the world, including the experience of other
people, is significantly informed by his works. This is presumably partly what Harold
Bloom means by his somewhat melodramatic claim that Shakespeare invented
human nature (in *The Western Canon* he quotes Emerson's comment: 'His mind is
the horizon beyond which, at present, we do not see'[1]). For Bloom, Shakespeare
displays, *inter alia*, 'cognitive acuity'.[2] It is amusing to see Terry Eagleton, whom
we would think of as one of Bloom's opponents, saying, rumbustiously, something
not dissimilar:

> Though conclusive evidence is hard to come by, it is difficult to read Shakespeare
> without feeling that he was almost certainly familiar with the writings of
> Hegel, Marx, Nietzsche, Freud, Wittgenstein, and Derrida. Perhaps this is
> simply to say that though there are many ways in which we have thankfully
> left this conservative patriarch behind, there are other ways in which we have
> yet to catch up with him.[3]

This may be simple to say, but the implications are surely considerable, and perhaps
unexpected: we do not feel quite this way about Ben Jonson or even Milton, hugely
intelligent though they were both.

But Shakespeare the philosopher, that is surely a step, or two, too far. Would we not do better to remember the stern injunction that G. E. Moore borrowed from Bishop Butler as his epigraph for *Principia ethica*: 'Everything is what it is and not another thing'?[4] Well! those thinkers whom for convenient shorthand we term 'postmodernists' make their living by arguing that identity of this kind — I was going to say does not exist. For them, categories such as 'literature' and 'philosophy' are always ripe for deconstruction. Richard Rorty, for example, in an essay on Derrida, suggests that philosophy is simply another kind of writing, with its own (contingent) history and conventions.[5] He enlists the authority of the later Wittgenstein for the view that philosophy, like language, is 'just a set of indefinitely expansible social practices, not a bounded whole whose periphery might be "shown"'.[6] (is 'just' quite the *mot juste*). And in general Rorty likes to argue that philosophers should abandon their search for progressive truth along with the metaphysics and ontology that underpins it, and become more like literary or cultural critics. This is a (much) more relaxed version of the position espoused, with pain and passion, by Nietzsche[7] — Nietzsche and water, one might even say.

I strongly suspect that Rorty is not among A. D. Nuttall's favourite philosophers. Certainly, one can find oneself irritated at times by a sort of cheerful anti-intellectualism in Rorty's over-ready dismissal of many traditional philosophical topics and problems, in particular any that savour of foundationalism or metaphysics. (Wittgenstein, a philosopher whom Nuttall clearly reveres, also makes moves of this kind, arguing, for example, that philosophy leaves everything as it is, but no one could accuse him of undue cheerfulness in so doing.) There is something too complacent in Rorty's conservative liberalism or liberal conservativism; for example, he assumes that, when it comes to ethical and political arrangements, we in the liberal West are, as it were, at the end of history.[8] At one astonishing moment in *Contingency, Irony, and Solidarity* he writes that 'the sciences are no longer the most interesting or promising or exciting area of culture', recommending that we switch attention to 'the areas which *are* at the forefront of culture, those which excite the imagination of the young, namely, art and utopian politics'.[9] The young, in my experience, are as likely to be interested in sex and rock music, not perhaps without reason, but it is hardly our job positively to encourage them in that. And one problem for the arts and humanities may be that they are still in 1900 in their understanding of matters scientific. At such moments Rorty reminds one of the sophists as characterized by Plato in Walter Pater's sense of it:

> And here the charge of Socrates against those professional teachers of the art of rhetoric comes to be, that, with much superficial aptitude in the conduct of the matter, they neither reach, nor put others in the way of reaching, that intellectual ground of things (of the consciousness of love for instance, when they are to open their lips, and presumably their souls, about that) in true contact with which alone can there be a real mastery in dealing with them. That you yourself must have an inward, carefully ascertained, measured, instituted hold over anything you are to convey with any real power to others, is the truth which the Platonic Socrates, in strongly convinced words, always reasonable about it, formulates, in opposition to the Sophists' impudently avowed theory and practice of the *superficial*, as such. Well! we all always need to be set on our guard against theories which flatter the natural indolence of our minds.[10]

Nuttall himself defends disciplinary boundaries, while always willing to cross them. In the preface to his superb collection *The Stoic in Love*, he tells us that the 'most elegant' of the Yale Deconstructionists (I take this to be have been Geoffrey Hartman) reproached him with the words: 'You always prefer philosophy to Theory' (Nuttall adds, 'I cannot be sure that those were the exact words (though I am fairly sure that I "heard" the capital "T" of "Theory")'). This is a charge that Nuttall was, and is, more than happy to accept:

> The accredited areas of negotiation between disciplines — aesthetics, say, or sociology or literary theory — have always seemed less exciting to me than the business of discovering unlooked-for connections between fundamentally autonomous modes of discourse. I would rather link Sterne with Hume than Macherey with Miller.[11]

At the University of Sussex, where Nuttall then taught, there were admirable course units called 'Topics', jointly taught by representatives of two different subjects, History and Philosophy (say), or English and Religious Studies; and Nuttall preferred the meaning of 'interdisciplinary' as 'linking two disciplines' to 'operating in a field intermediate between two disciplines'. Rorty obviously would demur at the phrase 'fundamentally autonomous disciplines', as indeed would I.[12] At any rate, one can point out — and Nuttall would, I am sure, not disagree — that disciplinary arrangements are contingent, have a (changing and contested) history, can always be reorganized, often should be (Analytic Philosophy is to my mind a case in point, for reasons that will become clear in due course). Still, at any one historical time and place different disciplines may be said to exist, and have their own distinct modes of operation.

In view of such considerations, is it merely perverse to call Shakespeare a philosopher? The issue is partly about the mode of writing currently deemed appropriate for philosophy. Analytic philosophers, in my experience, like to say that they have a particular commitment to clarity — as though the rest of us devote our scholarly lives to deliberate obfuscation. Responding to Bryan Magee's claim that the sentences in her novels are 'opaque' ('rich in connotation, allusion, ambiguity') while in her philosophical writings they are 'transparent [...] saying only one thing at a time', Iris Murdoch comments:

> I am tempted to say that there is an ideal philosophical style which has a special unambiguous plainness and hardness about it, an austere unselfish candid style. A philosopher must try to explain exactly what he means and avoid rhetoric and idle decoration.[13]

It is difficult to quarrel with the virtues of clarity, but, as Martha Nussbaum observes, 'there might be other ways of being precise, other conceptions of lucidity and completeness that might be held to be more appropriate for ethical thought' than 'the conventional style of Anglo-American philosophical prose' (that is, 'a style correct, scientific, abstract, hygienically pallid', a style that is 'a kind of all-purpose solvent in which philosophical issues of any kind at all could be efficiently disentangled, any and all conclusions neatly disengaged').[14]

Christopher Rowe, a classical philosopher in the analytic tradition, goes so far as to argue that, while polyvalence or even undecidability might be valuable in a literary text, in philosophy of a 'pure' kind (Aristotle, for example) there is no room for more than a single correct interpretation; if more than one is found, that is due to a failure on the part of the commentators or a momentary lapse in clarity on that of the author. Any proliferation of meaning would be a distraction: 'with an Aristotelian text, polyvalence might even reduce its value'.[15] It is perhaps for reasons such as these that Nuttall insists that, for all the philosophical subtlety of his reading of it, *Timon of Athens* is not a philosophical treatise but a play.[16] Well! Plato's works are not treatises but dramatic dialogues, Lucretius's *De rerum natura* is not a treatise but an epic poem, and one of exceptional poetic richness and power.

Plato is certainly a problematic author for someone with Rowe's conception of philosophy. One solution is to say that Plato is not really a philosopher; and yet philosophy has been described as 'footnotes to Plato' (indeed to deny Plato the title is to turn your back on history altogether). Another is to separate the 'literary' bits of the dialogues from the 'philosophical'. This was the approach of Ian Crombie, who accordingly entitled his monumental work on Plato *An Examination of Plato's Doctrines*.[17] But once again I say that Plato wrote dialogues, not doctrines. I agree with Walter Pater that Plato, rather than providing a system of propositions, 'forms a temper'.[18] This formulation provokes a remarkable outburst from Richard Jenkyns, who accuses Pater of solipsism and intellectual frivolity,[19] yet it is consistent enough with the dialectical form of Plato's work. In their more plodding way today's interpreters of Plato are gradually catching up with Pater, recognizing that you should not just abstract pure doctrine from a Platonic text, rather you have to read the whole dialogue. The song of the cicadas may be as important to the meaning of the *Phaedrus* as more technical sections. One might argue that a certain kind of speculative thinking requires a more open-ended, dramatic form than a treatise could provide, that complex ideas require complex forms. There is also the issue of the different kinds of audience a philosopher might wish to address. Analytic philosophers can easily be accused of talking only to themselves. For me, one of the great scandals of the modern academy is the way that Anglo-American philosophers have, in the main, ceased all constructive engagement with the rest of the humanities, employing a special hermetic style (full of equations and virile language) and rejecting most continental philosophy as so much 'poetic bullshit' (the words are those of a colleague from a philosophy department). Unsurprisingly, the hungry sheep look up and are not fed, and the way is left clear for 'Theory'.

Plato is a master of metaphor, and, at least since Aristotle's *Poetics*, metaphor (which involves making new connections) has often been seen as a privileged site of the poetic. Metaphor disrupts existing categories, and assertion of its omnipresence fits well with a postmodern deconstructing of boundaries. Yet we do not need to go the whole way with Nietzsche and say that all language is metaphorical, to suggest that philosophers can no more do without metaphor than the rest of us (even if the metaphors are in practice often 'dead' metaphors, as when, say, something is said to 'illuminate' a topic). Recent work on metaphor, for example that of Lakoff and his associates, tends to underline its cognitive function.[20] Metaphors, on this model, complicate meaning while constituting a potential source of philosophic insight. For all her insistence on the plain style in philosophy, Iris Murdoch understood their philosophical importance: 'Metaphors are not merely peripheral decorations or even useful models, they are fundamental forms of our awareness of our condition'.[21]

Style, or form, cannot of itself determine whether something is a work of philosophy or not. Analytic philosophers not only prescribe a particular mode of writing (one that excludes from their consideration Nietzsche, Heidegger, Derrida, and many others), they also read past texts in a different way from literary critics.[22] Responsible literary reading has, to my thinking, to be attentive to form and content together (however precisely we define them); the distinctiveness of the writing cannot simply be ignored. In *The Stoic in Love* Nuttall observes:

> New moments are hard to find in the history of ideas. Even Hume, I learn, followed unwittingly in the footsteps of Nicolas of Autrecourt. But the world of style renews itself miraculously over and over again. The parallels between Donne's ideas and those of his predecessors have been meticulously traced. But no one had ever written like *that* before.[23]

Pater I know is a critic Nuttall dislikes, but in *Plato and Platonism* he makes the same point. What is new in Plato is only 'the life-giving principle of cohesion', the form; 'the seemingly new is old also, a palimpsest, a tapestry of which the actual threads have served before'. And Pater concludes, provocatively, that 'in the creation of philosophical literature, as in all other products of art, *form*, in the full signification of that word, is everything, and the mere matter is nothing'.[24] This has considerable implications for the interpreter. Following the comparative failure of his *Treatise of Human Nature*, the later Hume employed a relaxed essay form, marked by an 'idiom of innocent amiability', for his philosophical works.[25] As Fred Parker points out, to read these just as if they were treatises is to make a mistake, indeed a *philosophical* mistake, since Hume's change of direction 'bears on the relation between philosophizing and living': 'Hume has some stringent reasons for thinking that arguments in philosophy are *only* arguments in philosophy unless and until their relation to experience finds expression'.[26] Hume's scepticism is thus as much a matter of 'style' as of 'doctrine', or rather the two cannot be disentangled.

The point holds, in my view, even when we are dealing with philosophy of the Aristotelian type in the form of a treatise. Take this sentence from an essay by Paul Guyer:

> Kant supposes that the pleasure in all beauty is intersubjectively valid — that is, that under ideal conditions any beautiful object ought to please all observers of it — and thus that a beautiful work of art, as the product of intentional activity, aims to produce an intersubjectively valid response and judgment; thus, a work of art aims to be a rule for all, something that all ought to find beautiful or otherwise appropriately satisfying.[27]

Guyer is perhaps the leading Anglophone authority on *The Critique of Judgement*, I am only an enthusiastic amateur; but nonetheless I say that this whole formulation seems to me most profoundly un-Kantian. Part of the problem is the word 'intersubjective', which is obviously not a Kantian word. The judgement of taste is not intersubjective; rather, it is, paradoxically, fully subjective and at the same time universal, in that it demands, though of course does not necessarily receive, the agreement of all (*The Critique of Judgement*, §7). 'Intersubjective' brings with it all sorts of characteristic intellectual baggage that may serve only to impede a fruitful understanding of Kant's arguments. Likewise, saying that 'all ought to find' a work of art beautiful sounds like a categorical imperative, which belongs to ethics not aesthetics in Kant's scheme. And Guyer seems also to be ignoring Kant's Copernican shift from the character of objects to judging subjects (Kant consequently never talks about what the artwork 'does' in anything like this way). What is happening here is that the text is being reconfigured to make sense according to a quite different logical scheme. As a result, the reading seems to me manipulative, disrespectful to Kant's words — *with the consequences that we are not encouraged to think differently*. Kant is assimilated to contemporary aesthetic positions rather than being allowed to challenge them. Now, of course, all interpretation involves translation, configuration in new words, but, in Guyer's breezy way of things, there is no recognition of the considerable problems of so doing. Such readings of past texts seem to me decadent (and not in the sense of Pater's 'comely decadence'), as the translation is made into the supposed language of eternity. Analytic philosophers, indeed, often say that they are dealing with ideas and truth, not texts and history — but, like the rest of us, in practice they have to make do (if that is how you want to see it) with texts that are historically embedded. The result is the modern equivalent of the *Ovide moralisé*, another late and decadent body of interpretation, in the form of ahistorical allegory, a radical appropriation in which the words of the text and their usual connotations so to say disappear almost completely.

An instance of the results we get from these different kinds of reading is amusingly described by J. G. A. Pocock:

> in 1976 I attended two conferences marking the bicentennial of the death of Hume, and at each it was evident that for the philosophers present, to say 'Hume says' meant using the word 'Hume' as little more than a trigger that set in motion various language games they desired to play. They did not care or need to know about the historical David Hume who was born in 1711 and died in 1776 and performed many acts of various kinds between those dates. For the historians present, the word *Hume* was a historical expression denoting the life and actions of that individual, and they used it only to introduce historical statements. The difference between the two usages was so absolute that it caused no confusion, only noncommunication. Things might have been worse if it had been supposed that the philosophers were talking history, or that the historians were negating the statements of the philosophers.[28]

Or they might have been better. For Pocock, apparently, once we recognize that different language games are being played, no real harm is done. My feeling is that a great deal of harm is done (non-communication is not an especially desirable state, and in practice there will be confusion), and that we are unlikely to get adequate accounts of Hume until either the skills apportioned to historians, philosophers, and literary critics are united in a single interpreter, or the various disciplines start listening to each other. I agree with the current Archbishop of Canterbury that, if we are to be good readers (he is speaking of theologians, but the same applies to philosophers, or literary critics), we need to jettison 'the mythology of an essential core of truth from which accidental material and external forms may be stripped away', and learn to read patiently, diachronically, and with due attention to the surface and the form, 'a production of meaning in the only mode available for material and temporal creatures'.[29] Literary, scriptural, and philosophical thought can all best be approached as diachronic *process*.

Two philosophers in the Anglo-American tradition who have explored, productively, interfaces between philosophy and literature are Stanley Cavell and Martha Nussbaum. Cavell, a Harvard philosopher, has written *Disowning Knowledge* specifically on Shakespeare, while *The Claims of Reason* explores the sceptical (post-Wittgensteinian) position that underpins it. Cavell rightly points out that if Shakespeare is indeed 'the burden of the name of the greatest writer in the language, the creature of the greatest ordering of English', it is reasonable to suppose that his writing might engage 'the depth of the philosophical preoccupations of his culture'.[30] Certain doubts, however, arise when Shakespeare's philosophy of life turns out to be suspiciously close to Cavell's own. Cavell is indeed aware of the danger of using Shakespeare to illustrate philosophical positions already known, and seeks for a genuinely open and exploratory dialogue in which literature interrogates philosophy as well as vice versa, but his attempt to describe the relationship of his two books reveals, in its vacillations, a certain residual unease: 'I claim my text on Shakespeare's text as an enactment of (illustration of? evidence for? instance of? model for? image of? allegory of?) the theoretical movement of *The Claim of Reason* at large'.[31] Well, which of these, one feels entitled to ask?

I have similar reservations about some of Martha Nussbaum's philosophical readings of literary texts. In *The Fragility of Goodness* she advances two persuasive reasons why 'works of literature are an indispensable part of a philosophical inquiry', at least within ethics. First, literature provides richer, more nuanced material for analysis than the rather jejune and slanted *examples* typically employed within philosophical discourse. Secondly, moral enquiry involves the emotions as well as the intellect, something that is readily exhibited in novels and plays concerned with moral issues.[32] But Nussbaum's thoughtful account of the decision of Aeschylus's Agamemnon to sacrifice his daughter (one heavily influenced by ideas of 'moral luck' espoused by contemporary philosophers like Bernard Williams) gives little sense of the intransigent alterity of the world of the play, little sense of the fearfulness of the divine beings at work behind the action. Nussbaum's particular brand of liberalism sits rather more easily, perhaps, with the novels of Henry James, which she mines for improving philosophical insights in *Love's Knowledge*; but in elaborating these she can be said to miss the force of T. S. Eliot's observation that James 'had a mind so fine that no idea could violate it'.[33] Moreover, it is not always clear whether, in Nussbaum's view, literature is a useful ancillary to philosophy, or whether literature on occasion performs real philosophical work.

In *The Therapy of Desire* Nussbaum offers one of the best readings currently available of a play by Seneca. In the Renaissance many thought that the same author was not responsible for both the plays and the philosophical works; rather, there were two Senecas, Seneca *philosophus* and Seneca *tragicus*. Modern scholars are happy in general with a single author, but a (somewhat tedious) debate continues about whether the plays exhibit Stoic doctrine (as when, in *Thyestes*, the Stoic commonplace 'Only a wise man is king' generates the splendid scene in which Thyestes accepts from Atreus the conventional symbols of kingship) or are simply rhetorical exercises (whatever quite that means). Nussbaum reads Seneca's *Medea* as a significant contribution to philosophical thinking, one that shows, in opposition to a more Aristotelian conception, that love is 'a dangerous hole in the self, through which it is almost impossible that the world will not strike a painful and debilitating blow'.[34] Not only does the play make vivid and immediate ideas set out in the prose works, but in some respects it takes those ideas further, making unexpected connections between them. But even here there are times when Nussbaum skirts the banality of a newspaper's agony pages:

> His tragedies parade before us a series of loyal loving wives who are abandoned in middle age by opportunistic husbands — usually for a younger woman, sometimes for money, always with callous disregard for the wife's long years of service. The wife's intense, unabated love then produces an upheaval that leads to tragedy [...] Seneca forces us to see that it is the one who loves properly, loyally, the one who really understands what it is to value a commitment to an external object, who will be most derailed by a loss.[35]

Such a formulation surely misses the quiddity of Seneca's tragic world, one in which ordinary external social relationships of this kind give place before an extreme of interiority in which the mind becomes its own place, and frequently a place of lonely damnation. (Shakespeare reproduces the effect in the overheated and claustrophobic rhetoric of some of Macbeth's speeches.) But, of course, such shortcomings do not mean that philosophers should not be encouraged to work with literature, only that, like all of us, they must strive to read (in the full sense argued for in this essay) with more precision.

   Millicent Bell is surely right to say of Shakespeare that while 'his plays are never allegorical — they never dramatize directly the contest of ideas — yet in them ideas contend from line to line in the richest language the stage has ever known'.[36] Indeed, as with Plato's dialogues, it is the fact that the characters are *not* allegorical that makes the plays philosophically so compelling. For example, *Measure for Measure* is Shakespeare's play about justice, but the characters are truly themselves, never a mere excuse to make an extrinsic ethical point. Pater, in his superb essay of 1874 (the best of his Shakespeare essays), subsequently included in *Appreciations* (1889), makes this the basis of his 'art for art's sake' reading: the play takes us from justice in the abstract to what Pater calls the *poetical justice* suggested by the play's title. 'Justice' is an important notion for Pater's aesthetics (in his essay 'Style' he argues that good style is about choosing, with attentive precision, the exact single word that alone will convey the sense, while his title *Appreciations* may have been chosen because of its etymological derivation from the Christian Latin word *appretio*, 'to set at a price', to put a true value on something[37]). In Pater's account of it, aesthetics and ethics fuse in Shakespeare's vision of justice (it may be relevant that 'measure' is also a word used about verse):

> The action of the play, like the action of life itself for the keener observer, develops in us the conception of this poetical justice, and the yearning to realise it, the true justice of which Angelo knows nothing, because it lies for the most

part beyond the limits of any acknowledged law. The idea of justice involves the idea of rights. But at bottom rights are equivalent to that which really is, to facts; and the recognition of his rights therefore, the justice he requires of our hands, or our thoughts, is the recognition of that which the person, in his inmost nature, really is; and as sympathy alone can discover that which really is in matters of feeling and thought, true justice is in its essence a finer knowledge though love [...] It is for this finer justice, a justice based on a more delicate *appreciation* of the true conditions of men and things, a true respect of persons in our estimate of actions, that the people in *Measure for Measure* cry out as they pass before us; and as the poetry of the play is full of the peculiarities of Shakespeare's poetry, so in its ethics it is an epitome of Shakespeare's moral judgements [...] It is not always that poetry can be the exponent of morality; but it is this aspect of morals which it represents most naturally, for this true justice is dependent on just those finer *appreciations* which poetry cultivates in us the power of making, those peculiar valuations of action and its effect which poetry actually requires.[38]

If that is right (as I think it is), it an insight that can justly be called 'philosophical', and it anticipates more modern approaches to ethics by, among others, Michael Oakshott:

A morality is neither a system of general principles nor a code of rules, but a vernacular language. General principles and even rules may be elicited from it, but (like other languages) it is not the creation of grammarians; it is made by speakers. What has to be learned in a moral education is not a theorem such as that good conduct is acting fairly or being charitable, nor is it a rule such as 'always tell the truth', but how to speak the language intelligently [...] It is not a device for formulating judgments about conduct or for solving so-called moral problems, but a practice in terms of which to think, to choose, to act, and to utter.[39]

The difference is that, while Oakshott has to content himself with articulating general principles, Shakespeare shows us a vernacular language, and thereby, perhaps, teaches us, if we will let him, to think, to choose, to act, and, above all else, to utter.

In Shakespeare's mature plays, auditors, or at any rate readers, were certainly expected to follow complex exchanges of ideas.[40] An example is the argument between Polixenes and Perdita about planting gillyvors (*The Winter's Tale*, IV. 4. 70–108), which touches on a number of topics in the nature–culture debate. Polixenes neatly 'deconstructs' the distinction between nature and art, but at the cost of making nature a concept too all-embracing to be of much philosophical use; Perdita gamefully defends the undeconstructed distinction by an appeal to common sense and common linguistic usage, and to her own values and experience of life. Of course, the significance of the exchange is massively complicated by the dramatic situation (Perdita is a supposed shepherdess courted by a prince), not all of which is fully clear to the characters at this point.[41] A pastoral interlude is not necessarily the first place one would look for such philosophical sophistication, but it is a significant element here and elsewhere in this play. A number of plays written in the early 1600s, including *Measure for Measure* (probably first performed in 1604), are especially and throughout very much explorations of ideas (much more demandingly so indeed than anything by, say, Shaw or Brecht). For example, *Timon of Athens* (usually dated around 1604) takes as its subject matter the issue of giving and receiving gifts, a traditional topic of ethical enquiry, treated at length by Seneca in the seven books of his *De beneficiis*; for Nuttall, the play is 'a powerful philosophic meditation [...] on the word *grace*'.[42] *Troilus and Cressida* (registered in 1603) is even more concerned with the clash of idea on idea; the play could be regarded as an exploration of Troilus's sceptical question 'What's aught but as 'tis valued?' (II. 2. 52) — 'in no other Shakespearean play is there so much theory'.[43] It is uncertain whether *Troilus* was ever performed in Shakespeare's lifetime (the prefatory epistle to the 1609 Quarto claims that it was 'never staled with the stage, never clapper-clawed with the palms of the vulgar'), so perhaps in its present form it is a play for readers. Certainly, it would be hard to find a scene more philosophically demanding than the exchange between Ulysses and Achilles about reputation, value, self-knowledge, and time (III. 3). This is, as Barbara Bowen observes, both the play's 'most post-modern moment' and its 'most clearly *early* modern scene', one that is 'in dialogue with an intellectual tradition that includes Plato, Cusanus, Alberti, Erasmus, Montaigne, Machiavelli and a series of English writers in the *nosce teipsum* [...] school'.[44] To persuade Achilles to re-enter the battle, Ulysses starts by pointing out that reputation is relational and not merely intrinsic; but, as often happens in this play, ideas are then pushed to a point when a sceptical abyss starts to open up. In the event — and this is another feature of *Troilus* — the arguments, although they fully engross the characters at that moment, have no effect whatever on what subsequently happens.

Shakespeare, then, is interested in philosophical ideas, and so are a number of his characters. As my final example I shall bring forward a figure more improbable perhaps even than Shakespeare the philosopher, and that is Cleopatra the philosopher. Defeated politically and in battle, and deprived of her lover, Cleopatra prepares carefully for her victory over time and her near-apotheosis ('I have | Immortal longings in me', V. 2. 280–81), by means of a suicide that is explicitly Roman and Stoic. The certainty of death brings her a clarity of mind now that the rest of life has been cleared away (does Shakespeare always associate philosophy with stasis?). Previously associated, like the Egypt which she embodies, with the imagery of water, earth, and slime, Cleopatra now becomes all 'air and fire' (V. 2. 288). The philosophical pieces are carefully put in place, the indifference to fortune, the espousal of constancy.[45] Cleopatra says:

> My desolation does begin to make
> A better life. 'Tis paltry to be Caesar:
> Not being Fortune, he's but Fortune's knave,
> A minister of her will. And it is great
> To do that thing that ends all other deeds,
> Which shackles accidents and bolts up change. (V. 2. 1–6)

> He brings me liberty.
> My resolution's placed, and I have nothing
> Of woman in me. Now from head to foot
> I am marble-constant; now the fleeting moon
> No planet is of mine. (V. 2. 237–41)

Cleopatra's 'liberty' is both political, freedom from arbitrary tyranny (at the heart of Roman Republican elite identity), and part of her new-found philosophical stance, the wider freedom of mind that the Stoic sage alone can achieve. To the Stoic, virtue, not success, was what counted, and, as with Cato at Utica, the supreme test of virtuous constancy was how one faced death.

In an early scene Cleopatra says of Antony: 'He was disposed to mirth; but on the sudden | A Roman thought hath struck him' (I. 2. 82–83). A Roman thought is presumably one that is austere, responsible, virtuous, soldierly — but perhaps also pompous and boring. In my experience, audiences laugh in sympathy with Cleopatra at this point rather than being shocked by her levity; her irony implies that Roman virtue may not anyway be all that it seems. In this 'Roman play' (where Shakespeare imagines, with consistent plausibility, a society with cultural practices, values, and ethos in important respects different from his own[46]) we may ask who plays best the part of the Roman, and how this relates to those who attend to the play in the theatre. The dialectic of ancient and modern is triangulated by the further internal contrast between Rome and Egypt (the Romans are foreigners if seen from an Egyptian perspective). In the event Cleopatra plays the Roman in the guise of the Stoic hero. Actors, despised for their low social status, and the fact that they performed a variety of roles and thus might seem very signifiers of inconstancy, nonetheless aroused the interest of both Cicero and Seneca. Acting raises questions about the problem of personhood, inner and outer. The word *persona* in Latin can refer to an actor's mask and a role in a play, but also, via the idea of playing a part in life, to personality and personhood. Cicero sees constancy as 'the consistent playing of an appropriate role';[47] within Stoicism the sage plays for himself, in a radical internalization of traditional heroic virtue. In the final scene Cleopatra not only plays her new part with supreme conviction, she even reminds us that her part will in turn be acted on the stage (by a young male), an extraordinarily audacious metatheatrical turn that serves only to deepen the sense of the reality of what we see. Shakespeare must have been sure indeed of his boy actor to take such a risk at such a moment:

> The quick comedians
> Extemporally will stage us, and present
> Our Alexandrian revels. Antony
> Shall be brought drunken forth, and I shall see
> Some squeaking Cleopatra boy my greatness
> In the posture of a whore. (V. 2. 216–21)

Cleopatra becomes her role as Stoic suicide, and, in her version of performativity, her role becomes her. In a recent performance at Stratford, Frances de la Tour played Cleopatra as ageing, nervous, and always on the verge of hysteria. This is quite foreign to my sense of the play, and in particular of its last act. Cleopatra does not rush into suicide (an un-Stoic procedure), but only after delay and when it becomes clear that there is no honourable alternative takes her life serenely, with careful planning and execution, 'a lass unparalleled'. It is all very different from the premature, messy, or botched suicides of the Roman men, Cassius, Brutus, and Antony.

Cleopatra's suicide is like that of a virtuous Roman man, not a virtuous Roman woman, the latter represented by Octavia in this play. (True, Cleopatra modifies such a suicide, seeking to avoid unnecessary pain and using for her death stroke the sinuous and erotically charged snakes of Nile instead of the rigid Roman sword — changes that serve to make her death the more transfiguring, as it brings into focus much of the loveliest imagery of the play.) All this relates to a current issue in gender politics. Judith Butler has argued forcibly that gender is not merely a construct of culture but something we perform; we put on different gender roles as we might change our clothes, and this increases 'the performative possibilities for proliferating gender configurations outside the restricting frames of masculinist domination and compulsory heterosexuality'.[48] This is particularly evident in the case of cross-dressing; 'drag', indeed, becomes normative within Butler's account. At the conclusion of this play a young male actor performs Cleopatra performing her latest gender role as Roman suicide. This final scene might then be found one of gender liberation (Wilde's *The Portrait of Mr W. H.* provides a brilliant gloss on all this). True, Cleopatra has to die, but then that is the common lot of us all, whether Caesar or beggar. At least she has fully enjoyed life, and dies not only well in an ethical sense but flawlessly in an aesthetic one:

> 'All you have to do to see the Medusa is look her in the face', wrote Hélène Cixous. 'She isn't deadly. She is beautiful and she laughs.' So too this imaginary Cleopatra turns out, when viewed steadily, to be benign. True, she is a woman endowed anomalously with masculine power. True, she is an exotic outsider who calls into question the cultural dominance of the West. True, she is a sensualist celebrating the mortal sins of the flesh. Those who envisage her with minds cleared of sexual anxiety and racial arrogance, those who (unlike Baudelaire) can contemplate their own hearts and bodies without disgust, those who can lay aside a yearning for the ease and clarity of a moral sphere in which one side is always right and the other wrong, may see her beauty, and hear her tolerant laughter.[49]

Cleopatra defends her vision of life in an exchange with Dolabella of very considerable philosophical subtlety, which must be quoted at length:

CLEOPATRA   I dreamt there was an emperor Antony.
O, such another sleep, that I might see
But such another man!
DOLABELLA   If it might please ye —
CLEOPATRA   His face was as the heavens, and therein stuck
A sun and moon, which kept their course and lighted
The little O of the earth.
DOLABELLA   Most sovereign creature —
CLEOPATRA   His legs bestrid the ocean; his reared arm
Crested the world; his voice was propertied
As all the tuned spheres, and that to friends;
But when he meant to quail and shake the orb,
He was as rattling thunder. For his bounty
There was no winter in't; an autumn 'twas
That grew the more by reaping. His delights
Were dolphin-like; they showed his back above

	The elements they lived in. In his livery
	Walked crowns and crownets; realms and islands were
	As plates dropped from his pocket.
DOLABELLA	Cleopatra —
CLEOPATRA	Think you there was or might be such a man
	As this I dreamt of?
DOLABELLA	Gentle madam, no.
CLEOPATRA	You lie, up to the hearing of the gods.
	But if there be or ever were one such,
	It's past the size of dreaming. Nature wants stuff
	To vie strange forms with fancy, yet to imagine
	An Antony were nature's piece 'gainst fancy,
	Condemning shadows quite. (V. 2. 76–100)

In these dizzyingly ontological speculations Cleopatra argues that her imaginings about Antony soar far beyond anything that could be purely imaginary. The lines echo, and go beyond, one of the paradoxical hyperboles Enobarbus uses to describe Cleopatra herself: 'O'er picturing that Venus where we see | The fancy outwork nature' (II. 2. 200–01). In idealizing art-theory, paintings could be praised for surpassing nature; here, in a breathtakingly quick leap, Enobarbus says that Cleopatra in her own nature outdoes the outdoing splendours of the picturing imagination. To mount this philosophical argument, Shakespeare and Cleopatra employ metaphor and dialogue, both of which allow for an extension of meaning, the possibility of having something two or more ways, rather than the reducing of complexity to a single, unambiguous meaning in the manner of an analytic philosopher. Cleopatra's rebuttal of Dolabella is, as it happens, close to Anselm's ontological proof of the existence of God. A. D. Nuttall, who points this out, comments that Shakespeare at this moment has 'seen through seeing through things'.[50] Arguments of this kind make the position of the sceptic, or scoptic, who — like Iago or Edmund or Thersites — regards love, imagination, beauty, religious belief as mere mystifications to be exposed, look distinctly jejune. In *The Silver Chair* C. S. Lewis (another favourite of Nuttall's) puts an analogous point into the mouth of Puddleglum when, in a sequence that recalls the allegory of the cave from Plato's *Republic* and Spenser's Cave of Mammon, the Green Witch, in a version of reductive materialism, tries to persuade him and his friends that the things of the Underland where they are confined are the only reality:

> Suppose we *have* only dreamed, or made up, all those things — trees and grass and sun and moon and stars and Aslan himself. Suppose we have. Then all I can say is that, in that case, the made-up things seem a good deal more important than the real ones. Suppose this black pit of a kingdom of yours *is* the only world. Well, it strikes me as a pretty poor one. And that's a funny thing, when you come to think of it. We're just babies making up a game, if you're right. But four babies playing a game can make a play-world which licks your real world hollow. That's why I'm going to stand by the play-world. I'm on Aslan's side even if there isn't any Aslan to lead it. I'm going to live as like a Narnian as I can even if there isn't any Narnia.[51]

One would rather be wrong about the nature of things with Puddleglum, Cleopatra, and Keats ('The Imagination may be compared to Adam's dream — he awoke and

found it truth') than right — were they in the event to be proved so — with the
Green Witch or Richard Dawkins. One would at least have imagined something
richer and stranger than an ultimately disappointing 'reality'. Graham Bradshaw
supposes that in this elaborately dialectical play Dolabella's 'regretfully firm' reply,
'Gentle madam, no', must be accorded its full weight, as showing, in a pre-Freudian
way, that Cleopatra's dream is (just?) a compensatory fantasy.[52] No doubt all good
moralists will agree, but the emotional logic of this final scene convinces me far
otherwise.[53]

Shakespeare, then, is interested in philosophy, as he is in so many other things,
but, *pace* some of his interpreters, he does not 'have a philosophy' so to say (in the
sense that, for example, Ben Jonson advances a fairly monolithic ethical position).
For all his interest in Montaigne, I cannot even see him as a *consistent* radical sceptic
of a Montaignian kind, as does Graham Bradshaw, who treats all the mature plays
as perspectivist in character (as we have seen, Stanley Cavell has a somewhat similar
view).[54] *Troilus* has moved from being (unjustly) one of the least admired and
performed plays in the canon to become for many the quintessential Shakespearean
play. This, surely, is somewhat perverse: we should rather celebrate Shakespeare
for his variousness, his many-minded character. I therefore reiterate my previously
expressed view that Shakespeare, though wonderfully well read and intelligent, is
also something of an opportunist. And I likewise reiterate that this opportunism
is a strength, part of that comprehensiveness of which Dr Johnson spoke, which
makes his plays, as he argues, readable as 'compositions of a distinct kind; exhibiting
the real state of sublunary nature'.[55] T. S. Eliot thought Shakespeare's lack of a
coherent intellectual system a weakness in comparison with Dante's Thomism; I
argue that it is one source of his 'universality', his widespread transhistorical appeal,
his negative capability, his secular temper. All this is consistent with the general
character of Shakespeare's art. He is no Sophocles or Racine: one can re-order or
omit scenes in all of the plays without reducing them to chaos. Many of his best
readers, even those who have thought him the greatest poet of all, have noted this
unevenness, this comparative lack of concern with formal perfection. Even his
best work contains inconsistencies in the quality of writing; in that sense he is a
poet of the Longinian sublime, who soars above the rest but occasionally crashes
(and sometimes gets in a flat). George Steiner, invoking Wittgenstein, goes so far
as to complain of 'prolixity and repetitiveness' (a charge some might think better
directed at Steiner's own writing): 'the intrusion of vulgarity and waste motion
into even the major texts (how many of us have ever seen a production of *Othello*
which includes the wretched exchanges with the Clown?)'.[56] I myself share a
common (post)-Romantic preference for this kind of writing over something more
'classically' correct and consistent, but, to quote Bishop Butler again, everything is
what it is and not another thing. Shakespeare's interpreters, less fleet of foot than he,
are constantly pressing the plays too far in the direction of a consistently patterned
and narrow purposefulness.

Shakespeare, a linguistic Autolycus, is attuned to different 'language games', as
we have come to call them. Leonard Barkan calls him 'a kind of language sponge,
a picker-up of specialized lexicons from every conceivable stratum of his society'.[57]
Always interested in ideas, he is always also attentive to the questions of who

uses them, in what circumstances, to what ends, with what degree of conviction. He shows how men and women are involved in a multitude of influences and attitudes, and play many parts, which brings us back to acting and a fascination with a constantly changing world, under a fleeting moon. He knows that ideas, even or especially good ideas, do not necessarily, or even often, carry the day. In chapter 18 of Johnson's *Rasselas*, the Stoic philosopher, with evident sincerity, recommends others by means of 'invulnerable patience' to show 'indifference on those modes or accidents to which the vulgar give the names of good and evil'; but, confronted by the death of his daughter, he finds it simply insupportable: 'What comfort [...] can truth and reason afford me?'.[58] Shakespeare's plays are full of such moments when ideas conflict with personality or events, usually handled with rather more subtlety. In *Troilus*, when the master politician Ulysses presents complex philosophical arguments about degree or value, he is always manipulating others, and, ironically, his manipulations are, in practice, not particularly successful. The early modern ethical imagination was nourished by carefully selected fragments of ancient and modern moral wisdom culled in commonplace books and the like. In *Lear* such ethical nuggets ('ripeness is all', and so forth) are duly deployed but tested to destruction, perhaps to be found in contradiction with each other or with the logic of events.[59] Whether all this makes Shakespeare a philosopher will, of course, depend on one's notion of the nature and function of philosophy; but it certainly means that the attentive reader of Shakespeare has to be prepared to think, and to think hard.

Notes to Chapter 3

It was a great honour to be invited to speak at the colloquium marking Tony Nuttall's 'retirement'; ADN has had a great influence on my thinking, and career, since shared (glory) days at Sussex, in a faraway (intellectual) world. I am also most grateful to David Hopkins, Duncan Kennedy, Liz Prettejohn, and Tony Taylor for help with this essay.

1. Harold Bloom, *The Western Canon: The Books and School of the Ages* (London: Papermac, 1995), p. 179; see also his *Shakespeare: The Invention of the Human* (London: Fourth Estate, 1999).

2. *The Western Canon*, p. 46.

3. Quoted by Barbara E. Bowen, *Gender in the Theater of War: Shakespeare's Troilus and Cressida* (New York and London: Garland Science, 1993), p. 87.

4. See Iris Murdoch, *Existentialists and Mystics: Writings on Philosophy and Literature*, ed. by Peter Conradi (London: Chatto & Windus, 1997), p. 164.

5. Richard Rorty, 'Philosophy as a Kind of Writing: An Essay on Derrida', *New Literary History*, 10 (1978), 141–60.

6. Richard Rorty, 'Wittgenstein, Heidegger, and Language', in *Essays on Heidegger and Others: Philosophical Papers Volume 2* (Cambridge: Cambridge University Press, 1991), pp. 50–65 (p. 57).

7. See Alexander Nehamas, *Nietzsche: Life as Literature* (Cambridge, MA, and London: Harvard University Press, 1985): 'Nietzsche [...] looks at the world in general as if it were a sort of artwork; in particular, he looks at it as if it were a literary text' (p. 3).

8. See, for example, Richard Rorty, *Contingency, Irony, and Solidarity* (Cambridge: Cambridge University Press, 1989), pp. 63–64.

9. *Contingency*, p. 52.

10. Walter Pater, *Plato and Platonism: A Series of Lectures* (London: Macmillan, 1893), p. 104. Pater writes here with unaccustomed vehemence, perhaps as one accused himself of sophistry in his engagement with the young.

11. A. D. Nuttall, *The Stoic in Love: Selected Essays on Literature and Ideas* (New York: Barnes & Noble, 1989), p. vii.

12. See, for example, Rorty, *Contingency*, p. 76: 'The metaphysicians [...] think it essential to get the genres right — to order texts by reference to a previously determined grid, a grid which, whatever else it does, will at least make a clear distinction between knowledge claims and other claims upon our attention. The ironist, by contrast, would like to avoid cooking the books she reads by using *any* such grid (although, with ironic resignation, she realizes that she can hardly help doing so).'

13. Murdoch, p. 4.

14. Martha C. Nussbaum, *Love's Knowledge: Essays on Philosophy and Literature* (New York: Oxford University Press, 1990), p. 19.

15. Christopher Rowe, 'Handling a Philosophical Text', in *The Classical Commentary: Histories, Practices, Theory*, ed. by Roy K. Gibson and Christina Shuttleworth Kraus (Leiden: Brill, 2002), pp. 295–318 (p. 301). See also the review by Michael D. Reeve, 'Snow on Cithaeron', *Classical Review*, 54 (2004), 5–12.

16. A. D. Nuttall, *Timon of Athens* (Boston, MA: Twayne, 1989), p. xxi.

17. I. M. Crombie, *An Examination of Plato's Doctrines*, 2 vols (London: Routledge & Kegan Paul, 1962–63).

18. Pater, *Plato and Platonism*, p. 171.

19. Richard Jenkyns, *The Victorians and Ancient Greece* (Oxford: Blackwell, 1980), pp. 253–63. Jenkyns refers to Pater's 'unphilosophic mind' (p. 253); this is a common misconception — in fact Pater was exceptionally well informed about philosophy, including German idealist philosophy.

20. See, for example, George Lakoff and Mark Johnson, *Metaphors We Live By* (Chicago and London: The University of Chicago Press, 1980), and *More than Cool Reason: A Field Guide to Poetic Metaphor* (Chicago and London: The University of Chicago Press, 1989) ('Metaphorical understanding [...] is endemically conceptual in nature', p. 50); Paul Crowther, 'Literary Metaphor and Philosophical Insight: The Significance of Archilochus', in *Metaphor, Allegory, and the Classical Tradition: Ancient Thought and Modern Revisions*, ed. by G. R. Boys-Stones (Oxford: Oxford University Press, 2003), pp. 83–100. An influential paper for the development of this view of metaphor was Paul Ricœur, 'The Metaphorical Process as Cognition, Imagination, and Feeling', *Critical Enquiry*, 5 (1978), 142–59; also pubd in *On Metaphor*, ed. by Sheldon Sacks (Chicago and London: The University of Chicago Press, 1979), pp. 141–57.

21. Murdoch, p. 362.

22. The two things are of course connected, and follow from ignoring the point that 'style itself makes its claims, expresses its sense of what matters' (Nussbaum, *Love's Knowledge*, p. 3).

23. *The Stoic in Love*, p. 55.

24. *Plato and Platonism*, pp. 3–4.

25. Fred Parker, *Scepticism and Literature: An Essay on Pope, Hume, Sterne, and Johnson* (Oxford: Oxford University Press, 2003), p. 172.

26. Parker, p. 138.

27. Paul Guyer, 'Originality: Genius, Universality, Individuality', in *The Creation of Art: New Essays in Philosophical Aesthetics*, ed. by Berys Gaut and Paisley Livingston (Cambridge: Cambridge University Press, 2003), pp. 116–37 (p. 126).

28. J. G. A. Pocock, 'Texts as Events: Reflections on the History of Political Thought', in *Politics of Discourse: The Literature and History of Seventeenth-Century England*, ed. by Kevin Sharpe and Stephen N. Zwicker (Berkeley and London: University of California Press, 1987), pp. 21–34 (p. 33).

29. Rowan Williams, 'The Discipline of Scripture', *On Christian Theology* (Oxford: Blackwell, 2000), pp. 44–59 (p. 55). A similar approach is recommended, with more philosophical argument, by Paul Ricœur in 'Toward a Hermeneutic of the Idea of Revelation', in *Essays on Biblical Interpretation*, ed. Lewis S. Mudge (London: SPCK, 1981), pp. 73–118.

30. Stanley Cavell, *Disowning Knowledge in Six Plays of Shakespeare* (Cambridge: Cambridge University Press, 1987), p. 2.

31. Cavell, p. 12; see also pp. 1–4.

32. Martha C. Nussbaum, *The Fragility of Goodness: Luck and Ethics in Greek Tragedy and Philosophy*, rev. edn (Cambridge: Cambridge University Press, 2001), pp. 14–16 (the quotation is from p. vii). For Agamemnon's choice, see ch. 2.

33. T. S. Eliot, 'In Memory', *Little Review*, 5.4 (1918), 44–47 (p. 46).

34. Martha C. Nussbaum, *The Therapy of Desire: Theory and Practice in Hellenistic Ethics* (Princeton, NJ: Princeton University Press, 1994), p. 442.

35. *The Therapy of Desire*, p. 446.

36. Millicent Bell, *Shakespeare's Tragic Skepticism* (New Haven and London: Yale University Press, 2002), p. 5.

37. Compare too the modern financial sense of 'appreciative' — the sense that value increases.

38. Walter Pater, 'Measure for Measure', in *Appreciations: With An Essay on Style* (London: Macmillan, 1913), pp. 183–84 (my italics).

39. Quoted by Rorty in *Contingency*, p. 58.

40. Lukas Erne, in his *Shakespeare as Literary Dramatist* (Cambridge: Cambridge University Press, 2003), has argued that Shakespeare produced different versions of plays for performance and for reading; for the contrary view that the plays are directed primarily at theatre audiences see Stephen Orgel, *Imagining Shakespeare: A History of Texts and Visions* (Basingstoke: Palgrave Macmillan, 2003).

41. On this see A. D. Nuttall, *William Shakespeare: 'The Winter's Tale'*, Studies in English Literature, 26 (London: Arnold, 1966), pp. 44–45.

42. Nuttall, *Timon of Athens*, p. 141.

43. Bowen, p. 75; for philosophical argument in this play see, in addition to Bowen, Graham Bradshaw, *Shakespeare's Scepticism* (Brighton: Harvester Wheatsheaf, 1987), chs 1 and 4; Nuttall, *Timon of Athens*, pp. 97–99; Charles and Michelle Martindale, *Shakespeare and the Uses of Antiquity: An Introductory Essay* (London: Routledge, 1990), ch. 3, esp. pp. 99–112.

44. Bowen, pp. 98–99.

45. See C. and M. Martindale, pp. 181–89; Geoffrey Miles, *Shakespeare and the Constant Romans* (Oxford: Clarendon Press, 1996), pp. 186–88.

46. See A. D. Nuttall, *A New Mimesis: Shakespeare and the Representation of Reality* (London: Methuen, 1983), pp. 99–120; and C. and M. Martindale, ch. 4.

47. Miles, p. 19 (Cicero was not, of course, a Stoic, but he was sympathetic to some Stoic positions). For Seneca and acting see Catharine Edwards, 'Acting and Self-Actualisation in Imperial Rome: Some Death Scenes', in *Greek and Roman Actors: Aspects of an Ancient Profession*, ed. by Pat Easterling and Edith Hall (Cambridge: Cambridge University Press, 2002), pp. 377–94.

48. Judith Butler, *Gender Trouble: Feminism and the Subversion of Identity*, 10th anniversary edn (New York and London: Routledge, 1999), see esp. pp. 163–80 (p. 180): cf. p. 180: 'If gender attributes [...] are not expressive but performative, then these attributes effectively constitute the identity they are said to express or reveal'.

49. Lucy Hughes-Hallett, *Cleopatra: Histories, Dreams, and Distortions* (London: Bloomsbury, 1990), pp. 306–07.

50. A. D. Nuttall, *Two Concepts of Allegory: A Study of Shakespeare's 'The Tempest' and the Logic of Allegorical Expression* (London: Routledge & Kegan Paul, 1967), pp. 130–33 (p. 132).

51. C. S. Lewis, *The Chronicles of Narnia*, VII: *The Silver Chair* (London: Collins, 1997), p. 145.

52. Bradshaw, p. 36.

53. See Bloom, *Shakespeare*, p. 549: 'Whore and her aging gull is a possible perspective upon them [Antony and Cleopatra], if you yourself are a savage reductionist, but then why would you want to attend or read this play?'.

54. Bradshaw, p. 37: 'the directing intelligence at work within the Works is both more sceptical than his idealistic characters and more tentatively — sceptically — affirmative than his nihilists and dogmatic sceptics.'

55. Samuel Johnson, *Dr Johnson on Shakespeare*, ed. with an introduction by W. K. Wimsatt (Harmondsworth: Penguin, 1969), pp. 72, 62.

56. George Steiner, 'A Reading against Shakespeare', in *No Passion Spent: Essays, 1978–1996* (London: Faber, 1996), pp. 108–28 (p. 127); see too David Hopkins, '"The English Homer": Shakespeare,

Longinus, and English "Neo-Classicism"', in *Shakespeare and the Classics*, ed. by Charles Martindale and A. B. Taylor (Cambridge: Cambridge University Press, 2004), pp. 261–76.

57. Leonard Barkan, 'What Did Shakespeare Read?', in *The Cambridge Companion to Shakespeare*, ed. by Margreta de Grazia and Stanley Wells (Cambridge: Cambridge University Press, 2001), pp. 31–47 (p. 45).

58. Samuel Johnson, *The History of Rasselas, Prince of Abissinia: A Tale*, ed. R. W. Chapman (Oxford: Clarendon Press, 1927), pp. 84, 86.

59. The effect is to 'disturb the very structures of thought'; see Paul Hammond, 'The Play of Quotation and Commonplace in *King Lear*', in *Toward A Definition of Topos: Approaches to Analogical Reasoning*, ed. by Lynette Hunter (Basingstoke: Macmillan, 1991), pp. 78–129 (p. 80). (I owe this reference, and the general thought, to Fred Schurink.)

PART II

❖

INVESTIGATIONS

CHAPTER 4

False Trials and the Impulse to Try in Shakespeare and his Contemporaries

Subha Mukherji

Scenes of trial abound in Renaissance drama, and they have received a good deal of critical attention. Not so the curious phenomenon of the 'false trial', which, I shall argue in this essay, embodies the impulse to try. Both kinds of trial have epistemological implications in common. Trial scenes of early modern playtexts are structures of knowing. Legal procedure, like anagnoristic plots, proceeds from uncertainty or ignorance to knowledge or recognition. Dramatic plots presented as trials, however, often call into question the ostensible certainty of the knowledge arrived at through legal means.

Shakespeare's *All's Well that Ends Well* is such a plot. Helena uses external, concrete tokens such as rings to prove that her marriage to Bertram has been made indissoluble by sex, although he thought he was sleeping with Diana when he was in fact tricked into bed with his spurned wife Helena. Thus the play shares with many others an insight into the fragile relation between truths of intention and demonstrable proof, which in legal contexts often turned out to take the form of Aristotle's inartificial signs rather than the artificial or inherently probable proofs that he thought were superior.[1] But what is interesting about this play, unlike, say, *Measure for Measure*, is that this critique coexists with an understanding of probability not as a failure of certainty, but as a pragmatic, contingent alternative in tune with the human condition, a necessarily provisional but hopeful step towards knowledge, and a ground for trust. Amidst the precarious provisionalities that haunt the end of this play, we are reminded of the king's tentative acceptance of Helena's improbable promise of medical cure:

> More could I question thee, and more I must,
> Though more to know could not be more to trust:
> From whence thou cam'st, how tended on — but rest
> Unquestioned welcome, and undoubted blessed.
> *(All's Well that Ends Well, II. I. 205–09)*

Like a promise, one might say, marriage, happy endings to stories, and happiness itself are all, in a sense, absolute and ignorant — a leap of faith, like Pascal's wager with God.

Such a perspective may be related to the emergent understanding of probability in the period, when civil law and legal philosophy were still dogged by the idea of demonstrable certainty, while the common law of England was moving towards a precedent-based procedure founded on probable application of case law. In such plays as *All's Well that Ends Well* there are already seeds of the idea that questioning itself has its limits.[2] Indeed, the epistemological uncertainty at the end of the legal plots of drama can even provide, at times, a human refuge from the knowledge that characters resist, and struggle to bury or undo, as we see later in Henry James's novels. Shakespeare's Helena or Portia or indeed Duke Vincentio are as desperately in need of uncertainty as James's Millie Theale or Merton Densher or Maggie Verver. Their plays need it too to stay poised on the brink between comic resolution and terrible cognitions — truths much the same as those for the 'pity and dread' of which Maggie buries her eyes, which register them, in her husband's breast, at the end of *The Golden Bowl*. But the pointed coincidence of plots of knowledge with plots of law in early modern plays engaged with legal procedure underlines the crucial relation — not necessarily synchronic — between epistemology, legal thinking, and literary form in this period. And this is a relation to which false trials are as germane as real ones.

But if trial scenes are primarily interested in the nature of the knowledge gained, it is the role of the false trial to examine the routes leading to it. What, then, is this illusory process? A false trial is a test that one person puts another through, beyond necessity or the facts of the case; sometimes even as a pretence. A peculiar pain often attends upon it. A familiar example is the scene in *Macbeth* (IV. 3) where Malcolm slanders himself to test Macduff's integrity, faced with the future king of his country. When Macduff is finally reduced to despair, Malcolm reveals that he was but trying him (Macduff), and that Macduff's response has wiped all 'black scruples' (116) from his mind. From what we know, however, Malcolm has had no reason to doubt Macduff's integrity in the first place. The justification of the genuine anguish that the patriotic Macduff is dragged through is questionable. As Malcolm explains his 'false speaking', he registers Macduff's stunned silence: 'Why are you silent?'. Macduff answers soberly, 'Such welcome and unwelcome things at once | 'Tis hard to reconcile' (137–39).[3]

A slightly different but comparably odd moment occurs in *The Tragedy of King Lear* (1623), where Edgar, pretending to be poor Tom, stands on even ground with his freshly blinded and already grief-crazed father Gloucester, and tells him it is 'horrible steep' (IV. 5. 3).[4] He takes his time to create the vertigo effect, in a long speech ending with 'I'll look no more, | Lest my brain turn and the deficient sight | Topple down headlong' (22–24). As Gloucester is brought closer and closer to the temptation of leaping off what he thinks is the edge of the cliff, Edgar makes sure he does: 'You are now within a foot | Of th'extreme verge' (25–26). And so Gloucester takes the 'suicidal' leap and falls on flat ground. If this is farcical, the audience's sense of comedy is almost cruel, and shares the bizarre humour of Edgar's charade. Earlier, he himself has articulated a sense of the indecorum of such mirth: 'Bad is the trade that must play fool to sorrow' (IV. 1. 39). Edgar's aside tells us: 'Why I do trifle thus with his despair | Is done to cure it' (IV. 5. 33–34). This sanctimonious self-justification smacks of the same brand of righteousness evident in other dramatic situations where people try other people from a high moral ground, backed by the knowledge that the suffering they are putting someone else through will be revealed, eventually, to be causeless; it may even prove to be morally edifying. It also has a whiff of the obscenity of his later attempt at theodicy when he says to Edmund, of their father's blindness, that 'The Gods are just [...] | The dark and vicious place where thee he got | Cost him his eyes' (v. 3. 162–65). Edgar, presuming to teach his father a lesson in valuing life by making him go through a kind of death, performs an act here that is a variety of playing God — perhaps felt necessary by him precisely because of the absence of the gods. But it is also a sort of playing Devil. In fact this moment looks forward to another literary scene where one character tempts another to take a plunge. They too stand on a 'specular mount' (236), and the eloquent speaker points to and conjures up a compelling picture of the scene beyond. This time, however, the tempted one is the Son of God in Milton's *Paradise Regained*. The temptation there is different, but it is figured as a trial. Satan, 'the tempter proud' (IV. 569, 595), says, after Christ refuses to take the mental leap:

> And opportunity I here have had
> To try thee, sift thee, and confess have found thee
> Proof against all temptation. (IV. 531–34)[5]

False trials are used in drama to interrogate the legitimacy of certain epistemologies. They usually reside at the interface between law and the metaphor of law, in the fertile intermediate space between actual legal procedure and general thinking about ways of knowing, driven as they are by the impulse to ascertainment or discovery. After Shakespeare, false trials appear in a range of Jacobean and Caroline plays and harden into a recognizable dramatic pattern. But they are not only plot structures but structures of feeling. In fact the means of their moral investigation is markedly affective, arousing, registering, and using odd pain, sharp emotions, or articulate subjectivity to raise questions about judicial-epistemological processes and associated literary forms, even to judge them. Showing how the use of temptation as a tool to elicit truth or establish knowledge can slide precariously into temptation *to* knowledge, replacing the *need* to know with the *urge* to examine, their quasi-legal impetus puts motives and methods of knowing under the spotlight, and reflects on the implications of uncertainty, risk, and probability — not only how we deal with them, but also how we use them. Thus, they illuminate the intersection between aesthetics, human feelings, and ethics, for that is what morality in these plays is about. Bernard Williams, in his book *Morality*, comments on 'the combination [of] discovery, trust, and risk' that is 'central to [...] the state of being in love'.[6] This combination lies at the heart of my consideration of characters as they play games of knowledge, trying out artful devices to discover truths that will free them of risk and ensure trust. For in the active avoidance of social and emotional risk, there can be a fundamental obscenity that courts a different kind of risk — ethical risk, the risk of losing the art of trust altogether. Ensuring is not the same as enabling. And the 'will to truth' itself, as Nietzsche would say, 'must be scrutinized'; 'our business now is tentatively to question the will to truth'.[7]

Christ has seen through Satan's imaginative speech about classical civilization as 'false', 'fabling fell and smooth conceits' (*Paradise Regained*, IV. 291–95). But is there something potentially devilish about that act of temptation itself to a seventeenth century imagination? The imagined edge of Dover Cliff is as insubstantial as Satan's Athens — 'built on nothing firm' (292). And Edgar does tell Gloucester later that there was a fiend on the top of the cliff, egging him on, standing exactly where Edgar himself was standing — close at Gloucester's ear. The spatial perception enables Gloucester to remember and identify this 'thing': 'He led me to that place' (*Tragedy of King Lear*, IV. 6. 77, 79). When the tempted is a human subject and thus not proof against temptation, the trial can take on a hint of perversity, as does Duke Vincentio's knowing trial of the fallible Angelo, whom he knows to be both a 'seemer' and an absolutist and therefore liable to be tripped up (*Measure for Measure*). It is the asymmetry in knowledge that makes such trials insidious. Meanwhile, let us hold on to the image of someone standing on the edge of a cliff, for it is suggestive of the process itself, a process that is existentially precipitous, with all the danger and all the attraction that entails. It is an image to which we, with Shakespeare, will return.

Trying in Plays, and in 'General Learning'[8]

It is this urge for truth that drives the distinct trials that two husbands put their wives through, in Massinger's *The Picture* and Ford's *The Lady's Trial*. In *The Picture* Mathias, a knight about to set off for the wars, leaving his loving and beloved wife Sophia behind, finds himself 'strangely troubled' (I. I. 109).[9] Fully aware that he nourishes a fury 'with imagind foode | [...] [for] suspition, she was ever | Or can be false heereafter', he nevertheless asks his friend Baptista, 'a generall scholer [...] deeply read in Nature's secret', to use his 'Art' to resolue [him]' (110–21). Sophia's normally inaccessible interior is analogized with the 'Nature' that Baptista is trained to search out. Baptista resists, but Mathias 'must know farther', for 'What one proofe | Could she give of her constancy, being vntempted?' (137, 141–42). 'These doubts must be made certainties' (150), he declares, his words suggesting almost a sense of the artifice of certainty, a product of 'making'. Temptation is posited, meanwhile, as a catalyst in the invention of certainty. But this is not just the idiosyncratic view of a paranoid husband, but part of a shared discursive culture. It is resonant of well-known attitudes to the quest for truth, such as Bacon's principle of natural philosophy in *The Advancement of Learning*:

> For like as a man's disposition is never well known till he be crossed, nor Proteus ever changed shapes till he was straitened and held fast; so the passages and variations of nature cannot appear so fully in the liberty of nature, as in the trials and vexations of art.[10]

This in turn reflects an idea already in circulation (see Fig. 1). Bacon uses the same image in *Parasceve* — 'the vexations of art are certainly as the bonds and handcuffs of Proteus';[11] and in the *Great Instauration* he reiterates that the truths of nature are most certainly manifest 'when by art and the hand of man she is forced out of her natural state, and squeezed and moulded', for only then can the mysteries of a 'labyrinthine' world be properly discovered.[12] Baptista's methods are seen by Mathias as an invincible combination of human control and art, although Baptista warns him of the limits of both (I. I. 155–61).

Symb. LXI.

FIG. 1. Truth as Proteus bound in chains and handcuffs,
waiting to be discovered by wise reason
Achille Bocchi, *Symbolicarum quaestionum* (1574), p. cxxxxi

So, in the end, Baptista devises a picture of Sophia for Mathias to take with him. If it keeps its original colour, that would mean that Sophia was innocent in fact as well as untempted. If it turns yellow, she was courted but unconquered. If it turns black, that would mean she was overcome. But even in this apparently accurate device there are crucial flaws. For instance, the 'black' would signify that 'the [...] fort by composition, or surprise, | Is forc'd *or* with her free consent surrendered' (I. I. 185; my italics). There is, of course, a vital difference between the two, which is underlined by the almost casuistical conversations characters have with themselves as well as each other on whether, between sinning in wishes and sinning in fact, there is a moral difference. Sophia is indeed tempted, by false reports of Mathias's infidelity, and she describes the effect of these 'strong imaginary doubts and fears' as a 'suddaine precipice' (II. I. 48–49). Interestingly, she sees this as pulling her down, against the upward motion of her prayers, and does not yield, for she recognizes, from her inner knowledge of Mathias's character, that these reports are most improbable. Mathias, on his part, is also tempted, and then also resists. But his grounds, far from being argumentative, are external to the nature of things (*rerum natura*), circumstantial, and artificial in a non-Aristotelian sense. When the picture turns yellow with a few dark lines, and Baptista interprets this as Sophia being false in her consent but not yet in fact, Mathias imagines the rest and swears he will kill her. Ironically, he uses the same image as Sophia: 'I am thrown from a steepe rocke heading into a gulph of misery' (IV. I. 54–55). But when the picture reverts to its original colour, he is entirely satisfied of her innocence. It is the logic of this inference, and the gratuitousness of the exercise, that Sophia chastises in the little trial *she* stages on his return (V. 2. 30). By this time aware of the full story, she pretends to have really 'turnd monster' — false and 'perverse' (V. 3. 93, 38) — and taunts Mathias when he is mystified:

> Whie? You know
> How to resolue yourselfe what my intents are,
> By the helpe of *Mephostophiles* and your picture,
> Pray look vpon it again. (V. 3. 76–79)

When Mathias finally recognizes the perversity of his methods and finds Sophia less than convinced by the change, he burns his picture as 'proofe' of his lesson in trust (V. 3. 213). Sophia, unlike Mathias, is aware of the deeper illegitimacy of 'bare suspition' as a motive for enquiry (III. 6. 67), and, while still in its grip, pre-emptively asks forgiveness mentally: 'For my certaine resolution [...] if in the search of truth | I heare or say more than becomes any virtue | Forgive me my Mathias' (III. 6. 24–28). The recurrent word 'suspicion' has legal resonance, as reasonable suspicion was specifically listed in English legal handbooks of the period as an admissible criterion for arrest,[13] and provided moral sanction for pre-trial examination, especially in crimes difficult to be witnessed.[14] So, as Barbara Shapiro demonstrates, '"suspicion" had become a legal category' by the mid-sixteenth century.[15] It is the presumption of the rationality of suspicion that Massinger's play puts to the test.[16]

Presumptive evidence is challenged again in Ford's *Lady's Trial*, but this is a curious play, with a more focused interest in the murky waters of motives behind trying, rather than the commoner dramatic preoccupation with motives behind actions tried. Again, we have a husband (Auria) leaving his wife (Spinella) for the wars. The main trial in this play is that of Spinella by her husband, whose friend Aurelio has brought a charge of adultery against her, having found her in a chamber alone with Adurni. At the time of their discovery, Adurni was indeed professing love to her, but she had resisted with spirit. Instead of believing Aurelio, Auria — remarkably — professes complete faith in his wife's virtue. He is articulately aware of the circumstantial nature of Aurelio's evidence, calling it a 'slovenly presumption' that is 'punishable by a sharp rebuke' (III. 3). And yet he orchestrates, deliberately and elaborately, a trial where he affects indifference and mistrust of his wife and challenges her to defend her case publicly: 'Keep fair, and stand the trial' (v. 2).[17] Aurelio admits *his* motive was a 'rash and over-busy curiosity', which he tries to justify by calling it 'honest doubt' (v. 2). But what was Auria's motive? Why does he put her through it?

The play's explanations of this tortuous route are several. When Auria hits upon the plan of staging the trial he exclaims: 'That's the way; | It smooths all rubs' (IV. 1). Anxious to ensure both public opinion and personal conviction, incapable of risking either, he fails to 'hazard | All that is dearest to [him]' for Spinella's cause (II. 4), as Adurni does. It is as if the test or trial itself is the challenge that Spinella has to withstand to prove her innocence, once aspersions have been cast, irrespective of how flimsy the evidence is. As Spinella faints, Auria exclaims, 'I find thy virtues as I left them, perfect, | Pure, and unflaw'd: For instance, let me claim Castanna's promise', and he peremptorily offers her sister Castanna to Aurelio in marriage because that 'rectifies all crookèd vain surmises' (v. 2). Here is a hint that despite his protestations to the contrary, he himself needed to secure — and offer — a demonstration of Spinella's innocence, having urged her at his departure to guard against being 'impeached' by popular speculation and presumptions (I. 1).

Ford's trial is touched too with the idea that drives Massinger's Mathias — that of temptation being a necessary test on the route to demonstrable truth. It is planted in the very first scene, where Aurelio warns Auria that Spinella has never been 'tempted | By trial of extremes', and expresses his 'honest doubt' about the consequences of Auria's departure. It is picked up again when Adurni explains why he tried to seduce the woman he so respected, making her 'an object | Of study for fruition', a subject of experiment: 'No beauty can be chaste unless attempted' (IV. 2). These two 'trials' or tests of virtue lead on to the actual 'trial' of Spinella by her husband in his domestic 'court'. When the loose ends are tied, Auria explains that he needed to spend time on the proceedings because he had 'fix'd on issue of [his] *desires*' (v. 2). And the desire was, in part, to tame the demon of the unchained Proteus, if only in the minds of others. Ford, incidentally, was no stranger either to legal thinking or to Bacon, having been a Middle Templar for almost fifteen years, and having taken the plot of *Perkin Warbeck* from Bacon.

But also informing Auria's trial of Spinella, unlike Mathias's of Sophia, is a zealous investment in process, as if that constituted a purification of truth. Spinella, and all else concerned, must go through the action of sifting, with a rigour out of proportion to the need to search. Troublingly hovering above the relatively simpler need of the trier — Auria — to resolve his own uncertainty is the Miltonic notion that 'that which purifies us is trial, and trial is by what is contrary'.[18] Mathias's belief, that only by resisting temptation can virtue be proved, admittedly smacks of the same idea; but his own genuine confusion and need for surety makes his impulse less dubious, more understandable. But the authority Auria assumes in order to exercise a sort of secular election and put his near and dear ones through a process they must live up to for the sake of demonstration and purification lies in the disturbing middle ground between aesthetic and ethical 'desire'; the uncertainty deliberately generated in the process supplants certainty with doubt as the object of 'making'.

Auria's instincts are anticipated in certain ways of thinking about legal procedure familiar to the period. The most obvious place to look is, again, Bacon, whose methods in natural philosophy were largely modelled on his principles of legal enquiry, derived from the heterogeneous legacies of common and civil law. Philosophy, he wrote, 'should be brought forth [...] out of [...] law-like, chaste and severe inquisition'.[19] Famously, he also specified that 'in the highest cases of treason, torture is used for discovery, not evidence'.[20] This is an intriguing distinction, to my knowledge so far inadequately explicated in the history of science. Discovery and evidence are both notoriously slippery words in the period, like testimony and fact. But where discovery is dissociated from evidence, it appears to refer to the process of uncovering itself and of establishing the facts. Evidently not referring to the discovery of the hidden law in this instance, although that is the most familiar Baconian use of 'discovery' in a legal context, the word applies to the discovery of 'facts', and perhaps also the agent's intention — a function of the confirmatory rather than informatory or evidentiary stage of a legal inquiry.[21] Bacon himself, of course, was obsessed with the process of searching truth: *Novum organum* actually has charts structuring the production of knowledge. Also, no private revelation was adequate at law any more than Nature's private responses to enquiry were, till both were publicly acknowledged and all ambiguities accounted for: 'if in any statement there be anything doubtful or dissatisfying, by no means would I have it suppressed or passed in silence, but plainly and perspicuously set down by way of note or admonition'.[22]

The idea that the impulse to try may be independent of the insufficiency — or indeed the sufficiency — of the information available recalls *The Winter's Tale*. Hermione's trial for adultery is not one of our false trials. But it does show how doubt takes on its own momentum, mistrust its own inexorable energy. So Leontes declares, 'There's no truth at all i' th' Oracle: | The sessions shall proceed', even when the oracle proclaims his wife's innocence (III. 2. 140–41), and presses on with his own mode of enquiry. One may indeed 'too much believe' one's own suspicion — a steep, perversely enticing climb, a process that can become compelling for its own sake, and overtake the original purpose of truth finding. And yet, as with the reason-robbed Leontes, it can come dangerously close to the rationalist legal impulse that outmoded the older form of trial by divine proof; a 'shift from consensus to authority', from trust to law, from faith to human interest.[23] After all, 'suspicion' had been initially developed as a legal concept by canon lawyers as one of the bases for a rational alternative mode of enquiry into the truth of a case, after the 1215 abolition of irrational proofs such as ordeals.[24] The hint of redundancy of evidence in *The Winter's Tale* not only finds an early expression in some of Bacon's more inscrutable statements on legal and scientific methods; the fierce teleological drive informing Leontes' legal process, and his righteous conviction, also remind us of the terms in which legal enquiry is described in Henry Swinburne's canon law treatise on spousals: 'By Distinctions we discern the Scent and Footsteps [...] of each Man's purpose and intent, thereby, like Blood-hounds, we are taught to trace and hunt out the very Center of each man's thought'.[25] The ferocity that could characterize the legal zeal to find truth often drew implicit sanction from the assumed rightness and necessity of the mission. But in dramatic plots of jealousy and doubt, it translates as psychological violence with potential for deep emotional injustice.

We have been warned by Peter Pesic not to take the analogy between experiment and judicial torture too far; he sees the bound Proteus as a figure for a more interactive wrestle with truth.[26] But it *is* Bacon's analogy; and as the scrupulous struggle of critics such as Elizabeth Hanson only makes clearer, Bacon himself struggles to harmonize the intersubjective model of the relation between nature and her discoverer with the more adversarial, purposive model; the neutral scientific approach with the interested one.[27] His articulate anxieties about using the inquisitory process improperly, in law or in natural philosophy, show his awareness of how easy it is to get it wrong when the matter goes out of the arena of precise scholarship into the muddled sphere of human transactions. Interestingly, one of the main points on which Pesic rests his thesis is a distinction between vexation and torture: 'In many passages the mental trials inherent in vexation distinguish it from the sheer brutality of torture'.[28] If anything, this makes Bacon more germane to our argument: what the plots of our plays are troubled by is precisely the precarious closeness between 'mental trials' and brutality. To move from Bacon's metaphors for natural philosophical enquiry to plays where people enquire into other people is to face the implications of metaphor itself, and what happens to it when translated into human action rather than applied to physical matter or 'nature'. 'Experiment' can become deeply dubious when the subject is human. In discussing motives of knowing in the *Filum labyrinthi*, Bacon warns against the inquisition 'of that which is known', rather than a 'discovery of the unknown' — Auria's obsession.[29] Just as, in *Advancement*, he warns: 'to be speculative into another man, to the end to know how to work him or wind him or govern him proceedeth from a heart that is double and cloven'.[30] Such conflicts are symptomatic of Bacon's double role as natural philosopher and lawyer, as well as being internal to his legal position: an advocate of common law also deeply learned in the Romano-canonical tradition, and at the same time an Inquisitor on behalf of the Privy Council and the Star Chamber. The last two offices involved examination and torture of witnesses and defendants,[31] and a collapsing of the roles of judge and jury kept scrupulously apart in common law.[32] This conflation is what Spinella accuses Auria of in Ford's play, for he, like Leontes, and like a Privy Councillor or Clerk of Star Chamber, becomes judge of both law and fact, converting the judge's role from an impartial referee into an active inquisitor and depriving the defendant of the benefit of jury.

Auria sets himself up, of course, as a superior wielder of method in the project of discovery — or uncovering — than both Aurelio, who convicts on adventitious evidence, and the common lookers-on, who might 'construe' guilt erroneously (*The Lady's Trial*, I. I). The wary references to presumption and to misconstruction of outward signs might suggest that Auria's own method of proving is 'direct' or 'inartificial' rather than artificial, that is, that he is resting his case on witness testimony or documents rather than on inherent and interpretable signs. Such a distinction would correspond to the early modern *legal* differentiation between direct evidence which constituted full proof, and circumstantial evidence — including probable inference from interpretable signs — which was inferior in law but nevertheless useful in cases of crimes hard to witness. But in fact Auria does not rest content once Adurni's confession — a direct and inartificial proof — has disproved Spinella's guilt. He proceeds to construct his own legal enterprise — Spinella's trial — so that the inherent nature of Spinella shows through her own legal performance till she faints; it is only then that he publicly declares her untainted (v. 7). He proves his distinction from the original prosecutor Aurelio not by producing witness testimony or facts or clues, but by presenting, through his fictive trial, a rhetorical argument that is inherently persuasive. Aurelio's use of manifest signs is relegated, meanwhile, to the domain of the inartistic, inadequate for inducing probability.

The implicit hierarchy, then, does not correspond to legal practice in Ford's England. Instead, it speaks to the original and value-laden distinction in rhetoric between the superiority of artificial proof or 'invention', constructed by the art of the orator, and the inferiority of external signs that the orator merely used. This goes back to Aristotle's division of proofs and signs into artificial and inartificial. In Aristotle the best means of recognition in dramatic plots are those based on 'probable incidents', and the worst are 'inartistic', based on material objects, divorced from rhetorical demonstration.[33] The categorization of proofs in the *Rhetoric* corresponds to this, although the hierarchy is implicit there.[34] The Aristotelian evaluation still hovered over early modern thinking through the accretions and translations of the rhetorical tradition, mainly via Quintilian, although in legal practice the hierarchy was switched around as the inartifical proofs were considered the surest. Auria's 'false' trial of Spinella, in making the difference between the legal and the purely rhetorical visible, embodies the potential for a dubious overlap between legal necessity and rhetorical temptation; the way in which the urge to invent, craft, and emplot a case was liable to exceed the needs of the 'issue of fact'. Spinella, expecting '[her] husband's clearest thoughts' to be opposed to other people's 'vain constructions' (II. 4), is confronted with his well-constructed tragicomic trial designed to discover the truth with maximum impact; indeed, to stage discovery itself.

For Auria is at once adjudicator and plot maker. What had been added to the Aristotelian tradition by this time was the Terentian notion that what is only probable, paradoxically, elicits belief in dramatic plots that are essentially controversial. Auria's marshalling of probability entails the deliberate and deliberative generation of uncertainty, which goes against the grain of the probability he is ostensibly trying to prove; to establish Spinella's innocence and correct disbelief, he torments her through a rhetorical elaboration of mistrust, using doubt as narrative capital. The 'desire' that he declares fulfilled through the trial, therefore, occupies the disturbing middle ground between ethical and aesthetic desire: uncertainty supplants certainty as the object of making. Thus, if *The Picture* goes half way towards the place from which, around 1654, Jeremy Taylor calls Augustine a 'good probable doctor', meaning a believable, trustworthy one, *The Lady's Trial*, written a decade later, subjects the desire for demonstration, and the anatomy of doubt, to moral examination.[35] If Massinger is content to ironize assumptions of certainty, Ford takes the further step of exposing the moral dubiousness of probability as a function of artifice. And this on the eve of the early triumphalist discussions of experiment and probability that led to the formation of the Royal Society.

A variety of critical voices within the play all focus on the surplus that constitutes the falsity of Auria's procedure, condemning not just 'brittle evidence' (IV. 2) but the tyranny of the sifting process and the emotional injustice of a needless trial. The final confrontation between the fictive pleasure of Auria's process and the reality of Spinella's articulate pain raises questions about the ethics of such judicial plotting. She comments on it with poignant dignity: 'It was to blame. But the success remits it'. But not before the protraction of the trial tipped her over the edge and caused her, Hermione-like, to faint upon hearing the words 'Auria, unkind, unkind' ('unkind' suggesting both cruelty and unnaturalness). Inasmuch as Auria's investigation is pointedly 'artificial', and part of a discursive culture of discovery, the illusory trial ends up being its emotional critique.

The Labyrinth of Knowledge

Tortuous, roundabout paths to truth, as we have seen, can only artificially be separated from the idea of torture in emotive drama. But how did non-dramatic genres invested or implicated in epistemology register such vexations, and how did these treatments relate to the drama's vision? In the context of writing about experiment, Bacon is wary about the applications of certain methods, and in the *Filum labyrinthi* strives to provide the 'filum' through the ethical and methodological pitfalls of straining after knowledge. The trouble is that the labyrinth itself becomes something of a moral maze. Indeed, the image of the labyrinth provides a telling clue to the place of such methods in seventeenth-century epistemology. Generally, it was a negative image of confusion, deceit, and incertitude — the space to which Milton's fallen angels were doomed; the figure that Calvin uses for 'each man's mind'.[36] Bacon calls the universe an obscure 'labyrinth', and laments the 'labyrinth of uncertainties' that the memorially accretive common law had become.[37] John Cowell in his legal Dictionary echoes this.[38] The image is used of canon law as well — witness Swinburne's offer of legal 'distinction' as the 'Thred which Ariadne gave [...] Theseus', to escape out of that dark and 'endless Labyrinth, wherein were so many difficult Turnings and intricate Returnings [...] but one only Out-gate'.[39] But when it comes to the path to knowledge rather than the epistemological quarry, there is a distinct idea shared by thinkers across the disciplines that difficulty and circuitousness are a function of ethical enquiry, a positive quality of search.

There was a discernible belief in the value of doubt as a hermeneutic and epistemological tool.

The labyrinthine, in this strand of thinking, becomes a positive image. In Donne's *Third Satire*, Truth stands at the top of a cragged hill, and 'hee that will | Reach her, about must, and about must goe'. Even Swinburne, by figuring the text of law itself as the labyrinth, puts value on the hermeneutic maze that needs to be cut through and made sense of in order to arrive at truth. Bacon himself, in *Novum organum*, invokes the 'labyrinth' as a necessary path towards truth. It is the way that is 'arduous [...] in the beginning' that 'leads out at last into the open country'.[40] Indeed, he makes a distinction between two methods of knowledge: a strenuous, rigorous pursuit of truth, which is the legitimate mode, and the other, condemnable desire of knowledge 'upon a natural curiosity and inquisitive appetite; sometimes to entertain their minds with variety and delight [...] as if there were sought in knowledge a couch'.[41] However, circuitousness and difficulty can also be the properties of a clever, ingenious, and self-delighting form. And when functioning thus, the labyrinthine can get *reconnected* with the dubiously pleasurable, and become a trope for the crooked and misleading. Bacon was not unaware of the 'natural but corrupt love of the lie itself' ('Of Truth'), and the role of fiction in epistemology.[42] George Herbert, in the distinct context of devotional poetry, suggestively teeters between the two implications of the circuitous aesthetic. His poetry records that process towards discovery which is the hermeneutic field that fallen man must plough before arriving at 'something understood'. Although we are inheritors of a certain illiteracy — 'Thy word is all, if we could spell' ('The Flower') — it is not enough to rest in the passive grace of revelation longed for in the 'Jordan' poems. The difficult act of interpretation becomes a necessary process, just as signification is a function of the fallen world: why else would God 'anneal in glass [his] story' ('The Windows')? This is in the spirit of Augustine, who thought that man needs to learn to read the divine metaphors by travelling the winding route from obscurity to discovery in proportion to what he has lost through the Fall. So Herbert's own figurations are as legitimate as our hermeneutic labours are necessary. But Herbert is both writer and reader. As a writer, indirectness becomes a function of playful intimacy with God, as well as of a text demanding rigorous interpretation. But as reader and devotee, he feels at the same time a weariness with the tortuous; an intermittent frustration, almost indignation, with the deliberate obscurity in which God clothes himself. Witness the anguished question in 'The Search', wrung from an uncomprehending subject incredulous of the severity, even perversity, of the test God puts him through:

> Where is my God? What hidden place
> Conceals thee still?
> What covert dare eclipse thy face?
> Is it thy will?[43]

So, even as the devotee often takes pleasure in prayer that works and winds its way up, in the 'crooked winding ways' of artifice ('A Wreath'), weaving a chiasmic wreath in the very act of rejecting the way that is not 'straight', there remains a longing for a straight path to knowledge, truth, and God:

> Yet through these labyrinths, not my groveling wit,
> But thy silk twist let down from heav'n to me,
> Did both conduct and teach me, how by it
> To climbe to thee.

There are, after all, two possible trajectories to labyrinthine journeys: into the heart of the labyrinth, and outside into free space. And if Shakespeare is half-remembering Arachne's spider-web while talking of Ariadne's thread in *Troilus and Cressida*, where Troilus mentions 'Ariachne's broken woof', that is a swift reminder of how the tremor of a single image, or mingled memory, can capture the closeness between the sinister labyrinth that traps and the *filum labyrinthi* that guides by virtue of its wielder's control over the maze.[44] What Yeats calls 'the fascination of what's difficult' is precariously poised, in epistemological ventures, between the rigorous and the perverse. The impulse that prompts 'false trials' is not unrelated to the purely fictive impulse and hard curiosity that Bacon labels as suspect. Romance heroines such as Cariclea in *Aethiopica* are addicted to this habit, driven to tell one intricate lie after another by an almost amoral caprice; Apuleius's adventures also have something of a desire for knowledge almost for the sake of it. And plots are spun out of these fictive mazes that tease with suspense and proliferate, with intricacy getting detached, in the process, from the ideal of discipline.

False Trials and Tragicomedy

Typically in the drama of the period, it is tragicomedies that use the formula 'I was but trying thee'. Being a form founded on the idea of *felix culpa* — 'happier much by [...] affliction made' (*Cymbeline*, v. 4. 108) — and, as such, licensing torment, it provides the perfect aesthetic structure for the false trial. According to Guarini, the Renaissance theorist of tragicomedy, the pain caused by tragicomic plotting is justified by the fact that it is all about the danger, not the death.[45] Yet this is an assurance available to the playwright and the inscribed artificer, but not to the characters. Thus the form can, and often does, suggest an aesthetic refusal of natural reality. But curiously, when tragicomedy turns self-referential, it becomes the very genre to question the relation between literary form and the ethics of emotion. By bringing alive the reality of the suffering that the characters undergo, without knowledge of the assured end, it draws attention to the emotional cost of ingenious plotting. And this begins with Shakespeare.

I want to dwell, in conclusion, on Shakespeare's *Cymbeline*, where the questionable legitimacy of such knowing trials is most sharply and self-consciously generic. The figure embodying this tendency is not the insecure husband Posthumus, but the Italian villain Iachimo, also the designated aesthete of the play. An early moment that anticipates his affiliation with the tragicomic impulse is his first meeting with Imogen. Iago-like, he plants doubts in her mind about her husband's disloyalty through a consummate interweaving of parentheses, aposiopeses, and subtle insinuation, hinting all along that she is to be pitied, for some reason too terrible to be uttered. Maddened by this, Imogen exclaims:

> You do seem to know
> Something of me, or what concerns me; pray you,
> Since doubting things go ill often hurts more
> Than to be sure they do — for certainties
> Either are past remedies; or timely knowing,
> The remedy then born — discover to me
> What both you spur and stop. (I. 6. 93–99)

The 'hurt' she talks about is the danger that is disacknowledged in the tragicomic comfort encapsulated by the physician Cornelius's description of his false poison: 'there is no danger in the show of death it makes'. But the power to withhold discovery, to spur and stop, and then to discover, belongs to narrative too and its arts of suspension. Dramatists themselves are dealers in, and manipulators of, doubt. This aesthetic implication is central to the idea of 'Iachimo'.

His pleasure in the exquisite, evident in the bedroom scene where he collects corporal tokens of Imogen's supposed infidelity with the eye of an art connoisseur, culminates, in the final scene of trial and confession, in his zestful, erotic recounting of the act of stealth he repents, which has cost Imogen all her pain (v. 5. 139–209). He goes about to expound his story at leisure, in the sensationalist style of an Italianate aria, while an assembly of characters 'stand on fire' (168), breathlessly awaiting disclosures that will change their lives. The potential perversity of this can only be sanctioned by a form that guarantees a happy ending but contains tragic experience, so that between the promise and its delivery there can be infinite and artful delay. Imogen, therefore, can wake up and lament, in the most surreally anguished poetry, over what she thinks is her husband's headless body, while the audience titters to see that it is only his gross double, the very Cloten she has scorned to look on (IV. 2. 296–332). But we know, as she does not, that her husband is alive. This makes the giggle an uncomfortable one. The queer, alienated, lyric power of Imogen's soliloquy, meanwhile, produces a bizarrely affecting dissonance, not unlike the sublime music given to the false lovers in Mozart's *Così fan tutte*, on which A. D. Nuttall has commented.[46] Guarini's aesthetic was centred on *rassomiglianza del terribile* — 'simulacrum of terror', or what he calls in *Il verato* (I) the 'fictive terror of someone else'.[47] Significantly, *Cymbeline* has an inset false trial within the larger dramaturgical pattern of tribulations, themselves false. When Imogen, gutted at first by Iachimo's lies about her husband Posthumus, ultimately refuses to believe him, he begs her pardon saying, 'I have spoke this' 'to *try* your taking of a false report' (I. 6. 173; my italics). All tragicomic triers (genuine or fake) have a moral excuse: Edgar does it to 'cure' Gloucester, Malcolm to ensure Macduff's honesty, and Auria and Aurelio both think the sufferings have made the resolution sweeter. Hence the claim, in Ford's subplot, that such unreal ordeals are 'harmless trials' (*The Lady's Trial*, I. 3). But the moral ground can often conceal an aesthetic agenda. When Adurni mutters about Auria's 'curious engines', the Genoese Auria responds smugly, 'Fine ones' (IV. 2).

Auria also claims he has deviated from the custom of his nation in not racing to revenge — for 'Italians use not dalliance, | But execution' (v. 1). And yet, in a sense, his aesthetic protraction of pain is as 'Italian' as it gets, tragicomedy being an Italianate genre. In *Cymbeline* Italy and Britain are reconciled politically, but remain opposed as aesthetic impulses. This opposition is focused again on Iachimo, embodying all the fascination of rivalry that Renaissance England felt for Italy. The subtle 'Italian brain' clearly belongs to the crook, but it is ten times more inventive and sophisticated than the 'duller [British]' (v. 5. 196–97): this Shakespeare knew, having taken his plot from an Italian novella. Iachimo is a modern Italian who has somehow swum into a Romano-British world. It was no accident that Italian poetics was associated in the English imagination with the labyrinthine narratology of Ariosto's epic. Giraldi's ideas on new epic forms were also in circulation. Italy was certainly *the* trendy place in terms of aesthetic self-consciousness. Of course, Ovid was always labyrinthine — a Roman Italian — before his time, the unclassical classical poet. Early on in *Cymbeline* Iachimo materializes in the bedroom of the English princess, physically popping out of the trunk (II. 2). But where does he really come out of? What else is almost surreptitiously half open in the scene? Ovid's *Metamorphoses*, of course, which the maidenly, unravished bride has been reading in bed, with the leaf 'turn'd down | Where Philomel gave up' (II. 2. 4, 45–46)! Could this be Shakespeare's joke about the erotics of Italy in the private and aesthetic imagination of English readers, and not just about the chaste Imogen's bedtime pleasure in Ovidian rape stories?

The Iachimo-impulse of a relishing protraction of tragicomic anguish does find schematic expression in the playwright's own indulgence at certain odd moments. Posthumus, mistaking Imogen for a page in the final scene, strikes her, saying, 'there lie thy part' (v. 5. 229). But the metadramatic joke, as well as the tragicomic habit of dicing with danger, is challenged by the heart-stopping directness of Imogen's response: 'why did you throw your wedded lady from you? | Think that you are upon a rock, and now | Throw me again' (261–63). Let us look back now on the cliff-hanging moment in *Lear*, and it will be discernible as an early example of putting tragicomedy itself on trial, and with it, the audience's capacity for balancing an aesthetic against an ethical response. What was a piece of action there becomes a highly conscious metaphor in the articulate pain of the quintessentially English Imogen, who, unlike Posthumus, never changed sides to fight for Italy. In *The Winter's Tale* the human cost of Time's work, and Paulina's, and tragicomic art's is captured in the single, eloquent detail of Hermione's wrinkles, noticed by Leontes when he looks at the false 'statue' in awe. The moral insurance of sixteen years that Leontes has indeed learned his lesson comes at a price, even if it is one tempered by forgiveness. In *Cymbeline*, however, the selfhood of the characters themselves rebels against such cost and resists it, as Grisell never did. It is ironic that tragicomedy was initially criticized both in Italy and in England for its exclusive investment in aesthetic delight and its detachment from moral issues.[48]

There are, then, two kinds of precipice. One is that of nature's and life's exciting uncertainty, which holds the promise of felicity as well as the risk of loss. From this we should have the capacity to take a Pascalian leap of faith, 'to give and hazard all' (*The Merchant of Venice*, II. 7. 16). But the other kind of rock-face — belonging to art — is the temptation we want to fly, the extreme verge of the cliff we cannot push others to, or off, with impunity.

Coda

While more obviously pre-empting the official narratives of the emergence of probability as a positive epistemological factor,[49] the other larger narrative these texts anticipate is that of risk. The plays discussed are deeply preoccupied with both dimensions of risk taking, just as they are concerned with both the excitement and the dubiousness of questioning. In abjuring one kind of uncertainty for another, they seem to be asking whether it is possible to salvage the art of hazarding, fading from an increasingly rationalistic, experiment-oriented culture,[50] from the realm of the irresponsible or the perverse, and restore it to a life lived with emotional and ethical lucidity. Perhaps to that extent they look forward to eighteenth-century novels such as *Clarissa*, in which risk becomes a condition of ethical investment in the sphere of human relations.[51] This has wider cultural implications for a society where lending money with interest had become acceptable in situations involving maritime risk.

A noticeable trend in plays involving false trials, especially from late Shakespeare onwards, is that what is put on trial is often the character or chastity of a woman, the trier being male. Critics who have noted and addressed the contested issue of women's sexual morality have also tended to see it as a vehicle of male ideology operating through dramatic plots. Lois Bueler's transhistorical study *The Tested Woman Plot*, which traces this plot structure masterfully from antiquity through Renaissance drama to the eighteenth- and nineteenth-century novel, sees it as a narrative code that is fundamentally concerned with the assertion of patriarchal order.[52] Lorna Hutson, in *The Usurer's Daughter*, argues that the burden of sexual errancy is placed on women for the persuasive Terentian plot in sixteenth-century England to work its ends legitimately, without giving up the productive structural deployment of uncertainty. Shakespeare is said to manage this by displacing moral accountability on the conduct of women: Hutson cites Isabella, Bianca, Luciana, and Desdemona, and suggests that they remain the vehicles of this uncertainty, subject to the playwright's narrative agenda.[53] The use of the specific motif of the false trial in the plays I look at challenges this thesis. The contemporary stereotype of female emotionality — uncontrollable, overflowing, inimical to reason — is harnessed in an entirely controlled way, whereby female resistance is made the agent of a precise questioning of such dealings in uncertainty. Women challenge the premises of investigative procedure as well as aesthetic and judicial dilation, and dislodge discourse from its 'position of mastery',[54] through articulate, affective subjectivity. Indeed, the woman sometimes becomes the agent of a counter-trial: as Sophia says in *The Picture*, she arranges for one 'to make [Mathias] know his fault and [her] just anger', calling upon her 'woman's wit' to do so (v. 2. 29–30). Her strange reception of Mathias and his royal guests is met in specifically gendered terms; Mathias exclaims at the 'bottomlesse hell | Of a false woman's heart' (v. 3. 113–14). Pointedly, Sophia does not forget and forgive when he vows to 'renounce [his] error' (163), but embarks on her own, gendered prolongation of his ordeal: 'the foule aspertions | In your unmanly doubts cast on my honour | Cannot so soon be washd of' (169–70). She eloquently expresses the paradox that though it is her sex that is 'subiect to suspitions and fears', she never set spies to survey her husband's actions when he went away to the wars; as justice, she demands a separation from bed and board till others intervene (171–80). To the very end she does not relent till Mathias can assure her that he will not act on jealousy 'hereafter', insisting that her forgiveness of 'what's past' is not enough (209). From being the subject of experiment, authority, and discovery, she becomes a 'subject' in the sense of being a site of feeling, agency, and action. This is a more self-conscious elaboration of the more fleeting and less judicial articulation of a female perception of emotional injustice in *Cymbeline*; and an active transformation of the way in which the price of trial is registered by the medium in *The Winter's Tale*. Even the most passive of women can occasionally surprise by articulating the perversity of affected trials. Jonson's Celia, in sheer disbelief of her husband Corvino's command to her to go and satisfy Volpone's desires, exclaims, 'Sir, let me beseech you, | Affect not these strange trials'.[55] She, of course, takes her cue from Corvino himself, who has, not long before this moment, explained to his terrified wife his volte-face from a raging jealous husband to one who has meanwhile discovered that taking her along to Volpone's house is the route to profit: 'I talked so but to try thee' (II. 3. 176). Notwithstanding the heartless comicality of this situation, the trope is not only morally unmistakable but recognizably gendered. Despite the metaphor and image of the tortured Proteus, the ancestry of the idea is not entirely gender-neutral: in Ovid, Peleus rapes Thetis — or rather, forces her to surrender — by restraining her with chains from transforming her shape and escaping.[56] It was Proteus himself who offered Peleus the secret recipe. The discourses of controlling nature, central to the developing methods and concepts of natural philosophy, were not entirely non-gendered either. Nature or physical matter was commonly referred to as *materia*, conceived as a feminine subject of discovery.[57]

Two broad movements are discernible in the post-Shakespearean plots of 'trying'. First, tragicomedy and specifically legal frameworks gravitate towards each other. Secondly, the false trial motif is placed at the heart of plots of love, and thus made explicitly affective; indeed, these plots are as consistently about love as much as they are about knowledge and the routes that lead to it. Thus they bring us to the threshold of the perception that comedic art and law and love all have something in common: they are all engaged in a subtle balancing act between discovery, trust, and risk. Ethical literature, legitimate knowledge, humane judgement, and the possibility of love are attainable — without sacrificing excitement — only when the balance is got right; when the process is examined and chastened as vigilantly as the end is sought. This is also, of course, a version of the Shakespearean juggling act between possibility, probability, and the improbable possible.

Notes to Chapter 4

An earlier version of this essay, 'False Trials in Shakespeare, Massinger, and Ford', appeared in *Essays in Criticism*, 56 (2006), 219–40.

1. *The Rhetoric and Poetics of Aristotle*, trans. by W. Rhys Roberts and Ingram Bywater, ed. by Friedrich Solmsen (New York: Random House, 1954): *Poetics*, 16, 1455a 16–21; *Rhetoric*, I.I.II,

1.37, 2.25.8. In Aristotelian terms, 'artificial' refers not to external objects but to arguments based on inherent probability or reasoning.

2. On the relation between uncertainty, law, and genre in *All's Well*, see Subha Mukherji, '"Lawfull Deede": Consummation, Custom and Law in Shakespeare's *All's Well that Ends Well*', in *The Cambridge Shakespeare Library*, ed. by Catherine Alexander, 3 vols (Cambridge: Cambridge University Press, 2003), I, 270–87.

3. For an interesting discussion of the scene between Macduff and Macbeth see Sally Mapstone, 'Shakespeare and Scottish Kingship: A Case History', in *The Rose and the Thistle: Essays on the Culture of Late Medieval and Renaissance Scotland*, ed. by Sally Mapstone and Juliette Wood (East Lothian: Phantassie, 1998), pp. 158–89.

4. References are to *King Lear: A Parallel Text Edition*, ed. by René Weis (London: Longman, 1993).

5. The Old Man in Marlowe's *Dr Faustus* uses the word 'sift' for Satanic attempts on his virtue, and associates 'trial' with God's testing of him through Satan: 'Satan begins to sift me with his pride | As in this furnace God shall try my faith': *Doctor Faustus*, ed. by David Bevington and Eric Rasmussen (Manchester: Manchester University Press, 1993), A-Text, v. 1. 114. And in Shakespeare's *Hamlet* the word is used by the purported villain of the piece, Claudius: 'Well, we shall sift him' (II. 2. 58).

6. Bernard Williams, *Morality* (New York and London: Harper & Row, 1972), p. 79.

7. Friedrich Nietzsche, *The Genealogy of Morals*, in *The Birth of Tragedy and The Genealogy of Morals*, trans. by Francis Golffing (New York: Anchor, 1956), p. 289.

8. Meric Casaubon's phrase: see his epistolary treatise on 'general learning', in Richard Serjeantson, ed., *Generall Learning: A Seventeenth-Century Treatise on the Formation of the General Scholar, by Meric Casaubon* (Cambridge: RTM, 1999), esp. 89–101.

9. References are to *The Picture*, in *The Plays and Poems of Philip Massinger*, ed. by Philip Edwards and Colin Gibson, 5 vols (Oxford: Clarendon Press, 1976), III.

10. Francis Bacon, *The Advancement of Learning*, II, in *The Works of Francis Bacon*, ed. by J. Spedding, R. L. Ellis and D. D. Heath, 14 vols (London: Longman, 1857–74), III, p. 333.

11. Bacon, *Parasceve*, in *Works*, I, 399; *Works*, IV, 257.

12. Bacon, *Works*, IV, 20; IV, 18.

13. See, for example, Henry Bracton, *On the Laws and Customs of England* (Cambridge, MA: Harvard University Press, 1968), pp. 404–48; and Barbara Shapiro, 'Rhetoric and the English Law of Evidence', in *Rhetoric and Law in Early Modern Europe*, ed. by Lorna Hutson and Victoria Kahn (New Haven and London: Yale University Press, 2001), pp. 54–72 (p. 62).

14. See Shapiro, 'Rhetoric', pp. 59–62.

15. 'Rhetoric', p. 61.

16. See Shapiro, 'Rhetoric', pp. 57–61 on the use of presumptive (or circumstantial) evidence in English law.

17. This consciously evokes treason or criminal trials, where defendants were not allowed counsel. On denial of the benefit of counsel to those accused of treason see Harry L. Stephen, 'The Trial of Sir Walter Raleigh', *Transactions of the Royal Historical Society*, 4th ser., 2 (1919), 172–87 (p. 184). See also Ferdinand Pulton, *De pace regis et regni* (London, 1610), esp. 184^v.

18. *Areopagitica*, in *Complete Prose Works of John Milton*, ed. by Don Wolfe and others, 5 vols (New Haven: Yale University Press, 1952–66), II (1959), p. 515.

19. Bacon, *Instauratio magna*, in *Works*, I, 144; IV, 32.

20. Bacon, *The Letters and Life of Francis Bacon*, ed. by J. Spedding, 7 vols (London: Longman, 1861–74), III (1868), p. 114.

21. See R. W. Serjeantson, 'Testimony and Proof in Early-Modern England', *Studies in History and Philosophy of Science*, 2 (1999), 195–236, on the separation, in dialectic, between proof and such amplificatory or confirmatory factors as testimony.

22. Bacon, *Parasceve*, in *Works*, IV, 261.

23. Gabriel Josipovici, *On Trust* (New Haven: Yale University Press, 1999), p. 98, in the context of a discussion of Richard's aversion of the trial by combat at the beginning of Shakespeare's *Richard II*.

24. See Shapiro, 'Rhetoric', p. 59.

25. Henry Swinburne, *A Treatise of Spousals* (*c.* 1600), ed. by Randolph Trumbach (London: Garland, 1985), p. 65. 'Distinctions' are legal categories and definitions devised for analysis and enquiry.

26. Peter Pesic, 'Wrestling with Proteus: Francis Bacon and the "Torture" of Nature', *Isis*, 90 (1999), 81–94.

27. Elizabeth Hanson, *Discovering the Subject in Renaissance England* (Cambridge: Cambridge University Press, 1998), pp. 122–49.

28. Pesic, pp. 88–89.

29. Bacon, *Filum labyrinthi*, in *Works*, III, 498.

30. Bacon, *Advancement*, in *Works*, III, 280.

31. See Julian Martin, *Francis Bacon, the State, and the Reform of Natural Philosophy* (Cambridge: Cambridge University Press, 1992), pp. 81–83.

32. On the jury system and its relative autonomy in English common law see Thomas Green, *Verdict According to Conscience: Perspectives on the English Criminal Trial Jury, 1200–1800* (Chicago: Chicago University Press, 1985), and *Twelve Good Men and True: The Criminal Trial Jury in England, 1200–1800* (Princeton, NJ: Princeton University Press, 1988); Barbara Shapiro, *A Culture of Fact: England, 1550–1700* (Ithaca and London: Cornell University Press, 2000), pp. 9–13.

33. Aristotle, *Rhetoric and Poetics*, 16, 1455a 16–21.

34. *Rhetoric*, 1.1.11, 1.37, 2.25.8; and cf. 1.2.4: 'where there is no certainty and there is room for doubt, our confidence is absolute'.

35. Jeremy Taylor, *The Real Presence and Spirituall of Christ in the Blessed Sacrament Proved against the Doctrine of Transubstantiation* (1654), in *The Whole Works of the Right Reverend Jeremy Taylor*, ed. by Reginald Heber, rev. by Charles Page Eden, 10 vols (London: Longman, 1849–54), VI (1852), 108.

36. John Calvin, *Institutes of the Christian Religion*, ed. by John T. McNeill, 2 vols (London: SCM, 1961), I, 64–65.

37. Bacon, 'Praefatio', *Instauratio magna*, in *Works*, I, 129; IV, 18.

38. John Cowell, *The Interpreter* (London, 1607), sig. ★3.

39. Swinburne, pp. 65–66.

40. Bacon, 'Proemium', *Instauratio magna*, in *Works*, I, 122; IV, 8.

41. Bacon, *Works*, I, 462; III, 294.

42. See Bacon, *Works*, VI, 377; see also John M. Steadman, *The Hill and the Labyrinth: Discourse and Certitude in Milton and his Near-Contemporaries* (Berkeley: California University Press, 1984), p. 3, but also, more generally, pp. 1–16 on the metaphors of the hill and the labyrinth.

43. George Herbert, *The English Poems of George Herbert*, ed. by C. A. Patrides (London: Dent, 1974).

44. *Troilus and Cressida*, v. 3. 152. The Riverside editors call this 'Shakespeare's error for the name of Arachne, who, according to Ovid [...] was turned into a spider by Pallas'. The New Cambridge editor suggests, more temptingly, that 'though "Ariachne" may be a slip or a spelling invented to fit the metre, it is more likely that Shakespeare conflated Arachne with Ariadne, the Cretan girl whose love for Theseus led her to give him a length of thread to help him find his way out of the labyrinth'. On how half-remembering can lead to a mingling of myths, meanings, and thereby genres in Shakespeare, see A. D. Nuttall, 'A Midsummer Night's Dream: Comedy as Apotrope of Myth', *Shakespeare Survey*, 53 (2000), 49–59, which is also brilliantly suggestive of how these little things in Shakespeare are rarely ever accidents.

45. Giambattista Guarini, *Compendio della poesia tragicomica* (Venice, 1601), III, 403.

46. A. D. Nuttall, 'The Winter's Tale: Ovid Transformed', in *Shakespeare's Ovid: The Metamorphoses in the Plays and Poems*, ed. by A. B. Taylor (Cambridge: Cambridge University Press, 2000), pp. 135–49 (p. 148).

47. Giambattista Guarini, *Il verato ovvero difesa di quanto ha scritto M. Giason Denores di quanto ha egli ditto in un suo discorso delle tragicomedie, e delli pastorali* (Ferrara, 1588), II, 259: to be referred to as *Il verato* (I), to distinguish it from *Il verato* (II), a second, longer treatise, *Il verato secondo* (written 1591 but published in Florence, 1593).

48. See, for example, Giason Denores's attack on Guarini in *Discorso di Giason Denores* (Padua, 1586), to which Guarini responded in *Il verato* (I), and in a longer treatise.

49. On the relation between the ideas of probability addressed in plays of the early seventeenth century and the official legal formulations of such ideas later in the period, in the writings of Matthew Hale and Geoffrey Gilbert, see Mukherji, *Law and Representation*, esp. 'Epilogue'. For histories of probability see Ian Hacking's outdated but still useful *The Emergence of Probability* (Cambridge: Cambridge University Press, 1975); Barbara Shapiro, *Probability and Certainty in Seventeenth Century England* (Princeton, NJ: Princeton University Press, 1983); James Franklin, *The Science of Conjecture: Evidence and Probability before Pascal* (Baltimore, MD: Johns Hopkins University Press, 2001). For useful correctives to Hacking and Shapiro see Serjeantson, 'Testimony and Proof'.

50. On experiment and the culture of fact, and the role of the Royal Society in the development of these, see Shapiro, *Culture of Fact*.

51. I am grateful to Yota Batsaki for alerting me in private conversation to this preoccupation in eighteenth-century fiction.

52. Lois Bueler, *The Tested Woman Plot: Women's Choices, Men's Judgments, and the Shaping of Stories* (Ohio: Ohio State University Press, 2001).

53. Lorna Hutson, *The Usurer's Daughter: Male Friendships and Fictions of Women in Sixteenth-Century England* (London: Routledge, 1994), pp. 163–223.

54. Luce Irigaray's phrase in 'The Power of Discourse and the Subordination of the Feminine', in *Literary Theory: An Anthology*, ed. by Julie Rivkin and Michael Ryan (Oxford: Blackwell, 1998), pp. 570–73 (p. 570).

55. Ben Jonson, *Volpone*, ed. by David Cook (London: Methuen, 1962), III. 2. 222–23.

56. Ovid, *Metamorphoses*, XI. I am grateful to Tania Demetriou for this reference.

57. The terminology and metaphors of natural philosophy have implications for the gendering of methodology in the seventeenth century. See Carolyn Merchant, *The Death of Nature: Women, Ecology, and the Scientific Revolution* (San Francisco: Harper & Row, 1980).

CHAPTER 5

Two Concepts of Reality in
Antony and Cleopatra

N. K. Sugimura

'The crown o' the earth doth melt': The Dissolution of Antony

In *Antony and Cleopatra* reality is 'a strange serpent' (II. 7. 48) indeed. While Roman reality is usually marshalled to the camp of the austere and civil, the constant, the reasonable, the hierarchical, and the temporal, Egyptian reality meanwhile sides with the playful, the over-abundant, the fluctuating, the passionate, the disorderly, and the eternal.[1] This division, supposedly arising from differences between 'Roman' and 'Egyptian' temperaments, actually underscores two different philosophical expressions of reality. In placing Antony in the context of Stoicism and Sartrian existentialism, on the one hand, and in aligning Cleopatra with both St Anselm and Simone de Beauvoir, on the other, it should be obvious that I am not making any historical claims for influence on Shakespeare's thinking. Although it is generally acknowledged that Shakespeare had familiarity with Stoic thought from sources like Plutarch and Montaigne, this essay is structured according to a conceptual (and not historical) framework. As A. D. Nuttall has demonstrated time and again, literature and philosophy talk to one another across the centuries. In Shakespeare we can read both the earlier and later history of philosophy. Such a reading not only assists our understanding of *Antony and Cleopatra*, but also sheds new interpretative light on the play's depiction of reality.

In Antony's cloud scene in Act IV, Stoicism readily lends itself to existentialism. Antony, who has fled and lost the Battle of Actium, now discovers that even Enobarbus, deemed to be his most faithful follower, has deserted him for Caesar (IV. 5. 11–17). As Antony watches Caesar's galleys conquer his own (IV. 12), he begins to suspect that Cleopatra has betrayed him as well — that she has 'pack'd cards with Caesar, and false-play'd my glory | Unto an enemy's triumph' (IV. 14. 19–20). Thinking himself bereft of honour, country, and, now, even his lover, Antony embraces suicide as the remedy for his current condition. Although not a fully fledged Stoic like Caesar in *Antony and Cleopatra* or Brutus in *Julius Caesar*, Antony is nonetheless a kind of 'lapsed' Stoic. Inculcated in him are the cultural pressures that Stoicism brings to bear on Roman society. When Cleopatra observes with frustration that 'a Roman thought hath strook him' (I. 2. 83), we have the distinct feeling this is not the first time that Antony yields to an acculturated understanding of the 'Roman' or Stoic mentality.

In Act IV Stoicism strikes Antony down. Here he experiences a type of existentialist crisis in which his personal self or essence — the one thing Descartes thought he could be sure of — is suddenly deemed insubstantial:

> ANTONY   Eros, thou yet behold'st me?
> EROS   Ay, noble lord.
> ANTONY   Sometime we see a cloud that's dragonish,
>   A vapor sometime like a bear or lion,
>   A [tower'd] citadel, a pendant rock,
>   A forked mountain, or blue promontory
>   With trees upon't that nod unto the world,
>   And mock our eyes with air. Thou hast seen these signs,
>   They are black vesper's pageants.
> EROS   Ay, my lord.
> ANTONY   That which is now a horse, even with a thought
>   The rack dislimns, and makes it indistinct
>   As water is in water.
> EROS   It does, my lord. (IV. 14. 1–12)

While Eros, in the dialogue, responds with 'Ay' to the contingency of the world, Antony, meanwhile, talks about contingency in so far as the dispersing clouds mirror — in the external, physical landscape — his feeling that his inner self is also 'dislimning', or dissolving.[2] The sense of self-effacement is strong, and recurs in Antony's lament, 'Here I am Antony, | Yet cannot hold this visible shape, my knave' (IV. 14. 12–14). At the core of this passage, then, is the Sartrian idea that being, or essence, melts away, annihilated in a moment ('That which is now a horse, even with a thought the rack dislimns'). As a result, impersonal existence is all that remains; Antony comes to be as 'indistinct | As water is in water'. Being-for-itself (the *pour-soi*) is swallowed up by the vast plenitude of being, or shocking, undifferentiated *en-soi* — the real.

The descriptive terms I have used here are Sartre's. In so doing, I have chosen the (perhaps more unfashionable) trend of using a language familiar to us in order to explore what Shakespeare is up to, rather than analysing Antony's sense of dissolution in the language of his contemporaries, in terms of Neostoicism. Yet the conceptual framework is seen to work because it responds to the psychology of Shakespeare's cloud passage, which feels like a description for an Existentialist Crisis straight out of modern literature. Shakespeare's emphasis on beholding and the process of dissolution, when compounded with his interest in performance, inclines to existentialism and Sartre's account of Bad Faith.

By examining Shakespeare's depiction of Antony through the language of existentialism, we discover that Shakespeare's play discloses vast inadequacies in Stoicism while, simultaneously, revealing problems latent in existentialism as well.[3] The Stoic practice of (obsessive) self-examination and evaluation naturally fosters a split between the inward-turning self and the projected outward self. As this separation is confirmed — that is, as the inner self slides away from the outward self, or externally viewed object — Stoicism begins to slip into existentialism. And this is why an existentialist like Sartre can provide an account of shame that is strangely congenial to Stoic thought and also to Shakespeare's depiction of Antony after the Battle of Actium.

For Sartre, shame is symptomatic of our realization that we have 'fallen' into the world as an object. We feel shame because it is 'before somebody'.[4] Antony's lines to Cleopatra, 'How I convey my shame out of thine eyes | By looking back what I have left behind | 'Stroy'd in dishonor' (III. 11. 52–54), invoke the Stoic doctrine that disgrace is an objective evil, worse than pain.[5] The idea is voiced in Sartre's statement, 'Wherever I am, *they* are perpetually looking at me'.[6] The remark displays the existentialist paranoid sensitivity to (brutal) objectification.

Sartre attempts to solve this problem by arguing that we locate a primary moral freedom in the potent darkness of our consciousness.[7] The strange vacancy of consciousness, the *pour-soi*, is said to be more truly constitutive of personality than the (fake) meanings we accrue through public behaviour. The latter acts are instances of *mauvaise foi*. They are remarkably similar to Stoic *officia*, or acts performed from an acculturated understanding of the good.[8] For the Stoic sage, acts done only according to custom are devoid of real virtue. Stoicism, which teaches one to separate value and object, thus warms to the existentialist project of bracketing off the world of meaning, thought, and essence from pure existence.

The problem that should immediately leap off the page at us is how, in existentialism or in Stoicism, we are to distinguish between 'fake' and 'real' acts. This is the difficulty Antony's imagery exposes. As Shakespeare underscores the impossibility of this task, it becomes increasingly apparent that Antony never succeeds in fleeing (what Sartre calls) Anguish. Antony never ceases *performing* for others, or even for himself.[9] The crisis comes to a head when, after Actium, he views his physical flight as an existential one: 'I have fled myself' (III .11. 8). In beseeching his friends to 'let [that] be left | Which leaves itself' (III .11. 19–20), Antony suggests that Eros is seeing only an indexical Antony — an object, a 'frail case' (IV. 14. 41). The imagery thus reflects Antony's sense that his descriptive content is dissolving as rapidly and randomly as the clouds he watches. Between the *je* and the *moi*, however, Shakespeare grants Antony a psychological, 'free-floating ego', which is able to observe the bifurcation between the objective and subjective 'I'. While the addition is alien to Stoicism, it is very familiar to existentialism. And it is precisely this role of consciousness in relation to being — which is so important to Sartre — that Shakespeare puts on stage.

At this point, a historical framework may be imposed alongside the conceptual one in order to elucidate Shakespeare's negotiation with these two philosophical systems.[10] One of Shakespeare's main sources, Montaigne, describes the (apparently) Stoic hero by emphasizing the notion that external greatness depends on inner virtue: 'externall accessions take both savor and colour from the internall constitution'.[11] But, notably, Shakespeare has Enobarbus's reflection on Antony turn Montaigne's thought inside out:

> I see men's judgments
> Are a parcel of their fortunes, and things outward
> Do draw the inward quality after them,
> To suffer all alike. (III. 13. 31–34)

Stoic philosophy, with its stern moral standards, appears to crumble under pressure after all. Antony's desperate hope that Caesar will engage him in hand-to-hand combat is proof enough for Enobarbus that 'Caesar [...] has subdu'd | [Antony's] judgment too' (III. 13. 36–37). According to Stoic doctrine, the loss of inner reason is the equivalent of losing the standard of the good: in Stoicism, Nature, which defines natural law and right reason, is harshly proscriptive. But this is because man has already *previously* prescribed to it this concept of rationality. As a result, the supposedly objective system folds into the subjective, into a dangerous relativism. As Stoicism veers into the waters of existentialism, the public face rapidly disintegrates; it too is shown to be another adopted role (the *en-soi*). And yet, in another twist, *this* too is revealed to have already discarded the *real* self (the *pour-soi*). With the anchor of reality — described either as Stoic right reason or existentialist consciousness — thus cast aside, the inner self becomes unmoored. Or, as Antony says, 'the rack dislimns' (IV. 14. 11).

Such a subjectivist stain in the external landscape was duly noted and commented on by Hazlitt in 1817: the 'dim, unstable, unsubstantial imagery' of the cloud scene created for Hazlitt the very 'semblance of reality'. The 'evanescent nature' of the clouds came to illustrate 'the total uncertainty of what is left behind', namely, those 'mouldering schemes of human greatness'.[12] Here, Hazlitt may be remembering Charmian's warning to Cleopatra: 'The soul and body rive not more in parting | Than greatness going off' (IV. 13. 5–6). Charmian's comment underscores her understanding that, in Stoic terms, the loss of greatness is equivalent to the loss of life.[13] For a Roman, the self, the soul, the essential being — what elsewhere Shakespeare called a 'glassy essence' (*Measure for Measure*, II. 2. 120) — subsists in virtue. But as Seneca wrote and Montaigne duly quoted, 'Vertue is desirous of danger'.[14] In Stoicism, as in existentialism, the subjective self gathers identity through its choices. As Sartre himself announced, 'man is condemned to be free'.[15]

Hence, in Stoic thought the rational and virtuous inner self gradually becomes the grindingly harsh mechanism responsible for evaluation, action, and the growth of one's consciousness.[16] This conception of *oikeiosis*, or the feeling of attachment to oneself — what Cicero termed in Latin as the *ipsum sibi conciliari* — grows to be the *amour de soi*. It encompasses self-consciousness and all the ethical principles that exist in accordance with natural law.[17] The play's emphasis on 'seeing oneself' depicts man's love not only for his own rationality, but also for the objective, rational system to which he and his reason belong.[18] The self-styled Stoic Brutus thus observes, 'The eye sees not itself | But by reflection, by some other thing' (*Julius Caesar*, I. 2. 52–53). Here, the 'other thing' supposedly speaks on behalf of those exterior moral precepts that impose themselves on the inner self. The (outside) system is gathering an uncomfortable psychological force.[19] When Cassius remarks, 'Brutus, I your glass, | Will modestly discover to yourself | That of yourself which you yet know not of' (*Julius Caesar*, I. 2. 68–70), we detect that this system no longer merely reflects what Brutus *is*; it is also dictating what he will *become*.

In *Antony and Cleopatra* the mirror imagery returns with strong existentialist pre-echoes. Antony's fall, reflected sharply in the glass of Stoicism, becomes the Sartrian 'other' that serves as a mirror to Caesar. The shrewd Maecenas comments, 'When such a spacious mirror's set before him [Caesar], | He needs must see himself' (v. i. 33–34). That is, in the shards of Antony's greatness, Caesar observes his subjective self obliquely. Antony, who might otherwise have reduced Caesar to an object, has become the 'spacious mirror' that depicts the powerful force of contingency as it relates to the self. Here, as in the cloud scene, Shakespeare dramatizes the feeling that we are hurled into this world amid a flux of being. By way of the imagery, Stoicism rushes to meet its modern cousin, existentialism.

In fact, Antony's existentialism is itself an outgrowth of his estrangement from Stoicism, from the very system that purports to secure his sense of selfhood. The process of alienation is up and running as soon as the play begins, as Philo observes:

> Look where they come!
> Take but good note, and you shall see in him
> The triple pillar of the world transform'd
> Into a strumpet's fool. Behold and see.
> (*Antony and Cleopatra*, i. i. 10–14)

The emphasis here is placed on observation, on assessing the watched object in terms of its dissolution. Paraded across the stage in Act i are the physical embodiments of those 'signs' and 'black vesper's pageants' (iv. 14. 7–8) that Antony will later describe. The verbs all indicate that the Stoic system is not only *watching* Antony — 'look', 'behold and see' (i. i. 19, 14) — but also actively *assessing* what Antony has become now that he has divorced himself from it (it decrees he is 'a strumpet's fool'). Given that all actions are performances and thus preconceived roles, the only free actions appear to be themselves random and irrational. In this, Shakespeare is exploiting a crucial observation from his main source, Plutarch's *Life of Marcus Antonius*, namely, that Antony is no longer 'master of himself'.[20] Against the harsh austerity of Roman Stoicism, Plutarch underscores Antony's deviation from the principle of *oikeiosis*, or self-attachment, by implying the unknowing and uncontrollable power of love: he 'was not his own man, proving that true which an old man spake in mirth: that the soul of a lover lived in another body and not his own'.[21] In this we hear the pre-echoes of the fractured self, of the separation of soul and body, as described by Charmian.

The Stoic Romans thus rebuke Antony for choosing the 'irrational'. Rather than taking up the public face Roman Stoicism offers him, Antony adopts the role of a lover to an Egyptian queen; he becomes, in their eyes, the 'bellows and the fan | To cool a gypsy's lust' (i. i. 9–10). Viewed from this Roman perspective, Antony is indeed the 'noble ruin of her [Cleopatra's] magic' (iii. 10. 18), a shadow of the general he once was. The prophecy of self-alienation he articulated to Octavia — 'If I lose mine honour | I lose myself' (iii. 4. 22–23) — has come true: Antony is left 'branchless' (24). The movement in the cellarage in Act iv similarly does not 'sign well' for Antony. His Stoic *daimon*, Hercules, stalks off into the Egyptian night; as T. S. Eliot later reminisced, 'the God Hercules | Had left him, that had loved him well'.[22] Bereft of this symbol of his reason and his 'Roman-ness', Antony's sense of self is set free. In response, he craves external validation for what is fundamentally subjective. His exclamation, 'Eros, thou yet behold'st me?' (iv. 14. 1), desperately seeks proof for the continued existence of his subjective self. But the fear that it is gone is too great; Antony turns away from Eros to Death.

Once more, Stoicism finds expression in the language of existentialism. Sartre argued that, against the residuum of determinism thrown up by material things, our original consciousness asserts itself. In fixing ourselves irrevocably on a given course that answers to no predetermined reason, we choose ourselves and that self's descriptive content. Hence, Antony claims to be 'a bridegroom in [his] death' (IV. 14. 100). In choosing how to die, Antony argues he can master death and thereby bestow meaning on it and, retrospectively, his life as well.[23] Out of this freedom to act, he asserts a new identity: his command 'Seal then, and all is done' (IV. 14. 49) demands that 'facticity' bow to this realization of his own consciousness.[24] Death is seen to open out on to the fertile field of that rich Sartrian Nothingness which supposedly accounts for who we are. Here, then, Antony can heal his 'mangled shadow' (IV. 2. 27); Humpty-Dumpty can put himself back together again.

Shakespeare's cloud-scene thus dramatizes, on the one hand, how the trembling neurosis implicit in Stoic silence attempts to heal itself on the couch of existentialism. The inward voice imprisoned in the mind of the outwardly composed Stoic is unleashed by the existentialist. Yet Cleopatra provides us with a withering response to this solution: 'He words me, girls, he words me' (V. 2. 190). What later existentialists such as Sartre aim to *describe*, namely, that consciousness is our freedom to imagine what is *not*, Shakespeare's Antony attempts to *perform*. We find our Stoic-existentialist at the brink of death terribly cheerful:[25]

> Where souls do couch on flowers, we'll hand in hand.
> And with our sprightly port make the ghosts gaze.
> Dido and her Aeneas shall want troops,
> And all the haunt be ours. (IV. 12. 51–54)

Antony's vision of the afterlife is caught up in how future generations will *look at* him and Cleopatra.[26] The freedom of spontaneity accorded to the imagination by the existentialists rapidly falls to pieces. In reimagining *Aeneid* VI, Antony unites Dido and Aeneas in the bright Fields of Elysium, thereby erasing Aeneas's painful discovery of her in the *Lugentes Campi*, or Mourning Fields (*Aeneid*, VI. 440–41). Antony's art ravages Virgil's: in banishing former lovers — such as Dido's Sychaeus — and wiping away the Stoic's tears, Antony annihilates Virgilian pathos.[27] Yet the latter is effective precisely because it works in the opposite direction of the epic: love longs and weeps for what it was divinely ordained to lose. In Antony's vision, however, the imagined future is enlarged to encompass *all* times — past, present, and future — so that the *historic* past of the lovers is dismantled.[28] To reclaim the honour he has lost in *this* life, Antony must disassociate his future (imagined) self from the (present) historic one. He then goes one step further and denies even the existence of the latter. While the existentialist trick may appear to succeed on the surface, Shakespeare's imagery works hard to expose the failures beneath.[29]

At first, however, the imagery appears to support Antony's movement to the underworld. Antony and Cleopatra gain a 'sprightly port' (IV. 14. 52); the lifelike, high-spirited bearing they are given in the Underworld, which mimics their strutting magnificence in the world of the play, fleshes out their ghostly aspect.

Indeed, there seems to be no 'faded splendour' here.[30] Momentarily, at least, it appears that Antony has successfully created a 'new heaven, new earth' (I. I. 17–18). But he has 'found it out' at a disastrous cost: the empire of Love is built not just on the ruins of the *Imperium* but on reality itself. In his rewriting of Virgil, Antony relegates both history and Rome to a sterile world of 'facticity'. It was of this brute existence that Seneca wrote, 'it [is] not a bitter thing to live, but superfluous'.[31]

Thus, as Antony moves away from his past, he simultaneously tries to distance himself from existence. He therefore places himself and Cleopatra in a continuous present, in a realm of pure essence. In the world of art, the existentialist doctrine that existence (or things) precedes essence (or meaning) is overturned:[32] essence is not created but given in advance. Hence Antony's vision implies that, by passing through death, we enter a more real reality, *a realibus ad realiora*. (Never mind that this argument kills the chicken that lays the golden egg.)[33] Antony's vision, in other words, suggests that we (of this world) are the ghosts, or half-real glimmerings, shut up in darkness. The Senecan hatred of life and *libido moriendi* (death wish) rise to the fore.[34] In refusing to obey that 'violent school-mistris' of necessity (the phrase is Montaigne's), Antony follows the Senecan notion that man always has a way open to liberty through choosing death.[35] In Heidegger this thought is pushed to its extreme: 'authenticity and individuality' are realized only when we 'launch out towards death'.[36] The Stoic emphasis on virtue and reason endorse an *ars vivendi* which becomes an *ars moriendi*. The Stoic and existentialist alike end up applauding the 'Roman by a Roman | Valiantly vanquish'd' (*Antony and Cleopatra*, V. I. 56–57).

But in the play Antony's suicide goes horribly wrong; it becomes a miserably botched affair. Literary critics have long commented on how Antony's death scene feels like a 'fake' (or failed) Stoic suicide.[37] It thus draws our attention to the fact that the flight from this world, which supposedly runs to a greater reality, is actually *less* transcendent than it seems. In fact, Antony's vision of the afterlife depicts himself and Cleopatra in terms of an extended performance: 'We'll hand in hand | And with our sprightly port *make the ghosts gaze*' (IV. II. 52–53; my italics). All of hell is now an audience for the two lovers. The continued love drama in Hell, thus *observed*, replicates the way in which the two lovers, caught up in the action of the play itself, are always staging their movements for others. Death no longer appears to conduct us to a greater reality; rather, it seems to be a prolonged — or eternal — act of bad faith.

By becoming an object that is constantly gazed at — even in the world of art — Antony's ideal self is imagined in terms not of intrinsic value or depth, but according to the astounded reaction of those looking at him. And this merely repeats the movement of the clouds: Antony is finding his 'self' in what is outside the self.[38] Shakespeare is dramatizing a fundamental weakness in Antony's existentialist philosophy: the Sartrian watching Other, or ever-present gaze (and gazer), refuses to allow the afterlife to be separated from this one. The belief that in death or Nothingness we move to a truer reality, to a world of essence, is revealed as a trick — as an act of self-deceit or *mauvaise foi*. Antony's suicide becomes yet another hollow performance, draining meaning from reality as well as art.

In the shrillness of Antony's cry — 'Antony's [valour] hath triumph'd on itself'
(IV. 15. 15) — we detect his fear of this failure. The illeism of the line brings back
the troubled notion of consciousness: Antony's valour triumphs over itself only if
someone or something is present to *observe* the act. But just as the clouds appear
'dragonish' or 'sometime like a bear or lion' (IV. 14. 2–3), so also does the self appear
to 'mock our eyes with air' (7). That is, it is always fleeing observation. Any analysis
of the self assayed by language meets with an objectivity that is nothing more than
a hopeful posture, or imagined shape, created by us: it is all a mirage.

On the one hand, Antony, like Sartre, might welcome just such a weakness. After
all, it points to the unknowability of the subject, which Sartre embraced: 'The
individual disappears from historical categories [...] the individual — questioned
questioner, *is* I, and is no one [...] We can see clearly how *I* am dissolved [*je me
dissous*] practically in the human adventure'.[39] Yet the 'human adventure' falls
from action into contemplation — or, in the case of Antony, into the realm of
the imagination. The overwhelmingly subjectivist mode of thinking, which
characterizes Antony's vision (and Sartre's), means that existence ends up possessing
an essence; it is suddenly knowable. The two — existence and essence — are no
longer comfortably opposite. In the end, the Stoic (and existentialist) project of
shunning reality for some sort of authorial, primal nothingness cannot sustain itself:
'nothingness', once put in relation to itself and to others, becomes a 'something'
(albeit a highly negative something). In this way, consciousness, which is supposed
to elude thinghood by being an act of negation, finally submits to becoming an
object all over again. Through the use of one verb, 'gaze', Shakespeare drives the
point home. The second Antony introduces the aspect of performance into his
death vision; the public world he professes to leave behind rushes in, replete with
its various meanings.

Yet Antony's ability to recast the physical landscape in terms of his self's sense of
dissolution succeeds in expressing through imagery (if not in language) what Sartre
believed was inexpressible. The ignominy involved in enduring a Roman triumph
and 'th' inevitable prosecution of | Disgrace and horror' (IV. 14. 65–66) dictates
that suicide is the only solution for Antony — 'it must be', he argues, 'for now |
All length is torture' (IV. 14. 45–46).[40] But Antony's death vision makes us unsure
if his 'miserable change' (IV. 15. 51) actually comes to an end in death, as he claims
it does. Could it not be that the old role, complete with its limitations, is merely
being re-enacted in a new and different register?

Antony prematurely exorcizes this thought: he convinces himself that death is
a delightfully vivid object of, and expression for, freedom par excellence.[41] The
de rigueur icy coolness with which he regards and rejects this world is the stuff in
Stoic thought that Pascal detected and disliked. The Stoics, Pascal writes, 'know
only the greatness of man but not their humanity'.[42] Indeed, the comfort in the
idea that 'there is left us | Ourselves to end ourselves' (IV. 14. 22) is terribly cold.
Antony's vision of death, which argues that the truest realities are those that *are
not*, is strangely unsettling. The world of things is fled. This tastes of idealism:
the impoverished existentialist lowers his sail and hurries back to what is now
an underworld haven of Platonic Ideas. But, unlike Plato (or Cleopatra), Antony

leaves in his wake a metaphysical 'gap in nature' (II. 2. 218): individual meaning, or essence, cannot make a claim for reality in this world except by negation and Sartrian nihiliation. This is bleak metaphysics indeed.

For this reason, Sartre asserted, as did Heidegger, that 'this *nothing* is human reality'; *le néant* is something perpetually beyond being.[43] For most of us it seems counter-intuitive to claim that we can overcome existence by simply annihilating it.[44] But this is precisely the difficult form of transcendence that Sartre and Antony's language aims to assert. The problem it encounters is that we are unable to demonstrate in art — as in reality — that such a victory over existence is *not* done in bad faith. In fact, Antony's concern for the show he and Cleopatra will give to the gazing ghosts of hell is palpably rich in bad faith. As such, the vision turns to participate, once more, in the illusion of self-definition.

In addition, Antony's death vision, so predicated on the nihilation of his past, drags history into an imagined future. Whereas the true Sartrian subject acknowledges that he cannot know what he is or what he will become, Antony is tempted by and falls into using the language of differentiation and definition — 'all the haunt be ours' (IV. 12. 54). Death and the next world are suddenly posited as something *more* than things indifferent. The 'given' absurdity of Death is now invested with personal meaning — it is *their* haunt. And it is also Antony's shelter from the shame and remorse he associates with this, his historic self.[45] As the compulsion for flight in the form of suicide grows stronger, Antony's imagined ghostly self shackles itself to a preconceived identity. The self-conscious desire for artifice in Antony's death vision is not enough to sustain the illusion of freedom. Sartre's trick of removing death from one's subjectivity because it is thought of as already *beyond* subjectivity is undone and proved impossible in Shakespeare. Antony's death vision cannot help but be intensely subjective and personal. This, as Sartre acknowledges, is highly problematic: '[T]he one who tries to grasp the meaning of his future death must discover himself as the future prey of others'.[46]

It is telling, then, that much of Sartre's talk and Antony's imagery tenses at the suggestion that an invisible hunter is chasing down their philosophy. They seem aware that difficulties proliferate when the claim 'consciousness is nothingness' is said to be unfalsifiable. Karl Popper demonstrated that an unfalsifiable thesis is not strong but vacuous: if you cannot explain what it would be like for your proposition *not* to be true — that is, if you cannot say what would disconfirm it — you are saying nothing.[47] Perhaps this is why a sophisticated philosopher such as Hume avoided positing any ideas about what lay on the other side of consciousness. He noticeably avoids all of Sartre's strained and ever-weakening assertions about the nature of *le néant*.

The powerful image of Antony's artistic underworld which asserts, over-whelmingly, its own ontological primacy — just as Nothingness does in Sartre — is weakening. Although Antony's fiction may remain *beyond* or *above* our reality, much like Roquentin's beloved jazz song in Sartre's *La Nausée*, it is nonetheless a refuge from a very real past.[48] Antony may claim to love the poet Theseus hated as a creator of unrealities (*A Midsummer Night's Dream*, V. 1. 12–22), but his own dream of the afterlife meanwhile limps after existence. Eventually, the (artistic) unrealities become as rotten as the realities of this world, defined as objects subjected to the gaze of an invisible Other. Through Antony's excessive interest in role playing, authentic reality becomes lost in performance. Meaning dissipates. The song of the Negress in Sartre becomes, much like Antony's vision, the swansong of existentialism and, we might add, of Stoicism.

In his concern for how he and Cleopatra will appear to others, Antony's freedom of imagination is severely compromised. Appearance not reality is privileged. Shakespeare's imagery, in plumbing the depths of Stoic philosophy, draws up a dangerous relativism lurking at its core: performing a role, or participating in existence in itself (*en-soi*), appears just as real as the more mysteriously grand power of the *pour-soi*, of consciousness. Here we have the end to all moral postures (not just the despised constitutional *officia*) that the Stoic proudly adopts: they are *all* postures, *all* unreal. As everything tilts and finally careens into being regarded as performance, the philosophy of a dignified, austere man turns into a notably histrionic affair. These are soluble structures after all. Shakespeare's imagery of melting, so recurrent in *Antony and Cleopatra*, thus reinforces the notion that Stoicism is itself dissolving. In the failure to differentiate between acts of bad faith (*officia*) and those that are genuine, we detect more than a whiff of nihilism.

Unsurprisingly, Cleopatra smells it out as well: 'Si le nez de Cléopâtre eût été plus court, toute la face de la terre aurait changé' ('if Cleopatra's nose had been any shorter, the face of the world would have changed') — or so declared Pascal.[49] In her anguished cry, 'So it should be, that none but Antony | Should conquer Antony, but woe 'tis so' (IV. 15. 17), Cleopatra displays an acute awareness of the fundamental weakness implicit in Antony's philosophy. Entering *le néant* requires the dissolution of worldly reality in favour of a fictional Underworld, even though the latter is, in point of fact, no better than this one — 'but woe tis so'.

In order to keep his play from bottoming out, Shakespeare fills up this strange 'vacancy' (II. 2. 216) by doing away with the Stoic-existentialist problem of play-acting. Cleopatra turns to naturalism rather than to the sterility and artifice associated with Antony's art.[50] For Cleopatra, the priority of being is not, as Antony or Sartre would have it, in Nothingness. While Antony thinks of reality as dependent on a nihilation of being (the *être-en-soi*), Cleopatra, meanwhile, conceives of being — and all that can be thought of *as being* in a *positive* sense — as the best foundation for reality.[51] She demonstrates most effectively that reality itself is rooted in ourselves — in the positive, life-affirming power of the imagination. And this, as she shows us, unites existence with essence once and for all.

Cleopatra: Redefining 'the high Roman fashion'

In Enobarbus's famous description of Cleopatra, Shakespeare foregrounds the idea that she and her art exceed natural reality:

> The barge she sat in, like a burnish'd throne,
> Burnt on the water. The poop was beaten gold,
> Purple the sails, and so perfumed that
> The winds were love-sick with them; the oars were silver,

Which to the tune of flutes kept stroke, and made
The water which they beat to follow faster,
As amorous of their strokes. For her own person,
It beggar'd all description: she did lie
In her pavilion — cloth of gold, of tissue —
O'er-picturing that Venus where we see
The fancy outwork nature. (II. 2. 191–201)

The conceit feels familiar. But Shakespeare is, in fact, up to something new. Enobarbus's use of 'o'er-picturing' (199), a word usually applied to works of art, strengthens the sense that the entire passage is a moment of *ekphrasis*.[52] Reclining and surrounded by 'pretty dimpled boys, like smiling Cupids' (202), the scene is a tableau, a kind of Roman frieze — but one that *moves*. The tables are turned: reality is left gaping at art (213–18).

An objection may be raised at this point: it could be argued that, despite her attempts to frame herself as if she were a work of art, Cleopatra remains a living, human being — a very real thing. And so Enobarbus's description is a *façon de parler*. The idea of art excelling nature is, in this reading, patently sophistical. The objection has a certain strength to it. But there is also strength in the kind of philosophy working through Shakespeare's imagery: 'fancy', as Cleopatra illustrates, can 'outwork nature' by fashioning something that can then leap into our plane of reality.

In opposition to Sartre, who, despite his professed mistrust of words, really wanted to nail existences down, wriggling under a pin of words, Simone de Beauvoir believed that reality could not be summed up.[53] Enobarbus agrees with her — at least when he is speaking about Cleopatra. The only definition available for her as the highest reality *qua* perfection itself must be a non-conforming one.[54] While we might be uncomfortable with the idea that Enobarbus is speaking about differing levels of reality, the average Elizabethan accepted, unhesitatingly, the metaphysical ladder of perfections: a man is more absolutely real than a crocodile (see II. 7. 40), and a crocodile, in turn, is more absolutely real than 'Nilus' mud' (V. 2. 59). This ontological hierarchy accounts for the powerful conviction present in Enobarbus's statement that Cleopatra makes 'defect perfection' (II. 2. 231).

But Cleopatra herself outdoes even Enobarbus. She begins with a dream and wakes to find a truth:

CLEOPATRA	I dreamt there was an Emperor Antony.
	O, such another sleep, that I might see
	But such another man!
DOLABELLA	If it might please ye —
CLEOPATRA	His face was as the heav'ns, and therein stuck
	A sun and moon, which kept their course, and lighted
	The little O, th' earth.
DOLABELLA	Most sovereign creature —
CLEOPATRA	His legs bestrid the ocean; his rear'd arm
	Crested the world; his voice was propertied
	As all the tuned spheres, and that to friends;
	But when he meant to quail and shake the orb,
	He was as rattling thunder. For his bounty

> There was no winter in't; an [autumn] it was
> That grew the more by reaping. His delights
> Were dolphin-like; they show'd his back above
> The elements they liv'd in. In his livery
> Walk'd crowns and crownets; realms and islands were
> As plates dropp'd from his pocket.

DOLABELLA   Cleopatra!

CLEOPATRA   Think you there was or might be such a man
> As this I dreamt of?

DOLABELLA   Gentle madam, no.

CLEOPATRA   You lie, up to the hearing of the gods!
> But if there be, nor ever were one such,
> It's past the size of dreaming. Nature wants stuff
> To vie strange forms with fancy, yet t' imagine
> An Antony were nature's piece 'gainst fancy,
> Condemning shadows quite. (v. 2. 76–100)

We must note that Cleopatra does not ask Dolabella whether Antony existed, but whether her *dream* Antony did. Dolabella responds with an existential answer: there was, indeed, a real 'Emperor Antony', a soldier who was the 'triple pillar of the world' (i. 1. 13). But Cleopatra is not interested in a correspondence between her propositions and Enobarbus's world of facts. Her strident reply is that, even if there never were, nor ever will be, an historical Antony corresponding to her dream-Antony, the fact remains that her vision of Antony is already 'past the size of dreaming'. This definition is crucial: it transforms an image into a 'strange form' of Nature. Cleopatra declares that, through her experience of the dream, the vision has entered worldly reality as 'nature's piece 'gainst fancy'. The intensity of the vision's coherence feels as if it takes on a necessary and real existence (unlike Antony's). In 'condemning shadows quite', the dream denounces as unsubstantial not only the creations of the imagination, but also the theory of reality derived from a correspondence between thoughts and things.[55]

As Charles Martindale has already observed (see Chapter 1 above), Cleopatra's argument is redolent of the philosophic position St Anselm advanced in his famous ontological proof for God. It should be clear at this point that I am not suggesting that Anselm influenced Shakespeare. But Anselm's argument, if momentarily adopted as a lens through which to view Cleopatra's speech, is useful for our understanding of Shakespeare: it draws out the important philosophical movement from concept to reality that is instinct in the play's imagery. I return again to my point that Shakespeare is always a step ahead of us. (Something similar could be said of A. D. Nuttall, who pointed out the relation between Cleopatra's imagery and Anselm's argument in his first book, *Two Concepts of Allegory*, published in 1967.)[56]

If we flick briefly to Anselm's *Proslogion*, we shall see that he argues (more or less) as follows: there is 'something than which nothing greater can be thought' (for Anselm, this being is God). Anselm then adds that we would generally agree that something is greater if it *really* exists than if it only exists as an image *in the mind*.[57] That is, if God did not exist, we could *mentally* make him greater by notionally attributing existence to him. But, *ex hypothesi*, God is greater than anything we can think or have thought. Therefore, he must already *have* existence — he *is* already there. Here we hit the trick of the ontological proof. Anselm cheerfully goes on to conclude that 'something than which nothing greater can be thought' must be the greatest thing, because it attains conceptual as well as actual existence. In other words, Anselm, like Descartes after him, ends up making existence perfection. (In fact, he subsequently writes that *necessary* existence is perfection.)[58]

Now there is an obvious difference between Cleopatra and Anselm in that Anselm's proof is for God's existence; Cleopatra, on the other hand, argues that the imagination has the power to add to reality — to form a sort of rape of the real.[59] But the conceptual similarity, or point of contact between the two, exists in their movement from *idea* to *reality*. In both Anselm and Cleopatra this jump is strange yet startlingly powerful.

Dorothy Emmet wrote that dreams certainly exist *qua* dreams.[60] They are, therefore, inescapably additions to the fabric of reality when they occur. G. K. Chesterton, in *The Napoleon of Notting Hill* (1904), demonstrates that the mere having an idea exerts crucial moral force.[61] He even implied that there is a certain self-evidence about ethical ideals. Once again, the good dreamed is a more substantial addition to reality beyond it, even if the thing imagined is said not to exist. But in Cleopatra's elegiac dream vision of Antony, Shakespeare appears to be asking, 'What happens if, from the *power* of a dream, we argue that the dream image attains real existence?'. In Cleopatra's dream, an idea of the imagination argues its way into reality as an object of truth. Even Dolabella, though unable to see Cleopatra's dream-Antony, acknowledges her vision's surreal and moving coherence:

> Would I might never
> O'ertake pursu'd success, but I do feel
> By the rebound of yours, a grief that [smites]
> My heart at root. (v. 2. 102–05)

Dolabella's response implies that, were this strange emotional ricocheting to take place, Cleopatra's dream (or at least part of it) would be shared with him. In doing so, it would attain at least a transphenomenal reality. But Cleopatra is not bothered by this distinction. She is satisfied with Dolabella's answer because he has used and argued from the crucial word — 'feel'. By carefully balancing Cleopatra and Dolabella's visions of truth against one another, the play regards both visions of reality as equally valid. Their similarity, we note, lies in their ability to argue things into reality from a sense of vivacity.

The main difference, then, between Dolabella and Cleopatra is that Cleopatra argues from the power of a dream impression. She philosophically maximizes, as Coleridge does, the power of the imagination.[62] Feeling gives rise to a phenomenal reality that makes shared reality look almost moribund. Antony, thinking Cleopatra dead, proclaims his 'torch is out' (IV. 14. 46); similarly, Cleopatra, speaking of Antony's death, tells Charmian and Iras, 'Look | Our lamp is spent, it's out' (IV. 15. 84–85). Without the other, each lover envisions the 'shore o' the world' as standing 'darkling' (IV. 15. 10–11). But Cleopatra's dream vision shoots it through with light: all is not 'naught' (IV. 15. 78). As her vision's coherence gathers force, we believe that her dream is, indeed, the very 'kind of thing that might be' (Aristotle).[63] Her concept of reality *should* exist.

When the Italian poet Angelo Poliziano, in his eulogy for Giotto, assumed the painter's voice and proudly proclaimed 'What my art lacked, Nature lacked too', he was applauding Giotto's sense of naturalism.[64] Naturalism in its most basic form says that reality is on the side of objective, natural phenomena. But Cleopatra overturns this idea: her imagination enlarges reality. From her dream vision she recreates Antony; in her death she also recasts herself. In the first instance this being is brought to life through the power of the imagination. Similarly, when she dies, she transfers her 'immortal longings' (v. 2. 281) to us. In both cases she predicates reality not on Nothingness but on a powerful conception of being. This is because in Cleopatra's version of reality being and meaning are derived from the power of the imagination. And, as Cleopatra emphasizes, imagining is an activity distinct from acting, from watching 'some squeaking Cleopatra boy my greatness | I' th' posture of a whore' (v. 2. 220–21). The metatheatrical allusion here underscores our sense of the difference between what is a 'play'-act (bad faith) and what is genuinely real.

Cleopatra, unlike Antony, has always been aware of this distinction. In Act I, when the two lovers quarrel, she rebukes Antony by sarcastically commenting on his ability to *act*: 'Good now, play one scene | Of excellent dissembling, and let it look | Like perfect honour' (I. 3. 78–80). Antony's angry response, 'You'll heat my blood; no more' and 'Now, by [my] sword' (I. 3. 80–81), lashes out and kills the banter. The Stoic, like the good existentialist, dislikes the uncomfortable idea that we perform acts of bad faith even when we think we do not. Cleopatra, it seems, has always been attuned to the fact that there exists a division between her earlier delight in play-acting (now seen as frivolous) and what appears to be play-acting. The latter, which actually jettisons performance, moves us into a greater mode of being, a new mode of reality.

Thus, when Cleopatra proclaims 'All's but naught' (IV. 15. 78), after Antony dies, she then asks whether it can be a 'sin | To rush into the secret house of death | Ere death dare come to us?' (IV. 15. 78, 81–82). We detect a very different tone here than that found in Antony's death speech. Her announcement to kill herself 'after the high Roman fashion' (IV. 15. 89) immediately feminizes and sexualizes death in an implicitly anti-Stoic, anti-Roman way. Death, as Cleopatra describes it, is 'as sweet as balm, as soft as air, as gentle' (v. 2. 311).[65] The strange Stoicism she invokes turns to find its yearned-for constancy in the realms of the imagination, in her ability to imagine freely and then become — or bring to life — *that* imagined something. In doing so, she more truly overcomes the problem of bad faith than anything created by Antony's philosophic imagination (or even Sartre's).[66] The phenomenal or binding power of a coherence theory of truth gradually trumps the world of fluctuating correspondences and an existential phenomenology: 'now from head to foot | I am marble-constant; now the fleeting moon | No planet is of mine' (v. 2. 239–41).

In contrast to Antony, then, Cleopatra is able to transcend the Stoic (and existentialist) problem of becoming a 'mere actor'. By creating herself out of herself, she always exceeds roles and representation.[67] It comes as no surprise, then, that Shakespeare gives Cleopatra the best lines in the play: she is the Sidneian poet, the creator of this autumnal Golden World.[68] Antony's art is beautiful but it divorces itself, like its creator, from this world. As an assertion of freedom, it thus shares the temperament of modern existentialists, who tend to think an act done for a reason is less free than an act 'unconstrained' by reason. The 'gratuitous crime' in Gide's novel *Les Caves du Vatican* is deemed more truly free than, for example, going into lunch because one is hungry.[69] Hume, who saw this coming, said it would lead to an absurd equation of the free with the random: the burblings of a madman would become paradigmatic free utterance.[70] This has radical consequences not just for ethics but for art. The haunting pathos of Cleopatra's elegiac lines for Antony would be bereft of meaning:

> The crown o' th' earth doth melt. My lord!
> O, wither'd is the garland of the war,
> The soldier's pole is fall'n! Young boys and girls
> Are level now with men; the odds is gone,
> And there is nothing left remarkable
> Beneath the visiting moon. (IV. 15. 63–68)

Shakespeare, like Hume, saw all this in advance. Art can never be purely random or wholly abstract; it must always start with something (or so said Picasso).[71] In confronting existence and responding to it, Cleopatra's art casts a bright light on what reality is and also what it means. Even death is made to seem a warm afterglow of this world's splendour. An astounded Caesar remarks: 'but she looks like sleep, | As she would catch another Antony | In her strong toil of grace' (v. 2. 346–48). Caesar draws our attention to the remarkable artistry in Cleopatra's death scene. As she prepares to die, Cleopatra herself recalls her spectacular entrance at Cydnus: 'I am *again* for Cydnus | To meet Mark Antony' (v. 2. 228–29; my italics). The sensuous exaltation of the dream has the effect of overturning phenomenal time — of making the dream world the richer reality. As such, both moments reflect Cleopatra's experimentation with a wholly new mode of art and concept of reality that transforms art into nature, dreams into realities.

In her assertion 'I have nothing | Of woman in me; now from head to foot | I am marble-constant' (v. 2. 238–40), the notion of transcendence strikes us as terribly serious. The being that ascends to greet Antony is greater than life itself: 'I am fire and air; my other elements | I give to baser life' (v. 2. 289–90). Even at the moment when she passes into Death, the redemptive power of creation, of transference, is present: she bequeaths 'the last warmth' of her lips to *our* world (v. 2. 291; my italics), thereby implying that she is *already* elsewhere even before she actually dies. Gliding beyond this world, she enters the eternity of myth.[72] Even her comment on Iras's death — 'If thus thou vanishest, thou tell'st the world | It is not worth leave-taking' (v. 2. 297–98) — reinforces the notion that *this* world is dispensable, once we have moved ourselves into a richer (alternative) reality.

In passing from our world and into the next, Cleopatra departs with the same imaginative force that brings her dream-Antony into reality. And yet while she is 'for the dark' (v. 2. 194), her sentiments and concerns remain vividly human. She worries, for instance, that the already dead Iras might steal a kiss from Antony: 'This proves me base. | If she first meet the curled Antony, | He'll make demand of her, and spend that kiss | Which is my heaven to have' (v. 2. 300–03). The humour warms the vision: Cleopatra hurries towards not death but a richer addition to, or *extension* of, this life. The moment of death is no more than a lying still (v. 2. 296), a removal from time, akin to the sleep she desired and described in Act 1: 'That I might sleep out this great gap of time | My Antony is away' (I. 5. 5–6). Death enables Cleopatra to complete her alchemical transformation. Empowered by the imagination, she depicts herself and Antony as moving between two planes of reality — this world and the next — and transcending both in the process.

In Cleopatra's death, then, the play implicitly endorses her concept of reality and notion of transcendence.[73] Her ability to deduce a vision's necessary and real existence from the felt vivacity of a dream impression creates, at the end of the play, the feeling that we have been persuaded to do the same. As such, the 'serpent of old Nile' (I. 5. 25) achieves for Antony — as well as for herself — a magnificent and immediately apprehensible transcendence that far exceeds anything found in Stoicism or in Sartre. Across the dark waters of death we hear a triumphantly beautiful chant as Cleopatra sings with Sophocles, 'I see with eyes shut, and I start up, more the watcher than the watched'.[74]

Notes to Chapter 5

1. Geoffrey Miles, *Shakespeare and the Constant Romans* (Oxford: Clarendon Press, 1996), p. 173.
2. A theme that recurs in *Hamlet*, III. 2. 376–82 and *The Tempest*, IV. 1. 150–56. On Antony as the largest fragment of Hamlet see Harold Goddard, *The Meaning of Shakespeare* (Chicago: University of Chicago Press, 1951), pp. 579 ff.
3. Robert Ellrodt, in 'Self-Consciousness in Montaigne and Shakespeare', *Shakespeare Survey*, 28 (1975), 37–50, observes that Montaigne arrived at the notion of an 'intense self-consciousness, which later led analysts like Amiel and phenomenologists like Sartre to claim that we never believe enough in what we believe' (p. 44).
4. Jean-Paul Sartre, *Being and Nothingness* (1943), trans. by Hazel E. Barnes, with intro. by Mary E. Warnock (London: Methuen, 1957; repr. with new Preface, London: Routledge, 2003), p. 299. Henceforth abbreviated to *BN*.
5. See, for instance, Cicero, *Tusculanae disputationes*, II. v. 13–14, in *Tusculan Disputations*, trans. by J. E. King, Loeb Classical Library, 141, rev. edn (London: Heinemann; Cambridge, MA: Harvard University Press, 1971).
6. Sartre, *BN*, p. 305.
7. Sartre, *BN*, p. 42.
8. Cf. Sartre's discussion of *mauvaise foi* in *BN*, pp. 70–94; see also the discussion Roquentin has with the Autodidact in *Nausea*, trans. by Robert Baldick (Harmondsworth: Penguin, 2000), pp. 172–77. On Stoicism and *officia* see Troels Engberg-Pedersen, *The Stoic Theory of Oikeiosis: Moral Development and Social Interaction in Early Stoic Philosophy* (Aarhus: Aarhus University Press, 1990), pp. 66–79, 96, 133–37; see also Cicero, *De finibus*, III. VI. 20–21 and III. XVIII. 59, in *De finibus bonorum et malorum*, trans. by H. Rackham, Loeb Classical Library, 40, 2nd edn (London: Heinemann; Cambridge, MA: Harvard University Press, 1971).
9. Sartre, *BN*, p. 68. The idea is present in the earlier critique of Stoicism available to Shakespeare in Montaigne, as Miles highlights (pp. 99–105): 'Montaigne [...] sees Stoicism in general as tainted by its concern with public performance'. The dangerous collapse of Stoicism into scepticism thus occurs, as Miles points out, when the Stoic notion of *homologia* is no longer taken as referring to an external right reason but is wholly internalized because of our problematic relationship with *decorum* (pp. 101–03).
10. For Shakespeare and the Classical tradition see T. W. Baldwin, *William Shakspere's Small Latine and Lesse Greeke*, 2 vols (Urbana: University of Illinois Press, 1944); on sources see *Narrative and*

Dramatic Sources of Shakespeare, ed. by Geoffrey Bullough, 8 vols (London: Routledge & Kegan Paul; New York: Columbia University Press, 1957–75), esp. vol. V: *The Roman Plays* (1964).

11. As quoted in Michel de Montaigne, *The Essayes of Michael Lord of Montaigne*, trans. by John Florio, 2 vols (London and Toronto: Dent, 1927), I, 40: 'That the taste of goods or evils doth greatly depend on the opinion we have of them'.

12. William Hazlitt, *Characters of Shakespeare's Plays* (Oxford: World's Classics, 1947), pp. 78–84.

13. See Marcia L. Colish, *The Stoic Tradition from Antiquity to the Early Middle Ages*, I: *Stoicism in Classical Latin Literature*, Studies in the History of Christian Thought, 34 (Leiden: Brill, 1985), p. 130. On greatness as derived from virtue in accordance with reason see Cicero, Paradox III. 22 in *Paradoxa stoicorum*, in *On the Orator, Book III; On Fate; Stoic Paradoxes; The Divisions of Oratory*, trans. by H. Rackham, Loeb Classical Library, 349 (London: Heinemann; Cambridge, MA: Harvard University Press, 1942), pp. 272–73. On Neostoicism in the Sir Philip Sidney circle and the popularity of figures such as Justus Lipsius and Philippe Duplessis-Mornay see J. H. M. Salmon, 'Stoicism and Roman Example: Seneca and Tacitus in Jacobean England', *Journal of the History of Ideas*, 50 (1989), 199–255, esp. pp. 205–07.

14. Montaigne quotes Seneca in *Essayes*, I, 276: 'Avida est periculi virtus'. For the idea in Seneca see 'On Providence', I. IV. 6, in *Moral Essays*, I, trans. by John W. Basore, Loeb Classical Library, 214 (London: Heinemann, 1957), pp. 26–27: 'Calamitas virtutis occasio est'.

15. Jean-Paul Sartre, *Existentialism and Humanism* (1946), trans. by Philip Mairet (London: Methuen, 1948), p. 34.

16. See S. G. Pembroke, 'Oikeiōsis', in *Problems in Stoicism*, ed. by A. A. Long (London: Athlone, 1971; repr. 1996), pp. 114–49 (p. 144).

17. The idea, though unnamed, is present also in Guillaume Du Vair's *La Philosophie morale des Stoiques*, which was translated in 1598 by one 'T. I. fellow of New-Colledge in Oxford' as *The Moral Philosophie of the Stoicks*; see pp. 29–30 of the Eng. trans.

18. See Engberg-Pedersen, pp. 70–75. On *oikeiosis* as a 'perception of what belongs' see Plutarch's *Moralia*, XIII, pt 2, ed. by H. Cherniss, Loeb Classical Library, 470 (Cambridge, MA: Harvard University Press; London: Heinemann, 1976), p. 455, note c and §1038C; see also Pembroke, pp. 114–19, 130, 132–41; and Margaret E. Reeser, *The Nature of Man in Early Stoic Philosophy* (London: Duckworth, 1989), p. 65.

19. See Gerard Watson, 'The Natural Law and Stoicism', in *Problems in Stoicism*, ed. by Long, pp. 216–38.

20. Plutarch was translated into French by Jacques Amyot (1559) and then, in 1579, into English by Thomas North.

21. See *Shakespeare's Plutarch: The Lives of Julius Caesar, Brutus, Marcus Antonius, and Coriolanus in the Translation of Sir Thomas North*, ed. by T. J. B. Spencer (Harmondsworth: Penguin, 1964), pp. 248, 258.

22. T. S. Eliot, *The Collected Poems, 1909–1962* (London: Faber, 1963), p. 32. The Shakespeare quotation is ''Tis the God Hercules, whom Antony lov'd, | Now leaves him' (IV. 3. 16–17).

23. Cf. Miles, pp. 184–85.

24. Edelstein agrees: 'The world is a brute fact, or mere factuality'; see Ludwig Edelstein, *The Meaning of Stoicism* (Cambridge, MA: Harvard University Press, 1966), p. 33.

25. Sartre owes much to Husserl's belief that consciousness is the 'intentional object' and that there is nothing, at the end of day, but consciousness. The more self-consciously Stoic vision of the underworld is in Cicero's 'Somnium Scipionus', *De republica*, VI. XIV–XXVI, in *De re publica; De legibus*, trans. by Clinton Walker Keyes, Loeb Classical Library, 213 (London: Heinemann, 1928).

26. In Robert Garnier's *Tragedie of Antonie, Donne into English by the Countesse of Pembroke* (London, 1595), Cleopatra, not Antony, is the one who envisions herself as a 'wandring shade' soon joining Antony 'under the *Cypres* trees thou haunt'st alone, | Where brookes of hell do falling seeme to move' (ll. 1972–74). Antony's 'haunt' becomes in Garnier the 'fields whereon the lonely ghosts do treade' (l. 1833). For Shakespeare's familiarity with Virgil see A. D. Nuttall, 'Virgil and Shakespeare', in *Virgil and his Influence: Bimillenial Studies*, ed. by Charles Martindale (Bristol: Bristol Classical Press, 1984), pp. 71–93.

27. In *Aeneid* VI, Aeneas, the Stoic hero, weeps twice: first, when, 'amid springing tears', he attempts

to comfort Dido (VI. 468); and, secondly, when, from afar, he follows her shade 'with tears' (VI. 476), in *Virgil, Eclogues, Georgics, Aeneid I–VI* with an English translation by H. Rushton Fairclough, revised by G. P. Goold (first published, 1916; Cambridge, Mass: Harvard University Press, revised with new introduction, 1999), p. 562 (Latin text).

28. See Sartre, *BN*, pp. 523–25.
29. Cf. Sartre, *BN*, p. 524.
30. John Milton, *Paradise Lost*, IV. 870, in *The Poems of John Milton*, ed. by John Carey and Alastair Fowler (London: Longman, 1968), p. 665.
31. Seneca, *Epistle*, XXIV, in *The Workes of Lucius Annaeus Seneca, Both Morall and Naturall*, trans. by T. Lodge (London, 1614), p. 207 [T2ʳ].
32. On essence after existence see Sartre, *BN*, pp. 490 ff, and *Existentialism and Humanism*, pp. 28–30.
33. This is Sartre's expression in *BN*, p. 314. This idea that we are conducted to a greater reality through death is also present in moments in *Aeneid* VI.
34. On Seneca and a terrorless death see, for example, *Epistle*, XXVI. 10; on the death wish see John M. Rist, *Stoic Philosophy* (London: Cambridge University Press, 1969), p. 249, and Seneca, *Epistle*, XXIV. 24, in *Ad Lucilium epistulae morales*, I, trans. by Richard M. Gummere, Loeb Classical Library, 75 (London: Heinemann; Cambridge, MA: Harvard University Press, 1953). Rist (pp. 250–55) notes that this overwhelming emphasis on death as freedom is absent in the earlier Stoics, like Zeno, as well as in Chrysippus and Epictetus.
35. For a similar idea in Montaigne see 'Uncertaintie of our Judgement,' *Essayes*, I, 47 (p. 319). See also Seneca, *De ira*, III. XV. 3–XVI. 1, in *Moral Essays*, I; and *Hercules Oetaeus*, ll. 1472–82. *Hercules of Oeta* and *Octavia*, ed. and trans. by John G. Fitch (Cambridge, Mass.: Harvard University Press, 2004), in *Tragedies*, vol. 2. Here, vol. ii, pp. 456–58 (Latin); 457–59 (English translation). See also *De Ira* III. xv. 3–XV. 1. 15 pp. 292–94 (Latin); 293–95 (English) in *Seneca's Moral Essays*, trans. by John W. Basore (first published, 1928; Cambridge, Mass.: Harvard University Press, 2003), vol. 1, pp. 106–355. Shakespeare would have assumed that Seneca the dramatist and Seneca the philosopher were one and the same.
36. Quoted in Mary Warnock, *The Philosophy of Sartre* (London: Hutchinson University Library, 1965), p. 71.
37. T. McAlindon, *Shakespeare's Tragic Cosmos* (Cambridge: Cambridge University Press, 1991), argues that it *is* Stoic (pp. 248–49). But his account of why Antony's death is not a moment of self-deception rests too easily on Cleopatra's supposed straightforward endorsement of it and Decretas's speech at IV. 5. 20–27.
38. Sartre, *BN*, p. 284.
39. Quoted in Christina Howells, 'Conclusion: Sartre and the Deconstruction of the Subject', in *The Cambridge Companion to Sartre*, ed. by Christina Howells (Cambridge: Cambridge University Press, 1999), pp. 318–52 (p. 342).
40. See Cicero's endorsement of suicide in *De finibus*, III. XVIII. 61.
41. The same thought is evident in Seneca's *Epistle*, LXX. 14–15.
42. Quoted in Edelstein, p. 93.
43. Sartre, *BN*, pp. 204–05.
44. Seneca's concept of freedom is similarly negative (see Rist, pp. 248–49).
45. See Sartre, *BN*, pp. 567–68 on how we 'die *into the bargain*'.
46. Sartre, *BN*, p. 564.
47. Karl Popper, *Conjectures and Refutations* (London: Routledge & Kegan Paul, 1972), pp. 33–65.
48. *Nausea*, pp. 248–53.
49. Blaise Pascal, *Pensées*, ed. by Philippe Sellier (Paris: Garnier, 1991), fr. 32. On Pascal's use of Cleopatra's nose see Richard Scholar, *The Je-Ne-Sais-Quoi in Early Modern Europe: Encounters with a Certain Something* (Oxford: Oxford University Press, 2005), pp. 162–73. I am grateful to the author for showing me this chapter prior to publication.
50. On the art–nature dialectic see McAlindon, pp. 236–40.
51. Sartre, *BN*, pp. 82, 103.
52. Compare Garnier's *Tragedie of Antonie*, where 'Nature by such worke | Herself, should seeme, in workmanship hath past' (709–10). That is, Nature is seen to surpass herself.

53. Anecdote reported in Warnock, *The Philosophy of Sartre*, p. 160.

54. On Sartre and 'positive conformity' see A. D. Nuttall, *A Common Sky: Philosophy and the Literary Imagination* (London: Chatto & Windus, 1974), pp. 163–99.

55. On coherence theories of truth see Dorothy Emmet, *The Nature of Metaphysical Thinking* (London: Macmillan, 1966), pp. 17–30, 77. The Coherence Theory of Truth in its most basic form states that if something is probable, it is because it is supported by another judgement. That is, one proposition makes another true. The Realist, or Correspondence Theory, demands that the truth of the proposition must be proved in relation not to another idea but to reality (pp. 78–95).

56. A. D. Nuttall, *Two Concepts of Allegory* (London: Routledge & Kegan Paul, 1967), pp. 130–31.

57. St Anselm, *Proslogion*, trans. by M. J. Charlesworth (Oxford: Clarendon Press, 1965, repr. 1979), pp. 116–19.

58. On existence as perfection see *The Philosophical Works of Descartes*, ed. by Elizabeth S. Haldane and G. R. T. Ross, 2 vols (Cambridge: Cambridge University Press, 1911–12; repr. with corrections, 1967), I, 182. For Descartes, existence necessarily pertained *only* to God's essence. On the difference in Anselm's proofs see Norman Malcolm, 'Anselm's Ontological Argument', *Philosophical Review*, 69 (1960), 41–62, esp. p. 46.

59. In this regard she is vastly different from Anselm, who thought of God as already in this world and sought to prove his existence.

60. Emmet, p. 16; see also Max H. James, 'The Noble Ruin: *Antony and Cleopatra*', *College Literature*, 8.2 (1981), 127–43 (p. 142).

61. G. K. Chesterton, *The Napoleon of Notting Hill* (London: The Bodley Head, 1968).

62. See Samuel Taylor Coleridge, *The Collected Works of Samuel Taylor Coleridge*, VII: *Biographia literaria, or, Biographical Sketches of my Literary Life and Opinions*, ed. by James Engell and W. Jackson Bate (London: Routledge & Kegan Paul; Princeton, NJ: Princeton University Press, 1983), p. 304.

63. Aristotle, *Poetics*, 1451a5; trans. by Ingram Bywater, in *The Works of Aristotle*, ed. by W. D. Ross, XII: *Rhetorica; De rhetorica ad Alexandrum; De poetica* (Oxford: Clarendon Press, 1924).

64. Quoted in Martin Kemp, *Behind the Picture: Art and Evidence in the Italian Renaissance* (New Haven: Yale University Press, 1997), p. 153.

65. A line of thought also emphasized by Charles and Michelle Martindale, *Shakespeare and the Uses of Antiquity: An Introductory Essay* (London: Routledge, 1990), pp. 184–89.

66. For arguments about Cleopatra's Stoic death see Goddard, pp. 584–89, especially in relation to his claim that she does not play-act her death scene; on her suicide as a complex union pointing to transcendence see McAlindon, pp. 252–56; Miles, pp. 186–88; and C. and M. Martindale, pp. 184–89.

67. These are different from acts of bad faith because, to use Sartre's example, the waiter in the café must adopt certain poses to be recognized as the role he fulfils — i.e., that of the waiter (BN, pp. 82–83).

68. These are no spring lovers, as Antony himself makes clear at IV. 8. 18–22.

69. Sartre, albeit in another context, also cites Gide, arguing that if 'pathos is free, it is a choice.' See BN, p. 484, and also Miles, pp. 105–08, who briefly touches on this existentialist principle in relation to Montaigne — and then Antony and Coriolanus.

70. David Hume, *A Treatise of Human Nature*, ed. by L. A. Selby-Bigge, 2nd edn, rev. by P. H. Nidditch (Oxford: Clarendon Press, 1978), bk 3, pt 1, §1, pp. 468–70.

71. Quoted in Herschel B. Chipp, *Theories of Modern Art* (Berkeley and Los Angeles: University of California Press, 1968), p. 270.

72. Goddard observes that Antony and Cleopatra 'seems to recede from mere history into myth, or, if you will, to open out and mount above history into a cosmic sunset of imagination' (p. 583). But where Goddard locates the alchemical power of transformation in Antony — a 'miracle that Antony, dead, performs on Cleopatra' (p. 584) — I see the process as belonging to Cleopatra, though perhaps triggered in response to Antony's Stoic-existentialism.

73. In this regard my reading complements that of Anne Barton, who analyses the play in terms of a 'divided catastrophe' and argues that it is unique among Shakespeare's plays in that we want Cleopatra to die. The divided catastrophe, according to Barton's reading, 'imposes a new angle

of vision, a change of emphasis which, while it need not conflict with the previous development of the tragedy, modifies our understanding of that development from a point beyond it in time'. See Anne Barton, '"Nature's Piece 'gainst Fancy": The Divided Catastrophe in *Antony and Cleopatra*', in *Essays, Mainly Shakespearean* (Cambridge: Cambridge University Press, 1994), pp. 113–35.

74. Sophocles, ed. and trans. by Hugh Lloyd Jones, III: *Fragments*, Loeb Classical Library, 483 (Cambridge, MA, and London: Harvard University Press, 1996), p. 357.

CHAPTER 6

Dreaming, Looking, and Seeing: Shakespeare and a Myth of Resurrection

Stephen Medcalf

I wish to make an attempt on two quarries: the first, Shakespeare's concern with the double theme of death and resurrection; the second, his creation of what T. S. Eliot calls 'the 'ultra-dramatic' — a dramatic action of beings who are more than human [...] or rather, seen in a light more than that of day'.[1] The two are closely related, for Eliot's example of the 'ultra-dramatic' is Pericles' recognition of his daughter Marina in Shakespeare's play *Pericles Prince of Tyre*; and *Pericles Prince of Tyre* is Shakespeare's dramatization of a Hellenistic romance of death and resurrection, the *History of Apollonius of Tyre*, which he seems to have loved.

Apollonius of Tyre is one of a number of romances composed in Latin or Greek probably from the time of the emperor Nero onwards.[2] They recount love affairs, their beginnings, thwartings, and final success, dangerous journeys to far countries, and apparent deaths that turn out to be illusions or mistakes. They do not seem to be Christian but emerge from the same world as Christianity. One notable contrast is that in all of them the deaths are only apparent, whereas all four Gospels stress an actual and proven death.[3] But although death may be simulated, it cannot, strictly speaking, be played or acted. True death followed by true resurrection is therefore not easy to portray, and even in the case of Christ or Lazarus in the Gospels, the passage from one to the other is not told. Nor is it attempted much in other literature. In English, unless we count the medieval portrayals of the Harrowing of Hell, we have a mere handful of works describing the world after death, such as Charles Williams's novel *All Hallows' Eve*, the third person narration of the raising of Lazarus by Browning in *An Epistle of Karshish*, and the dream of Newman's *Dream of Gerontius*. For the rest, and perhaps including the Harrowing of Hell and the narrations of such as A. J. Ayer (which are near-death experiences), we have only symbolizations, foreshadowings, and, as in the Hellenistic romances, simulations of death and resurrection.

Apollonius of Tyre was popular throughout Europe for over a thousand years, less because it images the resurrection than because it is a fairy story with the feature that Tolkien made diagnostic of fairy stories — the 'eucatastrophe', or unexpected happy ending, which can be taken as the symptom of a providential universe.[4] As William Golding was fond of quoting from Samuel Butler, 'As luck would have it,

Providence was on my side'.[5] The theology of some of the versions of *Apollonius* is not more serious than that. Where it is more serious, as in John Gower's handling both in his own person in his *Confessio amantis* and as chorus in Shakespeare's play, the moral has rather to do with the punishment of unnatural, and the reward of natural, love.

From its first version onwards the tale begins with the incest at Antioch of its king, Antiochus, with his daughter. Antiochus, to protect his love, devises a riddle, which anyone who would marry his daughter must solve or else die. Apollonius succeeds in solving the riddle, but, since it reveals the fact of incest, he knows that he has nonetheless incurred Antiochus's enmity. He flees, first home to Tyre, then to Tarsus and Cyrene; thereafter, in storms and sea wanderings, he wins and loses a wife and daughter. Antiochus and his daughter are killed by a thunderbolt from the gods, and Apollonius, believing his loves are dead, resolves to die at sea. His daughter escapes murder, kidnap, and a brothel, and when the sea tosses Apollonius up at Mitylene he finds her there. His wife, brought back out of the sea to life, has become high priestess of Diana at Ephesus. Bidden by an angel to tell his story in Diana's temple, Apollonius and his daughter are reunited there with his wife and her mother. The images that hold this fairy tale together are the two relations of father and daughter, and the sea to which Apollonius repeatedly entrusts himself, although it betrays him, until the time comes for the recognitions. There is a sense, in both the original and its versions, of the sea as fortune.

Shakespeare first used this story before 1594, at the very beginning of his dramatic career, in *The Comedy of Errors*.[6] He chooses only one thread from its elaborate tapestry — the separation, by the sea, of a wife from a husband, and her being found as a priestess, or rather abbess, at Ephesus. The image of death and resurrection is removed: Egeon the husband does not even believe his wife is dead, and only that of fortune and 'the always wind obeying deep' (I. I. 63) remains; there is no vision to lead Egeon to Ephesus, although Ephesus is, importantly for the comedy of mistaken identities in the play, a place of witches and sorcerers.

Yet what Shakespeare has taken from *Apollonius*, judiciously limited though it is, entirely transforms his principal source, Plautus's *Menaechmi*. Plautus's play is confined to the social and satiric; the separation of twins that occasioned the mistaken identities was caused not by the sea but by human folly or crime, and there is no reunion of husband and wife. In Plautus, the improbability of the whole story is excused by genre; Shakespeare makes it a major theme, and, with the aid of the sea and the suggestions of enchantment, turns it to providence and wonder. 'If I dream not', says the husband Egeon, 'thou art Emilia' (V. I. 354), anticipating the mood that Shakespeare will use more powerfully in the late plays. The shallow world of classicizing Renaissance comedy is laid aside for the eucatastrophe and more humane world of fairy tale.

It is fairy tale that, at first sight, seems to have attracted Shakespeare some sixteen or so years later, probably in 1608, when he dramatized the whole story of Apollonius in *Pericles Prince of Tyre*.[7] It is commonly thought that Shakespeare planned the entire play and wrote all of Acts III–V, but that Acts I and II, apart from some undeniably Shakespearean lines that flash out, are the work of George

Wilkins, though whether as collaborator or as botcher of a stolen text it is impossible to say. This need not trouble us unduly, as our prime concern is with Act V scene I (scene 21 in Gosset's Arden edition); the rest is important partly for support, but more for contrast.

Some features of the play, such as the bringing on of Gower to act as narrator and chorus, assert and excuse its fairy-tale aspect. But there is clearly an attempt through the body of the play to deepen the fairy tale by treating it as allegory or masque. The new names given to the two principal characters seem to show this. Marina for the Tharsa (or Tharsia or Thaise) of earlier versions is a response to the mystery of her life, 'born at sea' and 'found at sea' (21. 184–85). Pericles for Apollonius has been thought by some to come from the historic Pericles of Plutarch's *Lives* or from Pyrocles in Sidney's *Arcadia* because of a certain resemblance in their fortunes. But it seems more likely, in order to balance Marina, to be allegorical too, suggesting the *pericula* — the perils that come from the sea.

The masque-like aspect of the play, the quantity of spectacle in it, underlines the perils and the changes of fortune of Pericles: such is the procession of princes with *impresas* while Pericles is courting the princess of Cyrene or Pentapolis; and he himself bears as his device 'A withered branch that's only green at top, | The motto, *In hac spe vivo*' (6. 47–48), which resembles a shield displayed with many others at the palace at Whitehall (recorded in 1611);[8] but also the vision of Seth in the legend of the Cross of the Tree in Eden as blasted but with one branch carrying the cradle of the infant Christ.[9] There seems to be an attempt too at the beginning to suggest that Pericles is Mankind, when he describes his intention to win Antiochus's daughter by solving the riddle as the desire 'To taste the fruit of yon celestial tree' (1. 1. 64), as if the cause of his perils was the tasting of the fruit of the Tree of Knowledge.

But all this, including the last scene, where the thread of *The Comedy of Errors* is taken up and Pericles recovers his wife, is, like that play, only fairy tale and has to be accepted by an audience as such. Eliot speaks of a 'subterrene or submarine music' running through it,[10] and this is certainly present, much intensified, from Act III until the recognition scene. But it is different from the 'light more than that of day' that he describes in the recognition scene itself. Gower in the *Confessio amantis* concludes his vision of that scene:

> Fro this daie forth fortune hath sworn
> To set him upwarde on the whele
> So goth the worlde, now wo, now wele.[11]

Shakespeare's recognition scene, I hope to show, moves beyond the sphere of fortune. In dealing with it I shall do no more than affirm its dramatic qualities — the way, quite unexampled in any previous version, in which, detail by detail, recounted incident after incident, Pericles is brought back by Marina from the point of death. It is the ultra-dramatic, his recognition of her, and, in a sense, of himself as returned from death that I shall try to trace — the drawing out from the old story of Apollonius of a sense of passing beyond death.

There has already been a masque-like showing of his seeing Marina's tomb to demonstrate Pericles' certainty that her daughter is dead; and, in his despair, when

Marina speaks, he pushes her back. But when she invites his gaze, he is troubled by her likeness to his wife and in turn asks her, 'turn your eyes upon me' (21. 90). As they look at each other, he makes his first response to her claim to have suffered a grief equal to his, couched in the largely conventional quasi-Platonist ethics and iconography appropriate to a masque:

> Falseness cannot come from thee, for thou look'st
> Modest as Justice, and thou seem'st a palace
> For the crowned Truth to dwell in. (21. 109–11)

The effect, however, is not wholly conventional: for although 'modest' (which I take to have the Latinate sense of 'moderate, orderly') and 'crowned' look as if they could be interchanged, with Justice crowned and Truth modest, the whole description takes life from Marina herself. Pericles comes near to seeing her as an instantiation of both justice and truth in themselves. Even at its most conventional, Elizabethan and Jacobean iconography of the virtues normally has a logical basis in the Platonic view of values: that they are not only matters of choice, law, action or habit, but exist in themselves, transcendently, behind and above experience, so that they can be apprehended by dialectic ending in contemplation. In love poetry, moreover, the ultimate values of beauty and goodness may be seen perfectly embodied in the beloved, as in Shakespeare's Sonnet 53:

> Speak of the spring and foison of the year;
> The one doth shadow of your beauty show,
> The other as your bounty doth appear;
> And you in every blessed shape we know.

In fact this revolutionizes, while depending on, Plato's whole scheme. For, as Diotima in the *Symposium* outlines it to Socrates, although it is falling in love that first reveals what beauty is, to see beauty in itself involves seeing it as a universal, passing beyond the individual beloved. Shakespeare sometimes seems to adopt this more austere position, as in *The Phoenix and the Turtle*, and may have preferred it for some time.[12] But with Pericles' vision of Marina, he reverts to the vision of Sonnet 53, albeit now the relation is not between lover and beloved but between father and daughter. The style is carefully less metaphysical than in the sonnet: Justice and Truth are not Marina's shadows, she is simply as 'modest' as Justice and a palace for Truth to dwell in. The audience, however, in this masque-like speech must take some of the meaning of Truth and Justice from what they have seen of Marina's behaviour in the brothel, in scene 19. They know that she has the integrity that manifests Truth and Justice; they have seen her 'modest' in a wider sense than Pericles intends; and they know that she is a princess by birth and in disposition, and therefore deserves in her own right the epithet 'crowned'.

Pericles, however, must be accepting those values solely from her look, which reminds him of the wife whom he had seen as a man in love sees his beloved: 'For thou look'st', he says, 'like one I loved indeed' (21. 113–14). His vision provides the ground for a further revelation in her of the world where the Virtues exist as spiritual forces, in response to her claim that her sufferings, 'toss'd from wrong to injury', might equal his:

> Tell thy story;
> If thine consider'd prove the thousandth part
> Of my endurance, thou art a man, and I
> Have suffer'd like a girl; yet thou dost look
> Like Patience gazing on kings' graves and smiling
> Extremity out of act. (21. 126–28)

The tremendous image of these last three lines is metaphysical in both the philosophical and the literary senses. The phrase 'out of act' is relatively straightforward; there is a parallel in *All's Well that Ends Well*, when the King of France says of himself and Bertram's father that 'haggish age [...] wore us out of act' (1. 2. 29–30). Age robbed us of agency, of the strength to act. Patience's smile, then, likewise robs extremity of agency and, since extremity is only a state or activity, of its very actuality and existence. 'Smiling' must, like 'wore', be transitive. But what precisely is 'extremity'? The most natural explanation is that Pericles is referring back to the endurance of injuries and griefs shared with him by Marina. The closest parallel in Shakespeare to the usage here seems to be in the comparable resolving scene in *The Comedy of Errors* when Egeon, in distress at not being recognized by the man whom he believes to be his only son, exclaims: 'Not know my voice? O time's extremity, | Hast thou so cracked and splitted my poor tongue' (v. 2. 309–10). But since 'extremity' in *Pericles* is absolute, without any qualifying 'time's', we must interpret it absolutely — as extreme suffering, wrong, injury, or grief.

F. D. Hoeniger, adopting the similar interpretation, 'extreme calamity', in the second Arden edition, cites as 'the usual interpretation', which he rejects, 'smiling despair out of committing the extreme act [i.e. suicide]'. But this distorts the syntax unacceptably by forcing 'extremity out of act' into 'out of *committing* the extreme act'. Moreover, suicide is not here in question. Pericles never intended to commit suicide and still takes 'sustenance | But to prorogue his grief' (21. 19–20). The distinction in traditional morality between letting oneself die and the act of suicide is absolute: one might compare Lady Dedlock in Dickens's *Bleak House*, who believes it would have been wicked to throw herself into the Thames, but not wicked to walk until she dies.[13]

Like Pericles' first comparison of Marina to Justice and to Truth's palace, 'Patience smiling | Extremity out of act' rests on quasi-Platonic iconography, but extends the imagery and deepens its logic. One can see this by looking back half a dozen years to Shakespeare's use of the same image of an allegorical figure of Patience represented on a tomb, in *Twelfth Night*. There he mocks the girl who 'never told her love', 'pined in thought':

> And, with a green and yellow melancholy
> She sat like Patience on a monument
> Smiling at grief. (II. 4. 110–12)

But in *Twelfth Night* Patience smiles intransitively and without effect; in *Pericles*, transitively and triumphant. In *Twelfth Night* Patience, like the girl who is compared to her, does not disarm or obliterate grief. In so far as she is a character in a story told by Viola, the girl fades out of existence; in so far as she is Viola herself, she does

not behave like Patience at all, and wins Orsino, her love. The reason for Patience's
failure here is that she belongs to the kind of allegory which, as A. D. Nuttall argues
in *Two Concepts of Allegory*, is given life by ascribing their own attributes to the
qualities represented. Patience can be nothing but patient. This creates difficulties
when one quality is represented in its relations with another. One can present a
momentarily satisfying emblem of a patient Patience when all she has to do is sit
on a tomb. But what happens when, as in *Twelfth Night*, we ought to have shown
Patience triumphing over grief, or — as in an example that Nuttall takes from an
extended allegory that is a great storehouse of such cases, Prudentius's *Psychomachia*
— Patience triumphing over anger? 'The fact that *Patientia* defeats *Ira* by a process of
exasperation simply by standing still as the swords break over her head until *Ira*, in
despair, commits suicide', while an improvement on Modesty cutting Lust's throat,
is still, as Nuttall says, an embarrassment.[14] As he points out, there is an analogy here
with one of the logical difficulties that Plato raises against his own theory of Forms
— the difficulty of self-predication. This need not concern us, however, since the
difficulty is not present in the Patience of *Pericles*. For although, no doubt, Patience
smiling extremity out of act has as part of her nature what we normally identify as
patience in human beings, the point of the image is to direct our attention beyond
this to a power latent in such patience, though not always exerted by it. Its purpose
is to transform our notion of what an ideal patience might be like by demonstrating
what it is like in Marina. There is an overlap between what I shall say about Marina
and what Nuttall, exploring the uses of our capacity to image and symbolize, says
about some of the characters in Shakespeare's last plays, particularly in *The Tempest*.
It is the kind of imagination that he calls, in speaking of the island of *The Tempest*
and its likeness to the mind of man, 'pre-allegorical'. Even this attempt to describe
his theory distorts it, and I must refer the reader to the whole development of his
book — perhaps adding to it a reference to what has an affinity with his approach,
W. H. Auden's treatment of the characters of *The Tempest* in *The Sea and the Mirror*.[15]
I shall continue to use Eliot's term 'ultra-dramatic' to refer to what both Nuttall
and Auden intuit in *The Tempest*.

What, then, is revealed about Patience in and through Marina in these overlapping
modes? In *Pericles* Patience's smiling is the third in a sequence of overlapping acts.
First, there is Marina, 'looking', which is ambiguously either 'looking at' Pericles
or 'looking like' Patience: in the next line the ambiguity is resolved as 'look like',
but the other sense is given to Patience 'gazing'. 'Patience gazing on king's graves'
has the *visibile parlare* of the marble images of Humility in Dante's Purgatory, and,
like theirs, it is defined further.[16] Looking, gazing, and now smiling accumulate
an intentionality that robs extremity of its activity or even of its actuality. Yet this
is a paradox, because Patience as we know it is etymologically to do with *patior*
and passivity. Shakespeare here seems to presume the normal Aristotelian contrast
of passivity or potentality and act, and either to invert it or, if Patience is at once
receptive and active, to transcend it. T. S. Eliot, I think, is commenting on an
implicit metaphysicality here, when in his poem *Marina* he says that aggression,
vainglory, sloth, and lust 'Are become unsubstantial, reduced by a wind', taking
the odd word 'unsubstantial' — not 'insubstantial' — from scholastic philosophy

and 'reduced' from Edmund Husserl's phenomenology to suggest a suspension of existence.[17] This is what Patience does to Extremity. There is a parallel for Shakespeare's image and language about her 'smiling extremity out of act' in George Herbert's poem 'The Glance', in what the Reverend John Drury has drawn attention to (in an unpublished lecture) as 'lines of astonishing visual beauty':

> What wonders shall we feel when we shall see
> Thy full-eyed love!
> When Thou shalt look us out of pain.[18]

It may be only an analogy; or perhaps Herbert saw *Pericles* in his fashionable youth, and later recalled the effect of Marina's gaze on Pericles in order to express the effect of God's gaze on mankind at the end of the world. Either way, the parallel suggests how far Shakespeare's Patience adumbrates a heavenly power.

Patience here, then, is not like the melancholic Patience of *Twelfth Night*, or, as in Prudentius's *Psychomachia*, simply the universalization of some aspect of human psychology or behaviour. But I think there is still something Platonic about her, because Plato's forms serve at least two purposes: to account for universals, and to describe the ideas or values that lie beyond and give power to these universalized empirical features. It is the purport of the *Republic*, as of others of Plato's dialogues, that once one has become aware of such qualities as ideals, they transform our awareness of them as psychology or behaviour. The man who has emerged from the cave to see the world by the light of the sun will understand what lies behind the shadows when he returns to the cave. This may or may not turn to practical good: used to the sunlight, he may stumble among the shadows. We have seen Marina's particular kind of patience triumph in the brothel. But the problem of what would happen to the chaste maid in a brothel was a commonplace that troubled, for example, William Tyndale in his introduction to Genesis.[19] Pericles in this simile is aware of the ideal world, the world of which Tyndale and ourselves are perplexingly aware in the Beatitudes: 'Blessed are the meek: for they shall inherit the earth' (Matthew 5. 5). The ethics of Plato and of the Beatitudes have this in common: they assert perfect values in an imperfect world.

When Marina tells him her name, Pericles thinks he is mocked by some god, and she has to bid him to keep hold of the quality he has just invoked, echoing unknowingly what her nurse said when she first laid her in Pericles' arms: 'Patience, good sir, do not assist the storm'. 'Patience, good sir', says Marina, 'or here I'll cease', and she is once again triumphant; 'Nay, I'll be patient', he answers (11. 19; 21. 133–34).

The next detail that she reveals — that she is a king's daughter — persuades him that she may truly be his own daughter returned from the dead. Like the apostles of the risen Christ, he doubts if she is 'flesh and blood'; then, if she is not a 'fairy motion' (11. 21. 141–43); or, as in *The Comedy of Errors*, if he is not in a dream. T. S. Eliot, in *Marina*, explicitly picks up the phrase 'Have you a working pulse?', and expresses the change of focus beyond nature in what is to come: 'The pulse in the arm, less strong and stronger | Given or lent? More distant than stars and nearer than the eye'. Finally convinced of the truth of her return, Pericles pours out a series of images that show how it has transformed his world. First, the sea, emblem in the play as in *Apollonius* of Fortune, provides him with images of transcending the up and down, the to and fro of fortune, and, beyond this, of his own ecstasy — 'this great sea of joys rushing upon me'; and finally, as he addresses Marina, of death and resurrection: 'Thou that wast born at sea, buried at Tarsus | And found at sea again' (21. 180).[20] This latter image is preceded by one of something else beyond nature: 'Thou that beget'st him that did thee beget'. It evokes the relation of the Virgin Mary, 'doghter of thi sune', to God.[21] Given the present tense of 'beget'st', it must mean that Marina is like Christ after his resurrection (in an incident not in the Gospels, but widely believed, celebrated, and depicted in the Middle Ages) appearing to his mother, whose part is taken by Pericles.

Pericles asserts a further transformed relation of heaven to earth when he calls on Helicanus: 'Down on thy knees, thank the holy gods as loud | As thunder threatens us' (21.184–85); this is the same paradox as George Herbert will use a few years later to describe prayer — 'Reversèd thunder, Christ-side-piercing spear'[22] — although by then Shakespeare will have used the verb in the second part of Herbert's line for Prospero to say that prayer 'Pierces so, that it assaults | Mercy itself, and frees all faults' (*The Tempest*, Epilogue 17–18).

When Pericles at last reveals himself to Marina and she kneels to him, their relationship recalls, *mutatis mutandis*, that of an earlier recognition scene — of Cordelia by Lear, of which I shall say more below. The strange sequence of what he now says to Marina first suggests again the world of the Sermon on the Mount, of the command to be perfect as the Father in heaven is perfect, and of the meek inheriting the earth (Matthew 5. 5, 48), and then affirms his own recall to life: 'Thou hast been godlike perfect, the heir of kingdoms | And another life to Pericles thy father' (21. 193–94). He has still one more thing to say that takes him beyond nature. J. W. Mackail, in his *Lectures on Greek Poetry*, describing the uniqueness of Sappho, quotes Ἠράμαν μὲν ἐγὼ σέθεν, Ἄτθι, πότα, 'I was in love with you, Attis, once, long ago', and adds:

> just one sliding sigh and whisper of sound. Only one English poet has known
> the secret of this melody —
>> But what music?
>> My lord, I hear none.
>> None?
>> The music of the spheres.[23]

Difficult as it is to make such comparisons across languages and millennia, I suppose that Mackail is right. What he perceives about the phonetics of the lines goes with the suggestion of the repeated 'none', that if all the sounds of nature, that is, of nature on earth, fell silent, only then should we hear the music of the spheres. Of course, Pericles can still hear the noises of the earth, of people talking; but he is in ecstasy, for he seems first to hear the music just after he says 'I am wild in my beholding' (21. 209).

The music leads him into the slumber in which he beholds Diana. This piece of masque, which is unexampled in earlier versions, again directs Pericles to the sphere of the moon, which is the boundary of Nature. Both the dramatic and the ultra-dramatic tensions relax, and we are back with the allegorical pattern of the play in which Diana balances Neptune, the moon the sea, and Marina Antiochus's daughter; we are thus reminded of the suggestion at the beginning that Pericles has tasted of the fruit of the tree of knowledge, and we can give another traditional explanation for hearing the music of the spheres — that Pericles has been released by grace from the original sin that he fell into by tasting the fruit.

The recognition scene rises above the rest of the play. In it, Pericles' imagery makes him seem to reach through experience to what William Golding has called 'the seamy side, where the connections are'.[24] In this imagery there is an implied ethical and religious assertion that the kind of morality embodied in Marina, the morality of the Beatitudes, is a means to reach that other side.

Two or three years before he wrote *Pericles*, Shakespeare had given in *The History of King Lear* another recognition scene, that between Lear and Cordelia, and explored this kind of morality at the end of the play in relation to actual death. At about the same time as he wrote *Pericles*, or perhaps a little later, he seems to have reworked the play as the *Tragedy of King Lear*. In both versions the recognition scene is as ultra-dramatic as that in *Pericles*, and, as in that play, between a king and father and his daughter. I think too that it shows the story of Apollonius of Tyre in Gower's version working in Shakespeare's mind. For we have in it, as we do not have in any other version of the *Lear* story, the recall to life and the intense recognition whose imagery suggests that it is something more than natural.

In this scene (*History of King Lear*, scene 21; *Tragedy of King Lear*, IV. 6), indeed, we may recognize at work together Gower's *Apollonius*, the old *True Chronicle History of King Leir* (one of Shakespeare's sources for the Lear story), and the beginnings of *Pericles*. If, as is likely, the madness of Lear, which again is in no previous version of the story, derives from the likeness of the traditional tale to the fate of Sir Brian Annesley in October 1603, then one of the *données* of Shakespeare's play was the relation of a mad father to his loyal daughter. Sir Brian had three daughters: Grace Lady Wildgoose, Charity Lady Sandys, and the youngest and unmarried Cordel. Lady Wildgoose tried to have him certified insane so that her husband should administer his estate. Cordel defended him, pleading with Cecil that if he were unfit to manage his property it should be put into the friendly care of Sir James Croft; and she incidentally won her case, caring for her father until he died, and putting up a monument to him.[25]

There is in the old *Leir* a recognition scene of much less passion than Shakespeare's. It happens in France, where Leir, reduced to beggary but to nothing like the extremes of storm and madness, has gone to find Cordelia. She and her husband, the king of France, are in disguise, exploring the way of life of their subjects, and, recognizing her father, she reveals herself to him. Two heart-piercing moments from this play remain in Shakespeare's play and, although they do not appear in Gower, are repeated in *Pericles*. First, Cordelia says: 'But looke, deare father, looke, behold and see | Thy loving daughter speaketh unto thee' (*Leir*, 24. 203–04). Shakespeare curtails this in *Lear* to powerful effect: 'O look upon me, sir' (*History*, 21. 25; *Tragedy*, V. 1. 50), while in *Pericles* it becomes Marina's invitation to Pericles' eyes and his response (21. 74 ff.). Secondly, and immediately in the old *Leir*, Cordelia kneels to her father and he to her in a sequence that lasts over twenty-three lines and verges on the ludicrous, until she says: 'But I will never rise from off my knee | Vntill I have your blessing' (*Leir*, 24. 228–29). In Shakespeare's scene this is curtailed to: 'And hold your hand in benediction o'er me. | No, sir, you must not kneel' (*History*, 21. 26–27; *Tragedy*, V. 1. 51–52). In *Pericles*, again, it is recast to fit the gradual process of recognition. Pericles says: 'Now blessing on thee! Rise. Thou art my child' (21. 200).

The madness of Lear is responsible for a third deepening in the recognition scene that was not present in the old *Leir* but survives in *Pericles* to suit Pericles' recovery from despair. The father at the moment of recognition fears that he is mocked and will be laughed at. The feeling, in somewhat different ways, is associated with the naming of the daughter. Lear says: 'Pray do not mock me' (*History*, 20. 57; *Tragedy*, V. 1. 52). And then:

> Do not laugh at me;
> For as I am a man, I think this lady
> To be my child, Cordelia.
> (*History*, 20. 65–67; *Tragedy*, V. 1. 61–63)

MARINA	My name, sir, is Marina
PERICLES	O, I am mocked,
	And thou by some incensed god sent hither
	To make the world to laugh at me. (*Pericles*, 21. 131–33)

With these choices and abbreviations we see how Shakespeare gives to the recognition scenes of *Lear* and *Pericles* their ultra-dramatic quality by intensity of human emotion at something unhoped for. Another way, of which there is not even a hint in the old *Leir*, but which *Lear* shares with *Pericles*, is by imagery suggesting something beyond this world, and particularly beyond the dominion of Fortune, which *Pericles* (certainly) and *Lear* (probably) owe to the themes of Gower's *Apollonius*. We have seen how this works with Gower and in *Pericles*, and have noted in particular Gower's use of the wheel of Fortune at the recognition. Shakespeare replaces this in *Pericles* with hints of going beyond Fortune and Nature, where one can hear the music of the spheres. Something of this is at work in *Lear*.

The image of a wheel is used four times in *Lear*. The first time, by Kent in the stocks, is explicitly and simply the wheel of Fortune: 'Fortune, good night; | Smile once more, turn thy wheel' (*History*, 7. 166–67; *Tragedy*, II. 2. 163–64). The second, in the same scene, is the Fool's response to Kent's plight, and it enlarges on the image of a turning wheel with that of a wheel going down and up a hill, still that of Fortune: 'Let go thy hold, when a great wheel runs down a hill, lest it break thy neck with following it; but the great one that goes up the hill, let him draw thee after' (*History*, 7. 238–41; *Tragedy*, II. 2. 235–48). The fourth and last, beginning to bring the play to a close, is Edmund's acknowledgement that fortune, in whose close relative Nature he has not only placed all his trust but all his sense of himself and his system of values, has turned against him: 'The wheel is come full circle. I am here' (*History*, 24. 170; *Tragedy*, V. 3. 163). But in the third we have one of those superb fusions of trains of thought and imagery that, if we are to think with Shakespeare, we have to learn to respond to: the wheel of fire to which Lear feels himself bound, although indeed he is, at least for a time, about to be freed from it (*History*, 24. 42–46; *Tragedy*, IV. 5. 38–41). Almost the last words we heard Lear say when he was accosted by Cordelia's Gentleman were: 'I am e'en | The natural fool of fortune' (*History*, 20. 178–79; *Tragedy*, IV. 5. 186–87).

   This, along with his grief and his sense of mortality, continues in his mind and in the mind of Shakespeare creating him. But they are overtaken by an image of his sorrow and guilt at being the father of Goneril and Regan — the image of Ixion. Ixion tried to rape Juno and, when Jupiter substituted for her an image made of cloud, begot on it the race of centaurs:

> Down from the waist
> They're centaurs, though women all above.
> Beneath is all the fiend's. There's hell, there's darkness,
> There is the sulphurous pit, burning, scalding, stench,
> consumption.
> (*History*, 20. 119–24; *Tragedy*, IV. 5. 121–26)

Ixion was bound in punishment to an ever-turning wheel, in hell or in the heavens. The wheel of Fortune, Ixion's wheel, and the burning of hell take to themselves other wheels of torment, in apocryphal visions or stories of St Patrick's Purgatory, together with the actual sufferings of criminals broken on the wheel; and we have Cordelia breaking in on Lear's awareness, as Gloucester and her Gentleman had before, with their attribution to him of royalty, and his response:

> CORDELIA   How does my royal lord? How fares your majesty?
> LEAR   You do me wrong to take me out o' th' grave.
>   Thou art a soul in bliss, but I am bound
>   Upon a wheel of fire, that mine own tears
>   Do scald like molten lead.
> (*History*, 21. 42–45; *Tragedy*, IV. 6. 37–41)

There is no space here to do justice to the full power of this scene. Let us simply note Cordelia's annihilation of the jurisdiction of cause in personal relations in her phrase 'No cause, no cause' (*History*, 21. 73; *Tragedy*, V. 1. 69). Heart-rending as it is, it prepares for the scene in which Lear and Cordelia are brought in together as prisoners, which continues to correspond with the recognition scene in *Pericles*. The startling grace of 'No cause, no cause' is replaced by straightforward Stoicism. It is no longer through personal grace but through Stoicism that she now asserts her independence of Fortune:

> For thee, oppressed king, am I cast down,
> Myself could else outfrown false fortune's frown.
> Shall we not see these daughters and these sisters?
> (*History*, 24. 5–8; *Tragedy*, V. 3. 5–8)

Her father, however, believes that he has another way to rise above fortune. Like Pericles, he uses imagery of the contrast between this world, where change and Fortune rule, and the world beyond:

> We two alone will sing like birds i ' th' cage:
> When thou dost ask me blessing, I'll kneel down,

> And ask of thee forgiveness: so we'll live,
> And pray, and sing and tell old tales, and laugh
> At gilded butterflies, and hear poor rogues
> Talk of court news, and we'll talk with them too —
> Who loses and who wins, who's in, who's out,
> And take upon's the mystery of things,
> As if we were God's spies; and we'll wear out
> In a wall'd prison packs and sects of great ones
> That ebb and flow by th' moon.
> (*History*, 22. 11–19; *Tragedy*, v. 3. 9–19)

In this 'poignant picture of undramatic life', as Rowan Williams puts it, it seems for the moment 'simply possible to see freely, not to be caught up in the pathetic struggle for honour and precedence'.[26] But it is clear that Lear's vision is achieved only by losing sight of Goneril and Regan, and the scene rather suggests that his vision and Cordelia's need each other. In it we hear another Beatitude. Compare Lear's phrase, 'When thou dost ask me blessing, I'll kneel down | And ask of thee forgiveness', with Matthew's 'Blessed are the merciful: for they shall obtain mercy' (Matthew 5. 7).

It is this reciprocal blessing and forgiveness that enables them to make parallel statements about seeing in Cordelia's steely 'Shall we not see these daughters and these sisters?' and Lear's gentle 'take upon's the mystery of things | As if we were God's spies'. Is it to make too much of a pattern to say here, in the language we used about *Pericles*, that they see each other in the light of the Beatitudes and the world in the light of the Good? I should like to go a step further and propose that this scene gives a clue to the kind of transcendent patience which Pericles sees in Marina and which 'smiles extremity out of act': that is, that it reconciles Cordelia's uncompromising and active response to her sisters with Lear's meekly patient one, and is thus like the way in which not Lear but God himself must see 'the mystery of things', reconciling justice and mercy with love (*History*, 24. 16–17; *Tragedy*, IV. 5. 16–17).

But this recognition scene precedes, in *Lear*, the presentation of actual death. This too is not in any source of the *Lear* legend, which is very strange indeed. For not only in the five sources that Shakespeare probably used — Geoffrey of Monmouth's *History*, Holinshead's *History*, *The Mirror for Magistrates*, *The Faerie Queene*, and *The True Chronicle History of King Leir* — but in numerous other sources available to him and to his audience, Cordelia rescues Lear, sets him on his throne, and succeeds him when he dies. But the original story of Lear, though not quite a fairy tale, is very much a common type of folk tale with eucatastrophe, which, like the story of Apollonius, Shakespeare deepened. He wanted to portray Lear's death. One motive I take to be a parable implicit in the play. At the beginning we have explicitly two contrasting concepts of Nature as a goddess. Lear's ('Hear, Nature, hear; dear goddess hear') is of a hierarchic nature, in which parents and rulers have authority over their subjects and children; this is set against Edmund's ('Thou, Nature, art my goddess'), being a struggle for dominance in which the most powerful survive (*History*, 2. 468–69; *Tragedy*, I. 4. 254; I. 2. 1).[27] Both Lear and Edmund presume that right and value depend on Nature and the rewards given by Nature. They and their associates by the end are, so far as nature goes, defeated and disillusioned. There is an analogue for this in Glaucon's parable in Plato's *Republic*, which, ironically, purports to show that it is better to seem good than to be good. For, on the one hand, the man who enjoys all the practical benefits both of seeming good and of not being good will gain wealth, trust, and love, and, at the end, the blessing of the gods because of the sacrifices he has offered them. On the other hand, the man who remains good while never receiving any benefits from being good must, to put this to the test, 'be scourged, racked, fettered, will have his eyes burnt out and at last after suffering every kind of torture, will be crucified' (or 'impaled': the word can mean either).[28] As Caroline Spurgeon has pointed out, the dominant image of *King Lear* is of a human body being tormented, whipped, fettered, blinded, and ending with crosses and the rack.[29] The question is several times repeated: is this suffering the work of the gods? I think Shakespeare may have known Glaucon's parable. At any rate he had probably read some of Plato in Latin translation, for he echoes Plato's *Euthyphro* in *Troilus and Cressida* in dealing with the allied question of whether sanctimony is good because it is 'the gods' delight' or the gods' delight is in sanctimony because it is good.[30] But we do not need to suppose any direct influence to recognize that Shakespeare presents us with such a sequence ending in actual death. At the beginning of the play Lear is scarcely to be identified with the man who is good but does not seem so, and neither even is Cordelia. Rather, in the first scene we see her as good according to the law, as indeed she says ('According to my bond'; *History*, 1. 85; *Tragedy*, 1. 1. 93), rather than by grace as in the recognition scene. But from the recognition scene onwards they both must be taken as figures who follow the Good at all costs and without extrinsic reward. At the beginning of the play Lear's values, as we have noted, require the goddess Nature to validate, and this requirement is enlarged by his calling on the gods in the storm scene. But both these passages are set in careful contrast at the end with his 'And take upon's the mystery of things as if we were | God's spies', and the following 'Upon such sacrifices, my Cordelia, | The gods themselves throw incense'. The latter phrase, indeed, if Shakespeare had read the *Euthyphro*, looks like an allusion to the conclusion of that dialogue — that the gods admire piety and the other virtues because those virtues are good rather than rendering them good by their admiration of them. Lear's values now are simply the way in which not the gods but God sees the world.

The sacrifices of Lear and Cordelia seem to refer directly to Edmund's command to take them away. And it is not too much to say that this and its consequences proclaim the further application of the trials of Glaucon's parable. Shall we, when we see what happens to Lear and Cordelia, still assert that the Good seen in the recognition scene is good; that they are right and Goneril, Regan, and Edmund are wrong?

No doubt we shall. We are given our cue in the conclusion of the play, in its aspect as a parable about what the Good is, by Kent. There is a striking contrast between his two farewells to Lear. First, he sets the last action going by his arrival: 'I am come | To bid my King and master aye good night' (*History*, 24. 230–31; *Tragedy*, v. 3. 209–10). In the *History* the reason for this farewell is evidently that Kent is about to die, for when we last saw him, Edgar was saying as much (*History*, 24. 212–15). But in the *Tragedy* this whole speech of Edgar's is cut, and the audience is left to suppose either that Kent is about to die or that he knows of Lear's closeness to death — or most likely both. But in his second farewell, Lear's actual death has brought him to change his metaphor entirely: 'I have a journey, sir, shortly to go; | My master calls me, I must not say no' (*History*, 24. 316–17; *Tragedy*, v. 3. 297–98). In place of bidding good night and so asserting a separation, Kent asserts the continuance of his bond to his master. From Socrates to Wittgenstein, philosophers have asserted that whatever we think death is, there are moral demands that remain independent of it.

The presentation of a parable resembling Glaucon's is part of what renders the end of *Lear* 'ultra-dramatic'. But there is another consideration. Audiences and producers of our day tend to give a straightforwardly dramatic interpretation of the end of *Lear*, that is, that it represents Lear's coming to terms with the death of Cordelia. But that cannot have been the effect of the original production. Everyone in the first audience who knew any of the original sources will have expected Cordelia to live. And even those who did not know the original history will have shared one assumption that we do not have. We expect hanging, because it is done by breaking the neck, to kill. But they, used to hanging by strangulation and particularly to its most terrible form, in hanging, drawing, and quartering, will have known that hanging by itself does not necessarily kill. The trapdoor that ensures neck-breaking was not introduced until the later eighteenth century. In hanging, drawing, and quartering, the uncertainty of strangulation was deliberately exploited to recover the executed persons after they were turned off a ladder, if indeed even that mode of elevating them was used. For example, on 3 May 1606, within a year or so of the first writing of *King Lear*, Fr Henry Garnett was sentenced to hanging, drawing, and quartering for undivulged foreknowledge of the Gunpowder Plot. But the disembowelling was carried out only when he was dead, because the crowd, roused to sympathy by his demeanour, rushed forward when he was turned off, and pulled on Garnett's legs — 'something', as Antonia Fraser drily remarks, 'which was traditionally done by relatives in order to ensure a speedy death'.[31] The crowd knew, as the audience of *King Lear* will have known, that more than simple hanging was needed to ensure death. And in Cordelia's case, not only was the hanging planned to look amateurish so that she might seem to have killed herself, but Lear killed the hangman even in the act of hanging her. Finally, those of them who were devotees of Shakespeare will have remembered that he was capable of using the ambiguity of death by strangulation for dramatic effect, because he had done so already with Desdemona at the end of *Othello*.

The intention of the first production must have been for the audience to understand Lear's tests — 'Lend me a looking-glass' and 'This feather stirs' (*History*, 24. 257, 261; *Tragedy*, v. 3. 236, 240) — as part of their own doubt as to whether Cordelia can possibly be dead, and with a particularly Jacobean dramatic torment — 'I might have saved her' (*History*, 24. 266; *Tragedy*, v. 3. 245) — as being possibly true. At that production only the very hard-headed — those who would today say 'Of course the end is about Lear's reaction to Cordelia's death, because we know that Cordelia is dead' — would have gone out saying 'Of course Lear's reactions are deluded, because we know from history that Cordelia was alive'. But no one in that audience will have known *when* she dies.

This dramatic effect could work only so long as Shakespeare's ending of the story was not public knowledge, and it seems likely that this was one of the reasons for the substantial changes that Shakespeare made to the end between the *History* and the *Tragedy*. But in both versions it was clearly important to Shakespeare to make it seem possible that the play would end with the pattern of death and resurrection, and to keep it possible almost to the end. To this end he uses, as in *Pericles*, iconic visual effects.

There are two wonderful entries in the last scene. The first is the fairy-tale appearance, at the third sound of the trumpet, of the knight in full armour without a blazon to identify him. The purpose of this entry is to introduce the resolution of the parable about the good in so far as it concerns Edmund — and his values that repose on Nature's validation of success — in the struggle for dominance. His defeat by Edgar, his recognition that Fortune has abandoned him, and Edgar's story of their father's death, which 'shall perchance do good' (*History*, 24. 194; *Tragedy*, v. 3. 192), move him towards abandoning Nature as a foundation for value. The final push is given by the discovery that Goneril poisoned Regan for his sake and afterwards killed herself. 'Yet Edmund was beloved' (*History*, 24. 233; *Tragedy*, v. 3. 214); even he glimpses at the end Lear's and Cordelia's vision that the good is love.

His attempt to prevent the hanging of Cordelia, already perilously delayed, leads to the second iconic entry: 'enter Lear with Cordelia in his arms'. The iconic quality here is not from fairy tale but from religion. I side with those who have seen it as a *pietà*, Lear no less though no more than Pericles compared with Mary, Cordelia no less though also no more than Marina compared with Christ. With an agonizing doubt it introduces the possibility of resurrection, which, for the sheerly physical reasons we have outlined, dominates the last scene. It also offers another aspect of the resolution of Glaucon's parable: here is the Good incarnate, whatever Nature does with it.

This resolution has, of course, been prepared in the references that parallel Cordelia with Christ throughout the latter part of the play. It is a process that begins in the *History* (17. 31) when Cordelia's Gentleman describes her as one whose tears are 'holy water from her heavenly eyes', and whose emotions anticipate the reconciliation scene in their union of patience and sorrow:

> You have seen
> Sunshine and rain at once; her smiles and tears
> Were like, a better way. (*History*, 17. 17–20)

But this scene is cut from the *Tragedy*, perhaps for being otiose, and Cordelia herself appears in its place with what is unmistakably an echo of Christ's first saying in the Gospel of Luke, although it is not extended by any pattern in the play: 'O dear father | It is thy business that I go about' (*History*, 20. 194–96; *Tragedy*, IV. 3. 23–24).

But it is her Gentleman's description of her when he finds Lear that is picked up in the last scene:

> Thou hast a daughter
> Who redeems nature from the general curse
> Which twain have brought her to.

(*History*, 20. 194–96;[33] *Tragedy*, IV. 5. 201–03)

This seems to be an echo of St Paul's Epistle to the Galatians 3. 13 — 'Christ hath redeemed us from the curse of the Law' — but the Gentleman includes one of the themes of the play with 'nature', no source of value here, neither Lear's nor Edmund's goddess, but a creature that takes what valuation is given it. It can be cursed by Adam and Eve, or by Goneril; redeemed by Cordelia, or by Christ. Lear picks up the notion of redemption near the end:

> This feather stirs. She lives. If it be so,
> It is a chance which does redeem all sorrows
> That ever I have felt.
> (*History*, 24. 261–63; *Tragedy*, V. 3. 240–42)

Something of the light more than that of day which illuminated the recognition scene is renewed in the iconic quality of this scene, though turned to bleakness and pain, with Cordelia compared to the dead not the living Christ, except in so far as the audience credits the signs of her revival. For all its dreadfulness, the interchange of apocalyptic symbols between Kent, who thinks of the end of the world as an image for the end of Lear's life, Edgar, who points out the horror of the image, and Albany, who calls on the fall of the heavens implicit in it to happen now, sustains this grandeur:

> KENT   Is this the promised end?
> EDGAR   Or image of that horror?
> ALBANY   Fall and cease.
> (*History*, 24. 259–60; *Tragedy*, V. 3. 238–39)

Not improbably, coming as it does immediately on Lear's hope 'Why then, she lives', the particular description of 'the promised end' that Shakespeare evokes through Kent is St Paul's proclamation of the return of all the dead with Christ: 'Then shall be the end' (1 Corinthians 15. 24, Geneva version).

The grandeur and the more-than-natural light fade into pity with Lear's 'I might have saved her'. He tries for a moment to raise himself, as Othello does after Desdemona's death, by the memory of his own heroic past through the killing of the hangman: 'I have seen the day, with my good biting falchion | I would have made them skip' (*History*, 24. 272–73; *Tragedy*, V. 3. 251–52). But in comparison with the vision and the values that he had achieved in the reconciliation scene, this can only reduce Lear to the level of the unrepentant Edmund, building his values like someone from the heroic age on success. The imagery that follows returns Lear to Golgotha, but now not as Mary supporting Christ, but as an anonymous sufferer, a thief perhaps: 'I am old now, | And these same crosses spoil me' (*History*, 24. 273–74; *Tragedy*, V. 3. 232–33).

Up to this moment three things continue the sense of the poetry's pointing beyond the human: the imagery of Christ's Passion, the doubt whether Cordelia may not still be alive, and the splendour and rhythm of Lear's first four speeches, brief though they are. But now all three cease. Lear begins to break down into uncomprehending questions and incoherent responses: 'Who are you? | Mine eyes are not o' th' best, I'll tell you straight' (*History*, 24. 274–75; *Tragedy*, V. 3. 253–54).

Kent reasserts the reign of fortune, understressing the incoherence: 'If Fortune brag of two she loved and hated, | One of them we behold' (*History*, 24. 276–77; *Tragedy*, v. 3. 255).

In the *History*, representing those first performances when the death of Cordelia went against historical as well as against emotional expectation, every speck of imagery that might support this expectation is excluded, and each of Lear's broken remarks increases the desolation until he dies. If the text is reliable, his dying speech is rhythmically broken and flat. Only the second line continues with his old vehemence to its end; all the other lines tail off:

> And my poor fool is hanged. No, no life.
> Why should a dog, a horse, a rat have life,
> And thou no breath at all? O, thou wilt come no more,
> Never, never, never. Pray you, undo
> This button. Thank you, sir. O, O, O, O!
>
> (*History*, 24. 301–05)

'Pray you undo this button', recalling 'Off, off, you lendings' in the storm scene (12. 99), is entirely appropriate for Lear now stripped of his grandeur. There is only one thing left — the wish to die — and he expresses it: 'Break, heart, I prithee, break' (*History*, 24. 306). The effect is to remove any greatness, any light more than human. This too is appropriate even to the parable that at an earlier stage helped to add grandeur to the play; the more reduced at the end, the more removed from any consolation, even aesthetic, the more the parable of the man good without reward is enforced. Conversely, if the parallel with Christ is to be kept in mind (although the last trace of it faded from the text with Lear's 'these same crosses'), then it must be with a Christ without hope of resurrection so far as this play is concerned. The nearest parallel would be with St Paul's 'If in this life only we have hope in Christ, we are of all men the most miserable' (1 Corinthians 6. 19, Geneva version).

The *Tragedy* makes a radical change to Lear's death. Between his last two major speeches ('I'll tell you straight' and 'And my poor fool is hanged') there are some nine alterations, verbal or rhythmical, which bear witness to the care taken in overlooking the text, but do not affect the accompanying actions or their corresponding emotions. The last speech, however, is utterly transformed. It is not merely that Lear's last words, 'Break, heart, I prithee, break', are taken from him and given to Kent. The speech that led desolately down to them is given a new rhythmical grandeur by the addition of one syllable to the first line and the removal of two from the third, regularizing both; the extension of the fourth line to the astonishing, desolate but overpowering fivefold 'Never'; and the regularization again of the fifth with the omission of the inarticulate 'O, O, O, O'. Even 'Pray you, undo this button', which is no longer broken in the middle by a line-ending, has in this context more of the old Lear of excess than of the Lear of stripping and diminution — an effect that the *Tragedy* has anticipated by adding to 'Off, off, you lendings' in the storm scene the phrase 'unbutton here'. It now provides a bridge to a new outcry from Lear — may even, in view of what follows, represent a turning to Cordelia's body. For the *Tragedy* now gives Lear for his last words: 'Do you see this? Look on her, look, her lips, | Look there, look there'. The excitement of the fourfold 'Look', coming after the recovered majesty of the preceding lines, makes it impossibly difficult to read this, as would some interpreters, as drawing attention to Cordelia's dumb and unbreathing lips. To do justice to the repetition, it may seem most appropriate that he sees her lips moving, thus recreating the *History*'s effect of prolonging the audience's doubt as long as possible, and then recognizes that she is rendering up her spirit with her last breath. Whether it is played with Lear gazing throughout on Cordelia's face, or as Timothy West lately gave it,[33] with his looking up at 'Look there', as if he sees Cordelia's spirit rising before him, it must suggest that Lear at the moment of his death believes that he sees Cordelia alive. His 'Look on her' even suggests a response to her 'Look upon me, sir' in the recognition scene.

But at what he now sees, he dies. The two new lines give a shiver to the whole fabric of the play, but one for which in the *History* it seems to have been waiting. In place of Lear's dying in despair — 'Break, heart, I prithee, break' — his death now parallels that of Gloucester, whose 'flawed heart' in the *History*, as in the *Tragedy*, 'Twixt two extremes of passion, joy and grief, | Burst smilingly' (*History*, 24. 193, 195–96; *Tragedy* v. 3. 188, 190–91). But the light more than that of day shines on Lear's death as it does not on the third-person narrative of Gloucester's.

The ultra-dramatic quality in *Lear*, together with the intimations of Christ, may explain why *Lear* together with *Pericles* were chosen along with two more suggestively Popish Christian plays to entertain the gathering of recusants at Gowthwaite Hall in Yorkshire in the Christmas revels of 1609–10. It is, admittedly, not clear what text of *Lear* was used. One witness claimed, but with the obvious motive of supporting the legality of the performance, that they kept to the printed text, which would mean the Quarto of 1608, the *History*. And probably of all religious groups at that time, the recusants, with their exaltation of the sufferings of such as Fr Garnett, and the appetite for martyrdom of which John Donne speaks in describing his recusant boyhood, would have cared least whether there was a lightening of emotional mood in a story of the sufferings of the righteous in pagan times, when Christ was only figurally and symbolically presented. But it is doubtful how much weight can be placed on the one witness.[34]

If, as I conjecture from the tangled trails of bibliographers, Shakespeare made the changes embodied in the *Tragedy* (that is, the Folio text) in a copy of the Quarto of 1608, then they could have been made in the year in which he wrote *Pericles*.[35] Gary Taylor, with some persuasive though perhaps not final arguments, would prefer to place the *Tragedy* a little later, at the time of *Cymbeline*. He suggests, indeed, that we have in the Folio text an answer to A. C. Bradley's question as to what *King Lear* would have been like if Shakespeare had taken up the story later in his career, for instance at about the time he was writing *Cymbeline*. In *Pericles* and *Lear*, then, we have the most intense examples of Eliot's 'ultra-dramatic' in the recognition scenes, and, in the revised *Tragedy of King Lear*, Shakespeare's attempt to solve the intractable problem of presenting true death and true resurrection on stage. In *Cymbeline* and its successors, *The Winter's Tale*, *The Tempest*, and *King Henry VIII, or All is True*, the light of the ultra-dramatic is diffused more widely. In various ways Shakespeare presents the theme of true death to precede resurrection, notably by the poetic force of the dirge for Imogen and Ariel's mocking song 'Full fathom five'.

But he seems to avoid repeating a fully written recognition scene. The nearest is the recognition of Imogen by Posthumus at the end of *Cymbeline*, which is done with a deliberate swiftness that suits Imogen's characteristic speed in meeting an event. In *The Winter's Tale* the recognition of Perdita and Leontes is, equally deliberately, told in the third person. In *The Tempest* the recognition of Ferdinand and Alonso is subdued to the wedding of Ferdinand and Miranda. In the recognition of Hermione as statue and as herself by Leontes, and in the transformed scene in *Henry VIII* when Katharine sees her self in a masque welcomed into heaven, Shakespeare makes the main weight fall on the visual effect. But we have in all these plays the pattern set up in *Pericles* and derived from the story of Apollonius of extremity overcome by seeing — a seeing that Shakespeare tries many means to make his audience share. I recall a production of *The Winter's Tale* at Stratford, which I had enjoyed and was applauding judiciously at the end, approving particularly the epiphany of Hermione, when I was to feel myself humbled by an American girl in front of me, who wept and said: 'I've never seen anything so beautiful in my life'. She saw what Shakespeare had prepared for her.

Notes to Chapter 6

1. T. S. Eliot, unpublished lecture, 1937, quoted by B. C. Southam, *A Student's Guide to the Selected Poems of T. S. Eliot*, 6th edn (London: Faber, 1994), p. 246; see also C. L. Barber, 'Thou that Beget'st Him that Did Thee Beget', *Shakespeare Survey*, 22 (1969), 59–67.
2. Elizabeth Archibald, *Apollonius of Tyre: Medieval and Renaissance Themes and Variations* (Woodbridge: D. S. Brewer, 1991).
3. N. T. Wright, *The Resurrection of the Son of God* (London: SPCK, 2003).
4. J. R. R. Tolkien, 'On Fairy Stories', in *The Monsters and the Critics and Other Essays*, ed. by Christopher Tolkien (London: Allen & Unwin, 1983), pp. 109–61.
5. Personal communication from Mrs J. Carver.
6. See *Narrative and Dramatic Sources of Shakespeare*, ed. by Geoffrey Bullough, 8 vols (London: Routledge & Kegan Paul; New York: Columbia University Press, 1957–75), I: *Early Comedies; Poems; Romeo and Juliet* (1957), 10–11.
7. I have principally used the 3rd Arden edition — *Pericles*, ed. by Suzanne Gossett (London: Arden Shakespeare, 2004) — although I have not always retained her text. Gossett's division of the text is into scenes alone (and not acts).
8. Gossett, in *Pericles*, p. 247.
9. For example in *Cursor mundi* (1320–62), ed. by Richard Morris, Early English Text Society (London: Kegan Paul, Trench, Trübner, 1874–93), II (1875–76); and *The Cornish Ordinalia*, trans. by Markham Harris (Washington: Catholic University of America Press, 1969), pp. 22–24.
10. T. S. Eliot, Introduction to G. Wilson Knight, *The Wheel of Fire* (London: Methuen, 1930, repr. 1949), p. xix.
11. John Gower, *Confessio amantis*, VIII. 1736–38, in *The English Works of John Gower*, II, ed. by G. C. Macaulay, Early English Text Society (London: Kegan Paul, Trench, Trübner, 1901).
12. See Stephen Medcalf, 'Shakespeare on Beauty, Truth and Transcendence', in *Platonism and the English Imagination*, ed. by Anna Baldwin and Sarah Hutton (Cambridge: Cambridge University Press, 1994), pp. 117–25 (pp. 122–24).
13. Charles Dickens, *Bleak House* (London: Bradbury and Evans, 1853); see Lady Dedlock's letter to Esther in chapter 59.
14. A. D. Nuttall, *Two Concepts of Allegory: A Study of Shakespeare's 'The Tempest' and the Logic of Allegorical Expression* (London: Routledge & Kegan Paul, 1967), p. 37.
15. W. H. Auden, *The Sea and the Mirror* (London: Faber, 1945).
16. J. A. Burrow, *Gestures and Looks in Medieval Literature* (Cambridge: Cambridge University Press, 2002), pp.176–79 (referring to *Purgatorio*, 10. 28–99).

17. T. S. Eliot, *The Collected Poems, 1909–1962* (London: Faber, 1963), p. 115.
18. George Herbert, *The English Poems of George Herbert*, ed. by C. A. Patrides (London: Dent, 1974), p. 177.
19. William Tyndale, 'Prologue to the Book of Genesis', in *Doctrinal Treatises*, ed. by Henry Walter (Cambridge: Cambridge University Press, 1848).
20. See William Poole, 'All at Sea: Water, Syntax, and Character Dissolution in Shakespeare', *Shakespeare Survey*, 54 (2001), 201–12.
21. Geoffrey Chaucer, *Second Nun's Tale*, l. 36 (translating Dante, *Paradiso*, 33. 1); see also C. L. Barber, 'Thou that Beget'st Him'.
22. Herbert, p. 70.
23. J. W. Mackail, *Lectures on Greek Poetry* (London: Longman, Green, 1910), p. 105.
24. William Golding, *Darkness Visible* (London: Faber, 1979), p. 48.
25. See *Narrative and Dramatic Sources*, ed. Bullough, VII: *Major Tragedies* (1973).
26. Rowan Williams, 'God's Spies: Believers on Trial', in *Christ on Trial: How the Gospel Unsettles our Judgement* (London: Fount, 2000), pp. 95–118 (pp. 108–09).
27. See J. F. Danby, *Shakespeare's Doctrine of Nature* (London: Faber, 1959).
28. See Plato, *Republic*, 361e–362a.
29. Caroline Spurgeon, 'Leading Motives in the Imagery of Shakespeare's Tragedies', in *Shakespeare Criticism, 1919–1935*, ed. by Anne Bradby (London: Oxford University Press, 1936).
30. See Medcalf, 'Shakespeare on Beauty'.
31. Antonia Fraser, *The Gunpowder Plot* (London: Arrow, 1999), p. 266.
32. Reading 'one' for 'a,' and 'hath' and 'have'.
33. In Stephen Unwin's production, 2002–03.
34. Gossett, in *Pericles*, pp. 87–88.
35. See *King Lear: A Parallel Text Edition*, ed. by René Weis (London: Longman, 1990), pp. 4–5; Gary Taylor, '*King Lear*: The Date and Authorship of the Folio Version', in *The Division of the Kingdoms: Shakespeare's Two Versions of King Lear*, ed. by Gary Taylor and Michael Warren (Oxford: Clarendon Press, 1983), pp. 351–461.

PART II

❖

AFTERWORDS

CHAPTER 7

When Shakespeare Met Montaigne

Terence Cave

Shakespeare's plays, as the essays in this volume make abundantly clear, can be interpreted as staging certain kinds of philosophical problem — ethical, political, epistemological, even metaphysical — that still concern us nowadays. They can be shown to draw on philosophies of the ancient world — Platonism, Stoicism, scepticism — either directly, or as mediated by medieval and Renaissance thought. Or their scenarios can be likened to those of other kinds of intellectual argument, such as legal discourse and procedure. 'Thinking with Shakespeare', the phrase used here to encapsulate these features of the plays, avoids engaging with particular cross-disciplinary debates; it also seems to be consistent with Tony Nuttall's own work on ways of thinking with and through literature.

A vast and intractable question arises, however, when one begins to look more closely at the title of the volume: is thinking with Shakespeare in any sense different from thinking with literature in general? Of course there are distinctively Shakespearean themes, but do Shakespeare's plays make more thinking happen on the stage and in the audience than other literary works? As has already been recalled in this volume (it is virtually a topos of twentieth-century literary criticism), T. S. Eliot famously claimed that Dante was a great philosopher, Shakespeare merely a great poet. I imagine that most of the readers of these essays will disagree with at least the second part of Eliot's dictum, but is that kind of distinction valid at all? Isn't all literature a mode of thought, whether we are speaking of obvious cases like Diderot or George Eliot or Mallarmé, or less obvious ones like Jane Austen, Keats, Anthony Trollope or, for that matter, Joanna Trollope?

A provisional answer to that question might be: yes, in theory, but in practice some literary works, some authors, are more powerfully thoughtful than others. That Shakespeare is somehow in a class of his own as a thinker is an assumption without which this volume would never have been imagined and some of the finest readings in the history of Shakespeare criticism would fall to the ground. If purely aesthetic value judgements tend to be regarded with suspicion nowadays, this criterion — the 'thinking with' quotient of a given work or writer — would probably be admitted by most (certainly by Colin Burrow, among the contributors to this collection). However, I believe that it would be entirely wrong to define the difference in this respect between Shakespeare and (say) Massinger, or Anouilh, or even Schiller, by reference to some external philosophical system, which was what grounded T. S. Eliot's judgement. Shakespeare's drama is a paradigm of literary thoughtfulness precisely because he was not a 'philosopher' in the sense that Dante was.

How, then, should we go about imagining the kinds of thinking that happen in and through his plays? I suggest that we focus primarily not on particular ideas or fragments of philosophies or philosophical themes, but rather on what I would call the instruments of dramatic thought.

Several of the contributors remind us that Shakespeare often self-consciously dramatizes theatre itself, both the craft of acting and the imaginative resources of the playwright: examples include Hamlet's Mousetrap; the mechanicals' play at the end of *A Midsummer Night's Dream*; *The Taming of the Shrew* played by a company of actors for Sly; statements such as 'All the world's a stage' and 'If this were played upon a stage now, I could condemn it as an improbable fiction'; Prospero's later speeches in *The Tempest*, and so on. These examples could, of course, be interpreted simply as instances of a critical truism, widespread in the late twentieth century, that all literature is in some sense about itself, a critical strategy against which Tony Nuttall has often inveighed with good reason. It is more fruitful, I believe, to think of theatrical self-consciousness or self-representation as one of the imaginative structures and strategies by means of which the play of theme and the plot of poetic discovery are unfolded. In that sense it belongs not only with the activities of Oberon and Puck, as obvious forerunners of Prospero and Ariel, but also with the experiment of the Duke in *Measure for Measure*; the trials and false trials; the plots of mistaken jealousy; the behind-the-scenes work of Paulina in *The Winter's Tale*; the wager of Posthumus and Iachimo in *Cymbeline*; and the devices of the women: cross-dressing as in *As You Like it*, *Twelfth Night*, and *Cymbeline* again, the bed-trick devised by Helena and her friends in *All's Well*, and so on. Seen in this light, Prospero and his like are far more than self-indulgent representations of the author's power over his characters and their lives. They are, precisely, 'instruments of thought', second-level structures by means of which the characters are induced to reflect on themselves and their situations, and we, the audience, to embark on a parallel heuristic activity.

As directors and sub-directors of the action, such characters make things happen. They embroil the plot and then lay it open again, and in so doing they create powerful shifts of perception, often revealing *doxa* to be prejudice or naive credulity or dangerous hypocrisy or self-deception. They explore the possibilities of human behaviour, shining light into its pathologies and dead ends, and often (though of course not always) contriving strategies of healing and ways out and forward; they promote the resourcefulness that is proper to those who have nothing more to lose — those who 'expect nothing from life', as Gabriel Josipovici puts it. In that sense their function goes far beyond the plot-making activities of the tricksters and masters of intrigue who abound in seventeenth-century European drama, although, of course, such activities are part of the necessary substratum from which Shakespeare's experiments grow.

I mean 'experiment' here in the strong sense. It is not simply that Shakespeare experimented with the forms and potentialities of drama, but also that human nature and action become in his work the malleable materials of experimental reflection. The instruments of thought I have spoken of are the means by which a reflective suspension is brought about, sometimes for a scene or sequence of scenes, sometimes for the duration of a whole play: *The Winter's Tale* is a particularly complex example, staging erroneous conceptions and trials and virtual scenarios that test, on the vulnerable substance of life itself, how people respond, how they endure, how they might change.

Thinking with Shakespeare in this sense might, if one takes a step back and looks at the European scene, be seen to be strikingly close to thinking with Montaigne. More particularly, to thinking with the *Essais*, which were published on the threshold of Shakespeare's theatrical career and translated into English when that career was in full flow. Tony Nuttall has said of Shakespeare (the remark is echoed elsewhere in this volume) that he is always at least one step ahead of anything one might want to say about him, and those familiar with Montaigne will know that the same is notoriously true of the *Essais*. Furthermore, Montaigne's book is perhaps the only example in the whole history of European culture in which reflections on an indefinitely extensible range of topics, including ethical, political, and epistemological ones, are conducted in such a way that the activity of judgement is consistently foregrounded rather than the materials on which it operates, however important they may appear to be (some of them are in fact large fragments of philosophical discourse). In that way, foreclosure becomes impossible; appraisal, exploration, and experiment become the key mode of operation. The word Montaigne uses for this second-level activity is, of course, *essai*, here denoting not a genre characterized by informality but an activity of the mind and a particular way of writing. An *essai* is literally a trial, and Peter Burke's oral intervention in the symposium after Subha Mukherji's essay brought out this aspect of her theme. Shakespeare's trials, and the other procedures that operate in the same way, are his *essais*.

I do not wish to engage here with the eternal question of whether and how far Shakespeare was familiar with the *Essais*. I prefer instead to state my conception of thinking with Shakespeare in the form of a quasi-allegorical counter-factual story in which Montaigne, as the representative of a particular kind of discursive thought (essaying, trial-thinking), encounters and virtually changes places with Shakespeare, the thinking dramatist and poet.

I begin with a scene from history. In November 1623 John Donne fell dangerously ill with a fever. His own doctor attended him, but the king also sent his physician, Théodore Turquet de Mayerne, a Frenchman from a Protestant background and one of the most celebrated doctors of the age. It was thanks to his intervention, let us say, that John Donne recovered and lived another eight years, during which some of his finest work was produced; it was in fact in the midst of his convalescence that the famous sermon passage 'No man is an island' was written.

We now go back some thirty years: this is where the fiction begins. In 1591 Montaigne is visited by the same Turquet de Mayerne. Turquet will get his doctorate in medicine at Toulouse six years later, but he is already at this time a precociously brilliant student of diseases and symptoms. The object of the visit to Montaigne is to pay homage to the master whose *Essais* he has read in the 1588 edition, and whom he admires enormously; but he also wants to convince Montaigne that medicine is not such a useless science as he appears to think, and his plan is to diagnose Montaigne's own morbid symptoms and maybe even treat them. In this he is successful beyond expectation. At the time of the visit Montaigne is visibly and, as Turquet de Mayerne immediately sees, dangerously unwell. He stays with him for three months, talking to him about all kinds of things but also studying his diet and other habits. He prescribes a new sugar-free, salt-free, low-fat diet, including at least five portions of fruit and vegetables a day, together with some mild but regular exercise. Montaigne thinks all of this is rubbish, but he likes the young man, and he acquiesces in the treatment on the grounds that even highly implausible effects can be found in nature; soon he begins to feel a lot better. He does not know, although he suspects it, that Turquet has actually saved his life.

A few years later, having seen the revised edition of the *Essais* through the press, Montaigne decides that it is time for some travel. He gets out the diary of his previous journey to Italy via Germany and Switzerland, dusts it off, and thinks it might be worth publishing one of these days, perhaps together with a second journal to be composed during this new trip, which, he decides, will this time be northward to England and perhaps Scotland. Marie de Gournay agrees to accompany him. After some preparation — they make an attempt to teach themselves English, but without much success, as there are virtually no manuals of the English language on the market — they finally leave in the spring of 1599, by which time Montaigne is sixty-six and still going strong. They meet some important people, including Lord Bacon, whose brother Anthony Montaigne had met in France some years previously, and who persists in denying, much to Montaigne's amusement and Marie de Gournay's indignation, that his own *Essays* owe anything at all to Montaigne's book. They also meet John Florio, who is well advanced in his translation of the *Essais*. Florio gives them proper English lessons, and they make such good progress that after a mere six months they are able to go to the theatre, about which everyone in England seems to be enthusiastic. At first Montaigne thinks it a rather strange, disorderly kind of entertainment, not at all like his schoolboy experience of acting in the Latin tragedies of George Buchanan and Marc-Antoine Muret at the Collège de Guyenne, but he soon becomes fascinated by the plays of Shakespeare. He finds the history plays most accessible at first, and he begins to see already at this stage that the theatre provides its own way of 'essaying' things, presenting complex and problematic instances of human behaviour as material for reflection, and in such a way that the required narrative resolution is not accompanied by a facile resolution at that second-order reflective level. In short, he sees that what Shakespeare is doing is, *mutatis mutandis*, quite similar to what he himself was trying to do in the *Essais*.

We have very little evidence for the next two or three years. We know only, from a brief account in Marie de Gournay's travel diary (Montaigne's own had been abandoned after the first few months), that Montaigne met Shakespeare and had long conversations with him about the theatre, the essaying mode and the possible relation between them. Little, it seems, was said about scepticism, which they rapidly decided was tediously self-evident once you had seen the point of it. They spoke far more of the imagination and its ability to make things happen in the real world, and of how the mind may learn to turn back on itself and probe its own inner recesses. Above all, they talked of poetry, of how the poets can enable us, by a sudden shift in the mind's focus, to take flight from the uncertain, equivocal, everyday world and glimpse a possibility of transcendence, like the echo of a heavenly music.

The end of the story is well attested — at least with regard to the essential facts — from several contemporary sources. In 1609 Montaigne's health begins to decline, and even Turquet de Mayerne, who is now chief physician to James I, is able to provide only palliative measures. On February 28 of the following year, in honour of Montaigne's seventy-seventh birthday, Shakespeare arranges a private preview of his latest play *The Tempest*, which he thinks may also be his last. Physically moribund but mentally still alert, Montaigne is deeply moved. He recognizes, of course, the quotation from his chapter 'Des cannibales', deliberately placed as a token of homage to the French master, and is amused by the good-humoured caricature of himself as Gonzalo. But the great recognition comes in the final scenes when he perceives that Prospero embodies a unique fusion of his own mental world and Shakespeare's, as if the playwright were thinking with and through the *Essais*; and as he slips into his final coma, he realizes that Shakespeare's poetry — not that of Ovid or Lucretius or even Virgil — is the poetry of eternal reflection that he himself would have loved to write.

CHAPTER 8

The Last Word

A. D. Nuttall

When I was approached with the idea of a conference and a volume of essays to mark my retirement, I said I was delighted by the notion so long as the contributors talked about Shakespeare and not about me. Any impression of beautiful selflessness this may have created will now be shattered by this afterword, in which, alas, I shall refer with unseemly frequency to my own writings.

I expected a discussion of thinking in and with Shakespeare to be all about identity and selfhood. In the event it was all about the intractability of Shakespeare's genius, about flux, superfluity, and the status of imagination. Colin Burrow drew a contrast between the poetry of Michelangelo and Shakespeare's work. Michelangelo writes from a sculptor's drive to produce something of marmoreal permanence, having a beauty that transcends mortal mess. Shakespeare, conversely, is more than half in love with change itself, rejoices in the indefinite metamorphic multiplicity of the world. I respond warmly to this. It seemed to me to accord well with my idea that the work of Shakespeare, taken as a whole, could be described as 'Ockham's beard'.[1] 'Ockham's razor' is the famous principle of economy in explanation — 'Entities are not to be multiplied beyond necessity': exclude variables, isolate a single cause if you can, outlaw, wherever possible, overdetermination. It is a principle that has served science well, but perhaps there are other ways to be intelligent. It may be that we need, especially in the field of human affairs, the kind of person who cannot refrain from asking 'What else could be going on?'. Philosophers thirty years ago were scornful of Hamlet's remark 'There are more things in heaven and earth, Horatio, | Than are dreamt of in your philosophy' (I. 5. 166–67). Today I suspect the contempt is less automatic.[2]

But I worried about the picture of Michelangelo that seemed to be forming. If one thinks of his actual sculptures, Michelangelo stands out as the artist who made stone express not being but becoming. Think of the inchoate forms in the Rondanini Pietà, the slaves left struggling for ever in the rough matter from which they can never break free. Michelangelo has a central place in that Renaissance cult of the *non finito*, the unfinished work, of which Rudolf Wittkower wrote.[3] Croce and Collingwood, in their different ways, drew a strong distinction between the initial intuition in the artist's mind, and the mere banausic execution that followed. Michelangelo more than any other sculptor makes us respect or even revere the exciting recalcitrance of the material, the aesthetic life that springs not from the *concetto* alone but from the *concetto* physically engaged. I was ready, therefore, for a ding–dong argument. But then Burrow brilliantly detected, within the Michelangelo sonnet, a nostalgia for the *superchio*, that prior abundance that a successful act of shaping destroys. The poetry licenses the notion that there may be *many* forms latent in the marble. For Burrow, this counter-thought or counter-feeling is something magically asserted by poetry itself, against the wish of the great sculptor. *He* continues to desire a Platonic singleness and stability. I am not sure that I can believe this oddly mystical doctrine. Collingwood may have underestimated the force of physical execution in art, but this new view, conversely, gives (verbal) execution an unearthly autonomy. For me, mind and heart go together. The shift in the *Rime*, accurately detected by Burrow, is simultaneously a movement in Michelangelo himself — and the sculptures prove it.

There was a time when many Romans actually wished to be as like stone statues as possible. The development of Senecan Stoicism is oddly in line with what can be traced in the work of Michelangelo. That is to say, we find a movement from the static to the dynamic. Seneca shifts from praising the man wholly without passion to praising the man who heroically overcomes his passion. He even suggests before he has finished that the good Stoic should go *looking* for trouble ('Ideo ad offensiones', *De constantia sapientis*, 9. 3).[4] Shakespeare understood all of this, and went a stage further. If anything can redeem Brutus in *Julius Caesar*, it is his evident love of his wife, a love he struggles stoically to repress.

Shakespeare insistently reminds us of an ungovernable complexity some minds prefer to forget. Subha Mukherji writes of the legal and moral 'labyrinth', the interest in redundancy of evidence in Shakespeare's comic plots, of the fruitful chaos of memorially accretive English common law, and of the positive value that begins to be ascribed to circuitousness and difficulty in themselves. Gabriel Josipovici observes that when we see or read a Shakespeare play we 'experience far more than our critical or philosophical vocabulary seems able to articulate'.[5] Terence Cave notes that in both Shakespeare and Montaigne 'foreclosure becomes impossible; appraisal, exploration, experiment become the key mode of operation'. Charles Martindale also writes about 'polyvalence and even undecidability' but adds, fascinatingly, that we may err when we use Plato as the standard antonym to such things. The real Plato, as opposed to what we find in books about Plato, is an artist, a writer of dialogues, a lover of myth. One is reminded of Gilbert Ryle's suggestion that the characterization of philosophers as holding certain fixed positions, 'tenets', is a misleading fiction perpetuated by those who write histories of philosophy; real philosophers, he said, are always thinking, never still.[6] Charles Martindale's recuperation of Plato is analogous to the recuperation of Michelangelo I attempted earlier.

Noël Sugimura writes of 'the over-abundant, the fluctuating, the passionate, the disorderly, and the eternal'. She is here describing not Shakespeare's œuvre taken as a whole, but Egypt as it is presented in *Antony and Cleopatra*; but there is a clear overlap with the way others in this volume characterize Shakespeare himself. The surprise word in her list is 'eternal'. We commonly associate eternity, or at least timelessness, with Platonic forms, themselves (if Martindale will allow us to say so) paradigms of order. In *Antony and Cleopatra*, however, the Romans are indeed, antithetically, clear, hard in outline. The play's recurrent imagery of melting is associated precisely with the move southward and eastward from Rome to Egypt. Yet Roman rationality is, as Sugimura says, temporal; it is involved in astute political action, a technique for winning power struggles. Sugimura is right: Cleopatra is 'eterne in mutabilitie'.[7] They are far from innocent, but there is a hint of timeless Arcadia about the love of Antony and Cleopatra; she disengages him from the 'and-then-and-then-and-then' of political life, and they are in bliss, until so rudely interrupted by rational history.

On that arresting word, 'eternal', we reach the turning point of this essay. For if Shakespeare was eager to find a way of fusing rich disorder and eternity, he must love both; he must love — have an excited conception of — eternity. Here we suddenly hit an element deeply uncongenial to our twenty-first century culture. Any lecturer knows how easy it is to elicit warm come-back from one's audience by using words like 'fluid', 'protean', 'metamorphic', and be equally familiar with the immediate chill if, conversely, one speaks unironically of 'timeless truth'. There was a point in Burrow's essay where I wanted to say: 'Stop there. If you can detect a nostalgia for the *superchio* in Michelangelo, perhaps I may be allowed to find a nostalgia for the timeless in myriad-minded Shakespeare'. Burrow says Shakespeare's *Sonnets* are 'in love with change', but there is in them music of another kind:

> Love's not time's fool, though rosy lips and cheeks
> Within his binding sickle's compass come. (Sonnet 116)

It is good, as Burrow says, that Hermione's apparent assimilation to a statue does not hold, so that she becomes once more what she has really been all along, a living woman, but a kind of hunger for the cold eternity of stone can be felt in the *Sonnets*, in the sudden, eerie boast,

> Not marble nor the gilded monuments
> Of princes shall outlive this pow'rful rhyme. (Sonnet 55)

It may be suggested that there is an implicit contrast between pompous national memorials of the great and Shakespeare's 'rhyme'. I deny the suggestion. There is no contrast. We have a competitive field in which the monumental sculptor is defeated at his own game. This time the idea of the *paragone*, that contest of the arts Burrow evoked in his essay, operates not to soften but to harden all. When Shakespeare calls his rhyme 'pow'rful', he signals awareness that his words may be invidious — but he says them nonetheless. When the Roman poet of metamorphosis boasted, he did it differently; the last word of Ovid's huge poem is 'Vivam', 'I shall *live*'. I do not say that Sonnet 55 is typical of Shakespeare's practice; rather, I insist that Shakespeare's mobile polyvalence can include anything — even moments of anti-mobility. If we listen, we shall find this music of transcendence, which is now so antipathetic to our taste, everywhere in the comedies. True, the statue Hermione gives place to the real, aging, loved woman, but, 'in another part of the wood', Perdita's artful make-over in the pastoral revel of Act I, where she is queen of the sheep-shearing feast (IV. 4. 4), is less easily dissolved. 'Queen' and 'simple country girl' are natural opposites, but here the artful, festive pretence is truth-bearing: Perdita really is what the game would make her — nobly born, noble of bearing, noble of heart.

Mukherji refers to the 'queer, alienated, lyric power' of Imogen's soliloquy over what she believes is the body of her dead husband.[8] Shakespeare, it would seem deliberately, gives us overwhelming lyric beauty in exactly the wrong context. After all, the headless corpse before Imogen is really that of the contemptible bully Cloten. The point is still clearer if one looks at the song, sung over the body, just before Imogen's soliloquy: 'Fear no more the heat of the sun'. This was the poetry that reached me first, with complete power, when I had only just learned to read. 'Golden lads and girls all must | As chimney sweepers come to dust' haunted me. The effect of expending such splendours on Cloten is not to degrade the poetry but to exhibit its separate strength. It soars above circumstance.

At the end of *All's Well that Ends Well* Bertram is reunited with Helena, the lady he had unjustly scorned. Helena has won him, for a second time, by deception — by the bed-trick. Shakespeare goes out of his way to make us feel the theatricality, the contrived character of this denouement. We expect, from the happy ending of a love story, parties who have fallen deeply in love; and it is a condition of such falling in love that they should at least know each other. But Shakespeare withholds this satisfaction. He could easily have made Bertram regret his early rejection of Helena, made him realize that he had loved her all along. In Sidney's *Arcadia* (1593; I. vii), when Parthenia, having recovered her lost beauty, comes to Argalus, Argalus, not recognizing her, persists in his love to the supposedly dead Parthenia. But Bertram is entirely willing to marry, as he thinks, another lady altogether, minutes before he is united with Helena. His dazed capitulation is a point at which readers knit their brows but spectators in the theatre — watch them — suddenly smile. Shakespeare knew that they would. Again, the effect of the contrast between the general moral inadequacy of Bertram and the accomplished marriage is not to satirize marriage but to make us feel, 'Of course people are variously imperfect, but marriage is marriage, a good and happy thing in itself; it is the way the world continues'. There is a kind of transcendence here. Marriage itself is other than its accidents, in particular instantiations. So far, so Platonist. But the full Platonic *chorismos*, the separation of the Forms from human life, is avoided. The marriage of Helena and Bertram is a fully human thing. One is almost drawn to say that Shakespeare accords quasi-transcendent status to a social convention, a mere legal contract, but to employ these terms is to repress the intuition of glowing value in marriage, as Shakespeare presents it to us.

It is a strangely unsentimental ideal. Shakespeare, famous for his happy endings, refuses to say at the end of his comedies 'and they lived happily ever after', the second part of the standard formula. Touchstone and Audrey, joyously absorbed into the dance of weddings that concludes *As You Like It*, are actually promised a life of wrangling. It is as if Shakespeare has moved from 'Love's not time's fool' (Sonnet 116) to 'Love may be time's fool but there are human things that lie deeper than conscious personal relationships'. Yet *Antony and Cleopatra* (1606–07) is closer to the intuition of the sonnet — 'Eternity was in our lips and eyes' (I. 3. 35). Notice, however, that where physical lips are contrasted with the eternity of love in the sonnet, in the play we are offered a kind of fusion. This Shakespeare, he really *won't* keep still.

Both Martindale and Sugimura remind me that I once saw a certain similarity between Anselm's celebrated ontological proof of the existence of God and Cleopatra's reasoning in her reply to Dolabella. Shakespeare, I must concede at once, does not employ the logical conjuring trick that could still impress Descartes in the seventeenth century, when he wrote his Fifth Meditation. Anselm obtains, at the outset, an agreed definition: God is greater than anything we can conceive. He then extorts agreement that a real island is obviously miles better than a merely notional island. If God did not exist, we could imagine him greater by mentally ascribing to him the existence he lacks (an existent God is obviously miles better than a merely notional God). But we also agreed at the beginning that God is greater than anything we can imagine. So God must already *have* that existence we would have attributed to him. Therefore he exists. The rabbit jumps out of the hat.

The usual reply to Anselm is to say that his mistake is to make existence a predicate. After all, it is absurd to say that Mr Pickwick is a nicer person than Adolf Hitler, but Hitler finally wins the contest because *he* exists. Meanwhile, however, many people obstinately feel that real islands *are* better than merely notional islands. To those people one could say that the effect of Anselm's reasoning is not to establish the actual existence of God, but only to show that a God who met the requirements of the job, so to speak, *would have to be* real (not 'must be real, now'), could not be a useful fiction judiciously employed by human governors. I have granted that the peculiar logical hook in Anselm's argument is not there in Shakespeare. What nevertheless links them, as Sugimura says, is the sudden move from hypothesis to reality. Something similar can be found in Keats's letter of 22 November 1817 to Benjamin Bailey, the letter in which he compares the imagination to Adam's dream: 'He awoke and found it truth'.

For Cleopatra it is vividness that confers reality on the dream-image. This is an empiricist's criterion. When David Hume sought to distinguish mental images from percepts, he knew he could not base the distinction on the fact that percepts are 'of the real'. To say this is to imply that you can step outside the causal or representative theory of perception. The mind, for empiricists like Hume, is immediately confronted by an idea or image; this applies to, for example, visual perception; this 'idea' represents the distant object (or, more disquietingly, is caused by whatever is out there). You cannot check the accuracy of the presentation by going and having a look, because 'having a look' will always involve more intervenient ideas. Accordingly, Hume has to use an entirely ideational criterion. Percepts, he says, have more 'vivacity' than mental imaginings. So vivacity — vividness — is what does it.

So Cleopatra says to the unborn Hume, 'You may think my love vision of Antony is a delusion, not straight perception but a dream-image imposed by my unbalanced state of mind, but my "dream-Antony" is more solidly vivid than anything I have ever known; by your criterion, then, it must count as real.' The dream by its own inner power grows into truth.

Long before, in *A Midsummer Night's Dream*, Hippolyta thought the 'ontological status' of the marvellous night through which they had passed might be high. Theseus, that dominant male, explained to her that lunatics, lovers, and poets are composed of imagination and that imagination is delusion. His patronizing disquisition has found its way into innumerable anthologies of 'fine passages from Shakespeare'. Hippolyta, whose IQ is almost embarrassingly higher than Theseus's, lightly forgives his ungallantry (he, her lover, has just told her that all lovers are deranged) and thinks aloud:

> But all the story of the night told over
> And all their minds transfigured so together,
> More witnesseth than fancy's images,
> And grows to something of great constancy
> But, howsoever, strange and admirable. (v. 1. 23–27)

Her criterion is not vividness but coherency ('great constancy'), but the frame of the thought is empiricist, as in Cleopatra's speech. Another purely ideational way of distinguishing percepts from mental images is to say that percepts are more stably interlocked, one with another. By that criterion, Hippolyta suggests, the night's experience might count as real.

Anyone but Shakespeare having come up with as profound a notion as that he gives to Hippolyta or to Cleopatra would have taken a rest, and then set about corroborating the new insight. Shakespeare, instead, interposes a fascinating hesitation in both passages. Hippolyta, having urged the reality-claim of dream experience at an intellectual level well above the comprehension of Theseus, suddenly pauses — 'but, howsoever, strange and admirable'. She means, I think, 'Although I have emphasized coherence, I do not assert continuity with that other coherency of everyday experience; the midsummer night was, I still feel, amazing, separately marvellous.' It is as if we have not so much an extension of reality as a hinted plurality of 'realities'. In *Antony and Cleopatra* the hesitation takes the form of a catch in the dialogue. Having given her golden, autumnal picture of Antony, Cleopatra breaks off to look at the sturdy soldier she is actually talking to. She suddenly sees, perhaps, what such a man must be thinking. She asks him outright whether he believes that such a man as she has just described has ever existed. Very politely Dolabella says 'No'. Now comes the interesting moment. Cleopatra's instantaneous response is a loud 'You lie!'. But then, abruptly, she speaks in a different register: 'But if there were [...]'. This implicitly accepts that Dolabella has given what for him is a true answer, so that Cleopatra, in dialogue with him, must after all try to reach him by offering the whole vision as hypothesis. It is out of that modest hypothesis, however, that the strongest metaphysical claim at last emerges: 'past the size of dreaming'.

It is as if Shakespeare can retain sympathy for the Dolabellas of this world amidst the heady atmosphere of Cleopatra's philosophic vision. His 'Gentle madam, no' has its own quiet eloquence, its own modest force. These interposed hesitations are the most Shakespearean thing of all about these astonishing passages.

I began to argue with and learn from Stephen Medcalf on that October evening in 1955 when I ran into him — then a pallid, gawky youth — on a staircase in Merton College. Medcalf believes more than I do (he can believe six impossible things before breakfast). When he took Eysenck's test for 'tough-minded versus tender-minded', he proved to be so tender as to be off the scale. I am not sure that this places him at a disadvantage when it comes to understanding Shakespeare. Medcalf recently observed in a letter to me that Shakespeare was a moderate Anglican with a dash of Platonism. I responded that I had always believed him to be a Montaignian sceptic with a soft spot for the Old Religion. Medcalf then said, 'When people are challenged to say what Shakespeare's philosophy was, they always describe themselves.' He saw before I did that we had both just done exactly that. He finds in the last words of Lear in the Folio version an intuition of transcendent value, of Christian redemption. I have in general, through the years, fought this reading, insisting that what we feel most vividly at this point in the drama is that Lear is pathetically wrong in supposing Cordelia to be alive. I still think Medcalf takes too little account of the reversion to a primitive, pre-Christian retaliatory violence (*after* the luminous charity-towards-all of v. 1) when Lear instantly kills the man he finds hanging Cordelia. But Medcalf's link to romance and comedic materials is strong. I said earlier that the music of transcendence can be heard everywhere in the comedies, and argued that the general inadequacy of the human participants actually assists that intuition of transcendence. Could it be that the grim human chaos of *King Lear*, in like manner, finally operates not to crush but to isolate the separate fact of divine goodness? Those who argue, as I have done, for an anti-Christian *King Lear* point to the hideous absence of natural justice in the death of Cordelia (Dr Johnson found it almost literally unbearable), and to the fracturing of that charity-out-of-suffering that seemed so secure in v. 1. The strongest answer from the Christian readers was always, 'But Christianity has never said that everything comes right *in this world*; on the contrary, our life is a vale of tears, humankind is fallen'. When I felt surest of my anti-Christian reading, I always acknowledged that the play is not ethically nihilist: the words 'good' and 'evil' mean more, not less, to someone who has just read or watched *King Lear*. So, by parity of reasoning, perhaps I should concede that all the horrors we see in the play work to intensify a final intuition of goodness that must be in some way transcendent.

I am hesitating, but not conceding everything. The idea that life in this world is ordered by benign providence is smashed, I continue to think, in *King Lear*. And I still want to say that, although the play makes me believe in 'good', it does not make me believe in God.

Notes to Chapter 8

1. A. D. Nuttall, *A New Mimesis: Shakespeare and the Representation of Reality* (London: Methuen, 1983), p. 181.
2. See, for example, Patricia Hanna and Bernard Harrison, *Word and World: Practice and the Foundations of Language* (Cambridge: Cambridge University Press, 2004).
3. 'Individualism in Art and Artists: A Renaissance Problem', *Journal of the History of Ideas*, 22 (1961), 285–302, esp. pp. 299–302.
4. Seneca, *Moral Essays*, 1, trans. by John W. Basore, Loeb Classical Library, 214 (London: Heinemann, 1957).
5. I am uneasy that I have so little else to say in this piece about Gabriel Josipovici's brilliant essay on *Twelfth Night*. But I cannot resist one comment. I am shocked that Gabriel Josipovici, walker and dog-lover, should so readily prefer Feste to Launce. What can man do better than

lay down his life for his friend? What can a fool do better than take upon himself the sin, in fact committed by his dog, of pissing under the table (*Two Gentlemen of Verona*, IV. 4. 27)?

6. Gilbert Ryle, *Plato's Progress* (1966; Bristol: Thoemmes, 1994), p. 9.

7. Spenser, *The Faerie Queene*, III. vi. 47.

8. See my essay '*The Winter's Tale*: Ovid Transformed', in *Shakespeare's Ovid: The Metamorphoses in the Plays and Poems*, ed. by A. B. Taylor (Cambridge: Cambridge University Press, 2000), pp. 135–49 (p. 148).

BIBLIOGRAPHY

ANSELM, ST, *Proslogion*, trans. by M. J. Charlesworth (Oxford: Clarendon Press, 1965; repr. 1979), pp. 116–19

ARCHIBALD, ELIZABETH, *Apollonius of Tyre: Medieval and Renaissance Themes and Variations* (Woodbridge: D. S. Brewer, 1991)

ARISTOTLE, *The Works of Aristotle*, ed. by W. D. Ross, XII: *Rhetorica; De rhetorica ad Alexandrum; De poetica* (Oxford: Clarendon Press, 1924)

—— *The Rhetoric and Poetics of Aristotle*, trans. by W. Rhys Roberts and Ingram Bywater, ed. by Friedrich Solmsen (New York: Random House, 1954)

AUDEN, W. H., *The Sea and the Mirror* (London: Faber, 1945)

BACON, FRANCIS, *The Works of Francis Bacon*, ed. by J. Spedding, R. L. Ellis and D. D. Heath, 14 vols (London: Longman, 1857–74)

—— *The Letters and Life of Francis Bacon*, ed. by J. Spedding, 7 vols (London: Longman, 1861–74)

BALDWIN, T. W., *William Shakspere's Small Latine and Lesse Greeke*, 2 vols (Urbana: University of Illinois Press, 1944)

BARBER, C. L., 'Thou that Beget'st Him that Did Thee Beget', *Shakespeare Survey*, 22 (1969), 59–67

BARKAN, LEONARD, '"Living Sculptures": Ovid, Michelangelo, and *The Winter's Tale*', *English Literary History*, 48 (1981), 639–67

—— 'What Did Shakespeare Read?', in *The Cambridge Companion to Shakespeare*, ed. by Margreta de Grazia and Stanley Wells (Cambridge: Cambridge University Press, 2001), pp. 31–47

BARTON, ANNE, '"Nature's Piece 'gainst Fancy": The Divided Catastrophe in *Antony and Cleopatra*', in *Essays, Mainly Shakespearean* (Cambridge: Cambridge University Press, 1994), pp. 113–35

BELL, MILLICENT, *Shakespeare's Tragic Skepticism* (New Haven and London: Yale University Press, 2002)

BLOOM, HAROLD, *The Western Canon: The Books and School of the Ages* (London: Papermac, 1995)

—— *Shakespeare: The Invention of the Human* (London: Fourth Estate, 1999)

BOWEN, BARBARA E., *Gender in the Theater of War: Shakespeare's Troilus and Cressida* (New York and London: Garland Science, 1993)

BRACTON, HENRY, *On the Laws and Customs of England* (Cambridge, MA: Harvard University Press, 1968)

BRADSHAW, GRAHAM, *Shakespeare's Scepticism* (Brighton: Harvester Wheatsheaf, 1987)

BUELER, LOIS, *The Tested Woman Plot: Women's Choices, Men's Judgments, and the Shaping of Stories* (Ohio: Ohio State University Press, 2001)

BURROW, J. A., *Gestures and Looks in Medieval Literature* (Cambridge: Cambridge University Press, 2002)

BUTLER, JUDITH, *Gender Trouble: Feminism and the Subversion of Identity*, 10th anniversary edn (New York and London: Routledge, 1999)

CALVIN, JOHN, *Institutes of the Christian Religion*, ed. by John T. McNeill, 2 vols (London: SCM, 1961)

CAVE, TERENCE, *Recognitions: A Study in Poetics* (Oxford: Clarendon Press, 1988)

CAVELL, STANLEY, *Disowning Knowledge in Six Plays of Shakespeare* (Cambridge: Cambridge University Press, 1987)

CHESTERTON, G. K., *The Napoleon of Notting Hill* (London: The Bodley Head, 1968)

CHIPP, HERSCHEL B., *Theories of Modern Art* (Berkeley and Los Angeles: University of California Press, 1968),

CICERO, MARCUS TULLIUS, *De re publica; De legibus* (Cicero in Twenty-Eight Volumes, 16), trans. by Clinton Walker Keyes, Loeb Classical Library, 213 (London: Heinemann, 1928)

—— *On the Orator, Book III; On Fate; Stoic Paradoxes; The Divisions of Oratory* (Cicero in Twenty-Eight Volumes, 4), trans. by H. Rackham, Loeb Classical Library, 349 (London: Heinemann; Cambridge, MA: Harvard University Press, 1942)

—— *De finibus bonorum et malorum* (Cicero in Twenty-Eight Volumes, 17), trans. by H. Rackham, Loeb Classical Library, 40, 2nd edn (London: Heinemann; Cambridge, MA: Harvard University Press, 1971)

—— *Tusculan Disputations* (Cicero in Twenty-Eight Volumes, 18), trans. by J. E. King, Loeb Classical Library, 141, rev. edn (London: Heinemann; Cambridge, MA: Harvard University Press, 1971)

CLEMENTS, ROBERT JOHN, *The Poetry of Michelangelo* (London: Peter Owen, 1966)

COLERIDGE, SAMUEL TAYLOR, *The Collected Works of Samuel Taylor Coleridge*, VII: *Biographia literaria, or, Biographical Sketches of my Literary Life and Opinions*, ed. by James Engell and W. Jackson Bate (London: Routledge & Kegan Paul; Princeton, NJ: Princeton University Press, 1983)

COLISH, MARCIA L., *The Stoic Tradition from Antiquity to the Early Middle Ages*, I: *Stoicism in Classical Latin Literature*, Studies in the History of Christian Thought, 34 (Leiden: Brill, 1985)

COWELL, JOHN, *The Interpreter* (London, 1607)

CROMBIE, I. M., *An Examination of Plato's Doctrines*, 2 vols (London: Routledge & Kegan Paul, 1962–63)

CROWTHER, PAUL, 'Literary Metaphor and Philosophical Insight: The Significance of Archilochus', in *Metaphor, Allegory, and the Classical Tradition: Ancient Thought and Modern Revisions*, ed. by G. R. Boys-Stones (Oxford: Oxford University Press, 2003), pp. 83–100

Cursor mundi, ed. by Richard Morris, Early English Text Society, orig. ser., 57, 59, 62, 66, 68, 99, 101 (London: Kegan Paul, Trench, Tröbner, 1874–93)

DANBY, J. F., *Shakespeare's Doctrine of Nature* (London: Faber, 1959)

DESCARTES, RENÉ, *The Philosophical Works of Descartes*, ed. by Elizabeth S. Haldane and G. R. T. Ross, 2 vols (Cambridge: Cambridge University Press, 1911–12; repr. with corrections, 1967)

EDELSTEIN, LUDWIG, *The Meaning of Stoicism* (Cambridge, MA: Harvard University Press, 1966)

EDWARDS, CATHARINE, 'Acting and Self-Actualisation in Imperial Rome: Some Death Scenes', in *Greek and Roman Actors: Aspects of an Ancient Profession*, ed. by Pat Easterling and Edith Hall (Cambridge: Cambridge University Press, 2002), pp. 377–94

ELIOT, T. S., 'In Memory', *Little Review*, 5.4 (1918), 44–47

—— INTRODUCTION TO G. WILSON KNIGHT, *The Wheel of Fire* (London: Methuen, 1930, repr. 1949)

—— *The Collected Poems, 1909–1962* (London: Faber, 1963)

ELLRODT, ROBERT, 'Self-Consciousness in Montaigne and Shakespeare', *Shakespeare Survey*, 28 (1975), 37–50

EMMET, DOROTHY, *The Nature of Metaphysical Thinking* (London: Macmillan, 1966)

ENGBERG-PEDERSEN, TROELS, *The Stoic Theory of Oikeiosis: Moral Development and Social Interaction in Early Stoic Philosophy* (Aarhus: Aarhus University Press, 1990)

ERNE, LUKAS, *Shakespeare as Literary Dramatist* (Cambridge: Cambridge University Press, 2003)

FRANKLIN, JAMES, *The Science of Conjecture: Evidence and Probability before Pascal* (Baltimore, MD: Johns Hopkins University Press, 2001)

FRASER, ANTONIA, *The Gunpowder Plot* (London: Arrow, 1999)

GARNIER, ROBERT, *Tragedie of Antonie, Donne into English by the Countesse of Pembroke* (London, 1595)

GODDARD, HAROLD, *The Meaning of Shakespeare* (Chicago: University of Chicago Press, 1951)

GOLDING, WILLIAM, *Darkness Visible* (London: Faber, 1979)

GOWER, JOHN, *Confessio amantis*, in *The English Works of John Gower*, II, ed. by G. C. Macaulay, Early English Text Society, extra ser., 82 (London: Kegan Paul, Trench, Trübner, 1901)

GREEN, THOMAS, *Verdict According to Conscience: Perspectives on the English Criminal Trial Jury, 1200–1800* (Chicago: Chicago University Press, 1985)

—— *Twelve Good Men and True: The Criminal Trial Jury in England, 1200–1800* (Princeton, NJ: Princeton University Press, 1988)

GUARINI, GIAMBATTISTA, *Il verato ovvero difesa di quanto ha scritto M. Giason Denores di quanto ha egli ditto in un suo discorso delle tragicomedie, e delli pastorali* (Ferrara, 1588)

—— *Compendio della poesia tragicomica* (Venice, 1601)

GUYER, PAUL, 'Originality: Genius, Universality, Individuality', in *The Creation of Art: New Essays in Philosophical Aesthetics*, ed. by Berys Gaut and Paisley Livingston (Cambridge: Cambridge University Press, 2003), pp. 116–37

HACKING, IAN, *The Emergence of Probability* (Cambridge: Cambridge University Press, 1975)

HAMMOND, PAUL, 'The Play of Quotation and Commonplace in *King Lear*', in *Toward A Definition of Topos: Approaches to Analogical Reasoning*, ed. by Lynette Hunter (Basingstoke: Macmillan, 1991), pp. 78–129

HANNA, PATRICIA, and BERNARD HARRISON, *Word and World: Practice and the Foundations of Language* (Cambridge: Cambridge University Press, 2004)

HANSON, ELIZABETH, *Discovering the Subject in Renaissance England* (Cambridge: Cambridge University Press, 1998)

HAZLITT, WILLIAM, *Characters of Shakespeare's Plays* (Oxford: World's Classics, 1947)

HERBERT, GEORGE, *The English Poems of George Herbert*, ed. by C. A. Patrides (London: Dent, 1974)

HOPKINS, DAVID, '"The English Homer": Shakespeare, Longinus, and English "Neo-Classicism"', in *Shakespeare and the Classics*, ed. by Charles Martindale and A. B. Taylor (Cambridge: Cambridge University Press, 2004), pp. 261–76

HOWELLS, CHRISTINA, 'Conclusion: Sartre and the Deconstruction of the Subject', in *The Cambridge Companion to Sartre*, ed. by Christina Howells (Cambridge: Cambridge University Press, 1999), pp. 318–52

HUGHES-HALLETT, LUCY, *Cleopatra: Histories, Dreams, and Distortions* (London: Bloombury, 1990)

HUME, DAVID, *A Treatise of Human Nature*, ed. by L. A. Selby-Bigge, 2nd edn, rev. by P. H. Nidditch (Oxford: Clarendon Press, 1978)

HUTSON, LORNA, *The Usurer's Daughter: Male Friendships and Fictions of Women in Sixteenth-Century England* (London: Routledge, 1994)

IRIGARAY, LUCE, 'The Power of Discourse and the Subordination of the Feminine', in *Literary Theory: An Anthology*, ed. by Julie Rivkin and Michael Ryan (Oxford: Blackwell, 1998), pp. 570–73

JAMES, MAX H., 'The Noble Ruin: *Antony and Cleopatra*', *College Literature*, 8.2 (1981), 127–43

JENKYNS, RICHARD, *The Victorians and Ancient Greece* (Oxford: Blackwell, 1980)

JOHNSON, SAMUEL, *Dr Johnson on Shakespeare*, ed. with an introduction by W. K. Wimsatt (Harmondsworth: Penguin, 1969)

JONSON, BEN, *Volpone*, ed. by David Cook (London: Methuen, 1962)

JOSIPOVICI, GABRIEL, *On Trust* (New Haven: Yale University Press, 1999)

—— *The Singer on the Shore: Essays, 1991–2004* (Carcanet, 2006)

KEMP, MARTIN, *Behind the Picture: Art and Evidence in the Italian Renaissance* (New Haven: Yale University Press, 1997)

KERMODE, FRANK, 'O How Unlike the Father', *London Review of Books*, 15 October 1998, p. 14.

KERRIGAN, JOHN, 'Between Michelangelo and Petrarch: Shakespeare's Sonnets of Art', in *Surprised by Scenes: Essays in Honour of Professor Yasunari Takahashi*, ed. by Yasunari Takada (Tokyo: Kenkyusha, 1994), pp. 142–63

KRAUSS, ROSALIND, 'The Circulation of the Sign', in *The Picasso Papers* (London: Thames and Hudson, 1998), pp. 25–85

LAKOFF, GEORGE, and MARK JOHNSON, *Metaphors We Live By* (Chicago and London: Chicago University Press, 1980)

—— *More than Cool Reason: A Field Guide to Poetic Metaphor* (Chicago and London: Chicago University Press, 1989)

LEWIS, C. S., *The Chronicles of Narnia*, VII: *The Silver Chair* (London: Collins, 1997)

LOEWENSTEIN, JOSEPH, *Ben Jonson and Possessive Authorship* (Cambridge: Cambridge University Press, 2002)

McALINDON, T., *Shakespeare's Tragic Cosmos* (Cambridge: Cambridge University Press, 1991)

MACDONALD, RUSS, *Shakespeare and the Arts of Language* (Oxford: Oxford University Press, 2001)

MACKAIL, J. W., *Lectures on Greek Poetry* (London: Longman, Green, 1910)

MACLEAN, IAN, 'Foucault's Renaissance Episteme Reassessed: An Aristotelian Counterblast', *Journal of the History of Ideas*, 59 (1998), 149–66

MALCOLM, NORMAN, 'Anselm's Ontological Argument', *Philosophical Review*, 69 (1960), 41–62

MAPSTONE, SALLY, 'Shakespeare and Scottish Kingship: A Case History', in *The Rose and the Thistle: Essays on the Culture of Late Medieval and Renaissance Scotland*, ed. by Sally Mapstone and Juliette Wood (East Lothian: Phantassie, 1998), pp. 158–89

MARLOWE, CHRISTOPHER, *Doctor Faustus*, ed. by David Bevington and Eric Rasmussen (Manchester: Manchester University Press, 1993)

MARTIN, JULIAN, *Francis Bacon, the State, and the Reform of Natural Philosophy* (Cambridge: Cambridge University Press, 1992)

MARTINDALE, CHARLES and MICHELLE, *Shakespeare and the Uses of Antiquity: An Introductory Essay* (London: Routledge, 1990)

MASSINGER, PHILIP, *The Plays and Poems of Philip Massinger*, ed. by Philip Edwards and Colin Gibson, 5 vols (Oxford: Clarendon Press, 1976)

MEDCALF, STEPHEN, 'Shakespeare on Beauty, Truth and Transcendence', in *Platonism and the English Imagination*, ed. by Anna Baldwin and Sarah Hutton (Cambridge: Cambridge University Press, 1994), pp. 117–25

MERCHANT, CAROLYN, *The Death of Nature: Women, Ecology, and the Scientific Revolution* (San Francisco: Harper & Row, 1980)

MICHELANGELO BUONARROTI, *Rime*, ed. by E. N. Girardi (Bari: Laterza, 1967)

—— *The Poems*, trans. by Christopher Ryan (London: Dent, 1996)

MILES, GEOFFREY, *Shakespeare and the Constant Romans* (Oxford: Clarendon Press, 1996)

MILTON, JOHN, *Complete Prose Works of John Milton*, ed. by Don Wolfe and others, 5 vols (New Haven: Yale University Press, 1952–66)

—— *The Poems of John Milton*, ed. by John Carey and Alastair Fowler (London: Longman, 1968)

MONTAIGNE, MICHEL DE, *The Essayes of Michael Lord of Montaigne*, trans. by John Florio, 2 vols (London and Toronto: Dent, 1927)

MUKHERJI, SUBHA, '"Lawfull Deede": Consummation, Custom and Law in Shakespeare's *All's Well that Ends Well*', in *The Cambridge Shakespeare Library*, ed. by Catherine Alexander, 3 vols (Cambridge: Cambridge University Press, 2003), I, 270–87

MURDOCH, IRIS, *Existentialists and Mystics: Writings on Philosophy and Literature*, ed. by Peter Conradi (London: Chatto & Windus, 1997)

Narrative and Dramatic Sources of Shakespeare, ed. by Geoffrey Bullough, 8 vols (London: Routledge & Kegan Paul; New York: Columbia University Press, 1957–75)

NEHAMAS, ALEXANDER, *Nietzsche: Life as Literature* (Cambridge, MA, and London: Harvard University Press, 1985)

NIETZSCHE, FRIEDRICH, *The Genealogy of Morals*, in *The Birth of Tragedy and The Genealogy of Morals*, trans. by Francis Golffing (New York: Anchor, 1956)

NUSSBAUM, MARTHA C., *Love's Knowledge: Essays on Philosophy and Literature* (New York: Oxford University Press, 1990)

—— *The Therapy of Desire: Theory and Practice in Hellenistic Ethics* (Princeton, NJ: Princeton University Press, 1994)

—— *The Fragility of Goodness: Luck and Ethics in Greek Tragedy and Philosophy*, rev. edn (Cambridge: Cambridge University Press, 2001)

NUTTALL, A. D., 'The Argument about Shakespeare's Characters', *Critical Quarterly*, 7 (1965), 107–20

—— *William Shakespeare: 'The Winter's Tale'*, Studies in English Literature, 26 (London: Arnold, 1966)

—— *Two Concepts of Allegory: A Study of Shakespeare's 'The Tempest' and the Logic of Allegorical Expression* (London: Routledge & Kegan Paul, 1967)

—— *A Common Sky: Philosophy and the Literary Imagination* (London: Chatto & Windus, 1974)

—— *A New Mimesis: Shakespeare and the Representation of Reality* (London: Methuen, 1983)

—— 'Virgil and Shakespeare', in *Virgil and his Influence: Bimillenial Studies*, ed. by Charles Martindale (Bristol: Bristol Classical Press, 1984), pp. 71–93

—— *The Stoic in Love: Selected Essays on Literature and Ideas* (New York: Harvester Wheatsheaf, 1989)

—— '*Hamlet*: Conversations with the Dead', in *The Stoic in Love*, pp. 27–40

—— *Timon of Athens* (Boston, MA: Twayne, 1989)

—— '*A Midsummer Night's Dream*: Comedy as Apotrope of Myth', *Shakespeare Survey*, 53 (2000), 49–59

—— '*The Winter's Tale*: Ovid Transformed', in *Shakespeare's Ovid: The Metamorphoses in the Plays and Poems*, ed. by A. B. Taylor (Cambridge: Cambridge University Press, 2000), pp. 135–49

—— *Shakespeare the Thinker* (New Haven: Yale University Press, 2007)

ORGEL, STEPHEN, *Imagining Shakespeare: A History of Texts and Visions* (Basingstoke: Palgrave Macmillan, 2003)

PARKER, FRED, *Scepticism and Literature: An Essay on Pope, Hume, Sterne, and Johnson* (Oxford: Oxford University Press, 2003)

PASCAL, BLAISE, *Pensées*, ed. by Philippe Sellier (Paris: Garnier, 1991)

PATER, WALTER, *Plato and Platonism: A Series of Lectures* (London: Macmillan, 1893)

—— 'Measure for Measure', in *Appreciations: With An Essay on Style* (London: Macmillan, 1913), pp. 183–84

PEMBROKE, S. G., 'Oikeiōsis', in *Problems in Stoicism*, ed. by A. A. Long (London: Athlone, 1971; repr. 1996), pp. 114–49

PESIC, PETER, 'Wrestling with Proteus: Francis Bacon and the "Torture" of Nature', *Isis*, 90 (1999), 81–94

PLUTARCH, *Shakespeare's Plutarch: The Lives of Julius Caesar, Brutus, Marcus Antonius, and Coriolanus in the Translation of Sir Thomas North*, ed. by T. J. B. Spencer (Harmondsworth: Penguin, 1964)

—— *Moralia*, XIII, pt 2, ed. by H. Cherniss, Loeb Classical Library, 470 (Cambridge, MA: Harvard University Press; London: Heinemann, 1976)

POCOCK, J. G. A., 'Texts as Events: Reflections on the History of Political Thought', in *Politics of Discourse: The Literature and History of Seventeenth-Century England*, ed. by Kevin Sharpe and Stephen N. Zwicker (Berkeley and London: University of California Press, 1987), pp. 21–34

POOLE, WILLIAM, 'All at Sea: Water, Syntax, and Character Dissolution in Shakespeare', *Shakespeare Survey*, 54 (2001), 201–12

POPPER, KARL, *Conjectures and Refutations* (London: Routledge & Kegan Paul, 1972)

PULTON, Ferdinand, *De pace regis et regni* (London, 1610)

REESER, MARGARET E., *The Nature of Man in Early Stoic Philosophy* (London: Duckworth, 1989)

RICŒUR, PAUL, 'The Metaphorical Process as Cognition, Imagination, and Feeling', *Critical Enquiry*, 5 (1978), 142–59; also pubd in *On Metaphor*, ed. by Sheldon Sacks (Chicago and London: Chicago University Press, 1979), pp. 141–57

—— 'Toward a Hermeneutic of the Idea of Revelation', in *Essays on Biblical Interpretation*, ed. Lewis S. Mudge (London: SPCK, 1981), pp. 73–118

RIST, JOHN M., *Stoic Philosophy* (London: Cambridge University Press, 1969)[A]

RORTY, RICHARD, 'Philosophy as a Kind of Writing: An Essay on Derrida', *New Literary History*, 10 (1978), 141–60

—— *Contingency, Irony, and Solidarity* (Cambridge: Cambridge University Press, 1989)

—— 'Wittgenstein, Heidegger, and Language', in *Essays on Heidegger and Others: Philosophical Papers Volume 2* (Cambridge: Cambridge University Press, 1991), pp. 50–65

ROWE, CHRISTOPHER, 'Handling a Philosophical Text', in *The Classical Commentary: Histories, Practices, Theory*, ed. by Roy K. Gibson and Christina Shuttleworth Kraus (Leiden: Brill, 2002), pp. 295–318

RYAN, CHRISTOPHER, *The Poetry of Michelangelo: An Introduction* (London Athlone, 1998)

RYLE, GILBERT, *Plato's Progress* (1966; Bristol: Thoemmes, 1994)

SALMON, J. H. M., 'Stoicism and Roman Example: Seneca and Tacitus in Jacobean England', *Journal of the History of Ideas*, 50 (1989), 199–255

SARTRE, JEAN-PAUL, *Existentialism and Humanism*, trans. by Philip Mairet (London: Methuen, 1948); orig. pubd as *L'Existentialisme est un humanisme* (Paris: Nagel, 1946)

—— *Being and Nothingness* [BN], trans. by Hazel E. Barnes, with intro. by Mary E. Warnock (1958; London: Routledge, 2003); orig. pubd as *L'Être et le néant* (Paris: Gallimard, 1943)

SCHOLAR, RICHARD, *The Je-Ne-Sais-Quoi in Early Modern Europe: Encounters with a Certain Something* (Oxford: Oxford University Press, 2005)

SENECA, LUCIUS ANNAEUS, *The Workes of Lucius Annaeus Seneca, both Morall and Naturall*, trans. by T. Lodge (London, 1614)

—— *Ad Lucilium epistulae morales*, I, trans. by Richard M. Gummere, Loeb Classical Library, 75 (London: Heinemann; Cambridge, MA: Harvard University Press, 1953)

—— *Moral Essays*, I, trans. by John W. Basore, Loeb Classical Library, 214 (London: Heinemann, 1957)

SERJEANTSON, R. W., 'Testimony and Proof in Early-Modern England', *Studies in History and Philosophy of Science*, 2 (1999), 195–236

—— ed., *Generall Learning: A Seventeenth-Century Treatise on the Formation of the General Scholar, by Meric Casaubon* (Cambridge: RTM, 1999)

SHAKESPEARE, WILLIAM, *King Lear: A Parallel Text Edition*, ed. by René Weis (London: Longman, 1993)

—— *The Complete Poems and Sonnets*, ed. by Colin Burrow (Oxford: Oxford University Press, 2002)

SHAPIRO, BARBARA, *Probability and Certainty in Seventeenth Century England* (Princeton, NJ: Princeton University Press, 1983)

—— *A Culture of Fact: England, 1550–1700* (Ithaca and London: Cornell University Press, 2000)

—— 'Rhetoric and the English Law of Evidence', in *Rhetoric and Law in Early Modern Europe*, ed. by Lorna Hutson and Victoria Kahn (New Haven and London: Yale University Press, 2001), pp. 54–72

SIMMEL, GEORG, 'Sociability', in *On Individuality and Social Forms* (Chicago: Chicago University Press, 1971), pp. 127–40

SOPHOCLES, *Sophocles*, ed. and trans. by Hugh Lloyd Jones, III: *Fragments*, Loeb Classical Library, 483 (Cambridge, MA, and London: Harvard University Press, 1996)

SOUTHAM, B. C., *A Student's Guide to the Selected Poems of T. S. Eliot*, 6th edn (London: Faber, 1994)

SPURGEON, CAROLINE, 'Leading Motives in the Imagery of Shakespeare's Tragedies', in *Shakespeare Criticism, 1919–1935*, ed. by Anne Bradby (London: Oxford University Press, 1936)

STEADMAN, JOHN M., *The Hill and the Labyrinth: Discourse and Certitude in Milton and his Near-Contemporaries* (Berkeley: California University Press, 1984)

STEINER, GEORGE, 'A Reading against Shakespeare', in *No Passion Spent: Essays, 1978–1996* (London: Faber, 1996), pp. 108–28

STEPHEN, HARRY L., 'The Trial of Sir Walter Raleigh', *Transactions of the Royal Historical Society*, 4th ser., 2 (1919), 172–87

DAVID SUMMERS, *Michelangelo and the Language of Art* (Princeton: Princeton University Press, 1981)

SWINBURNE, HENRY, *A Treatise of Spousals* (*c.* 1600), ed. by Randolph Trumbach (London: Garland, 1985)

TAYLOR, GARY, '*King Lear*: The Date and Authorship of the Folio Version', in *The Division of the Kingdoms: Shakespeare's Two Versions of King Lear*, ed. by Gary Taylor and Michael Warren (Oxford: Clarendon Press, 1983), pp. 351–461

TAYLOR, JEREMY, *The Real Presence and Spirituall of Christ in the Blessed Sacrament Proved Against the Doctrine of Transubstantiation* (1654), in *The Whole Works of the Right Reverend Jeremy Taylor*, ed. by Reginald Heber, rev. by Charles Page Eden, 10 vols (London: Longman, 1849–54), VI (1852)

TOLKIEN, J. R. R., 'On Fairy Stories', in *The Monsters and the Critics and Other Essays*, ed. by Christopher Tolkien (London: Allen & Unwin, 1983), pp. 109–61

TYNDALE, WILLIAM, 'Prologue to the Book of Genesis', in *Doctrinal Treaties*, ed. by Henry Walter (Cambridge: Cambridge University Press, 1848)

VARCHI, BENEDETTO, *Due lezzione, nella prima delle quali si dichiara un sonetto di M. Michelagelo Buonarroti* (Florence, 1549)

WARNOCK, MARY, *The Philosophy of Sartre* (London: Hutchinson University Library, 1965)

WATSON, GERARD, 'The Natural Law and Stoicism', in *Problems in Stoicism*, ed. by A. A. Long (London: Athlone, 1971; repr. 1996), pp. 216–38

WILLIAMS, BERNARD, *Morality* (New York and London: Harper & Row, 1972)

WILLIAMS, ROWAN, 'The Discipline of Scripture', *On Christian Theology* (Oxford: Blackwell, 2000), pp. 44–59

——— 'God's Spies: Believers on Trial', in *Christ on Trial: How the Gospel Unsettles our Judgement* (London: Fount, 2000), pp. 95–118

WITTKOWER, RUDOLF, 'Individualism in Art and Artists: A Renaissance Problem', *Journal of the History of Ideas*, 22 (1961), 285–302

WRIGHT, N. T., *The Resurrection of the Son of God* (London: SPCK, 2003)

INDEX